# 'DEAR OLD KIT'

*The Historical Christopher Carson*

*Last known photograph of Carson, 1868.* (Courtesy of Kit Carson Museum)
*See page 231.*

# 'DEAR OLD KIT'

## The Historical Christopher Carson

*With a New Edition of the Carson Memoirs*

**By HARVEY LEWIS CARTER**

UNIVERSITY OF OKLAHOMA PRESS : NORMAN AND LONDON

By Harvey L. Carter

(Editor) *The Pikes Peak Region, a Sesquicentennial History*
(Colorado Springs, 1956)

*Zebulon Montgomery Pike: Pathfinder and Patriot*
(Colorado Springs, 1956)

*The Far West in American History*
(Washington, 1960)

*'Dear Old Kit,' The Historical Christopher Carson*
(Norman, 1968)

Library of Congress Catalog Card Number 68-15681
ISBN: 0-8061-2253-6



5 6 7 8 9 10 11 12 13 14

*To my dear grandchildren*
Scott Stratford Carter
*and*
Colleen Carter
*I dedicate this book about*
Kit Carson
*a nice guy who finished first*

# Contents

# Illustrations

# Maps

*"Dear old Kit, O wise of counsel, strong of fame, brave of heart and gentle of nature."*

—Edward Fitzgerald Beale

# Preface to the Paperback Edition

THIS IS A REPRINT, not a revised edition, of *'Dear Old Kit'* (1968). An effort has been made to correct typographical errors of the original edition, but with two exceptions, errors of fact have not been corrected or replaced by information learned since 1968. One exception occurs on page 43, where, thanks to the researches of David Weber, Carson's "Col. Tramell" is identified as Philip Trammell, not as Richard Campbell. The other is found on page 176, where the date for the death of Josefa Carson is corrected to read April 27, 1868, on the basis of a letter from Robert H. Whatley to Albert H. Pfeiffer, written the day after her death. For this information I am indebted to Mary Lund Settle. I wish to acknowledge also Janet Lecompte's identification of the trapper called Frederick (p. 80) as Justin Grosclaud, a Swiss with a French name, so that the Frenchman mentioned may well have been Frederick and not a separate person. The discovery and publication of a letter written by Jessie Benton Frémont to Carson at the time of the Navajo War is another contribution to our knowledge of Carson by Janet Lecompte.

Historians usually learn something as a result of publication that they wish they had known before. It is a great pleasure, nevertheless, for an author to gain valuable knowledge from interested readers. In two separate instances I was enabled by readers to take up cold trails and follow them to successful conclusions. After reading *'Dear Old Kit,'* Albert Brown, of Arvada, Colorado, told me that there were descendants of Carson's trapping partner, Dick Owens, living in the Denver area. Through them I was able to learn something of his earlier and later life, concerning which I had known very little (p. 73).

Richard Lemon Owings was born in Owings Mill, Maryland, in 1812.

He grew up near Zanesville, Ohio, and, in 1834, he went West with Caleb Wilkins. His name appears frequently in the Fort Hall ledgers as Lemon Owens or Owings. After his years with Carson he returned to his family in about 1850. They were located near Marion, Indiana, and here he married in 1854. He moved to Iowa during the Civil War and to Circleville, Kansas, in 1872. There he died in 1902, and there I visited his grave in 1971. True, this knowledge is not essential to a Carson biography, but it clears up the mystery of what became of his best friend.

A South Dakota reader, Dennis Ottoson, wrote to me in 1973 to suggest that Carson joined Thomas McKay in trapping the Humboldt River in 1836, not with Alexis Godey but with Antoine Godin. John Mostin in taking down Carson's dictated memoirs had written Antoine Godey, and it had always been assumed that he had meant to say Alexis. Ottoson's suggestion seemed plausible to me for two reasons. I recalled that Carson's memory for names was so remarkable that he made no other slips of this sort. I also recalled that Godin's name appeared frequently in the Fort Hall ledgers but that it was usually written as Goda, which would be pronounced about like Godey.

I made an intensive restudy of the Fort Hall ledgers and found no entries for either Antoine Godin or Christopher Carson during the period that McKay was gone on this expedition. Frémont hired Alexis Godey in 1843 at Fort St. Vrain and wrote that he "had been in the mountains for six or seven years." This would indicate that Godey did not become a trapper until 1837, at the earliest. This renders it virtually certain that Carson's companion on the Humboldt in 1836 was Antoine Godin, not Alexis Godey.

Carson's memory for people was infallible, but his recollection of chronology was not. Like most of us he had difficulty getting events in the proper years. The late Dale Morgan believed that Carson came out of the mountains in 1840, not 1841, but Carson was right in his recollection of that important event. Morgan based his opinion on the faulty recollection of another person. My detailed inspection of the Fort Hall ledgers led me to the conclusion that Carson worked for Donald McLean, of the Hudson's Bay Company, after he returned from the Humboldt excursion and that he did not join Bridger until December, 1836. Two instances of charges against Carson's account have to be attributed to his wife and to one other person for this to be true. So it is mentioned here only as a probability not a certainty.

Two other probabilities deserve mention. Thelma S. Guild, my coauthor of a biography of Carson (*Kit Carson: A Pattern for Heroes.* Lincoln: University of Nebraska Press, 1982; Bison Books, 1984), suggested that Carson's Arapaho wife accompanied him on his Humboldt River excursion. It was British policy to encourage Indian wives to accompany trappers, and there are other indications as well that render this a most likely probability. Pamela Herr, a recent biographer of Jessie Benton Frémont (*Jessie Benton Frémont: American Woman of the 19th Century.* New York: Franklin Watts, 1987), suggested that Jessie was the "reporter" who wrote and published the early newspaper account of Carson's life found in Appendix B of *'Dear Old Kit,'* but again there is no clinching evidence. These are matters that some future Carson scholar may determine.

The illustration (p. 97, but discussed on pp. 233–34) that I regarded as a picture of Carson and Frémont has been identified by others as a photograph taken by Matthew Brady of Kit Carson and Ward Lamon, head of the Secret Service during the Civil War. The curator of the Brady Collection cannot certify that it was taken by Brady himself, however, but only that it was collected by him. There is no evidence that Carson and Lamon ever met, and from knowledge of their lives, it is nearly certain they could not have done so. I would say that if the seated figure is Lamon, the other figure is not Carson, and that if the standing figure is Carson, the other figure is not Lamon. Since most of the copies extant were found in New Mexico, I am now inclined to believe that this picture may be Carson and Edwin O. Perrin, as Kenny and Loraine Englert believed it was in 1968.

My original edition of *'Dear Old Kit'* had to contend with the mythmakers who were not content with a hero as ordinary as the actual historical person but who wished to worship him as a superman who never failed and who could do no wrong. These people felt that my book was disrespectful to their concept of Carson by being so familiar as to refer to him as 'Dear Old Kit.' This reprint edition will no doubt have to contend with the new mythmakers who regard Carson as an inhuman monster who starved, beat, and killed untold numbers of Navajo Indians and enslaved those who survived. These people want a scapegoat where the earlier mythmakers wanted a demigod.

Carson became a hero by having the role thrust upon him. He recognized that it had been overdone, but he still tried his level best to live up to the reputation he had been given. How he would react to being cast as a villain, I do not know. I suspect that his feelings would be hurt but that he would be reluctant to admit it. My only wish is to assure readers that my original evaluation of Carson and the Navajo War stands in no need of change. The record is clear that Carson was more sympathetic to the Indians in later life than he was earlier and that he was never an Indian hater as were so many people in his time.

Harvey L. Carter

*Colorado Springs, Colorado*
*January 27, 1990*

# Preface to the First Edition

The late Professor Frederick Logan Paxson had a dictum to the effect that students never had good ideas about choosing subjects for papers in history. His system was to prepare a list of subjects and then to match the alphabetically arranged names of the members of his class against the alphabetically arranged list of subjects. One of the results of this arbitrary method of assigning papers at the University of Wisconsin in the year 1928 was to bring the names of Carson and Carter into juxtaposition as subject and writer, respectively.

I was pleased with my luck, for one of the books in my grandparents' home that I had read as a boy was Colonel Frank Triplett's *Conquering the Wilderness*. I thought that I had known all about Kit Carson for several years. However, I discovered that Triplett was not a highly reliable source and that a good many contradictory statements about Carson had been made by other authors.

Professor Paxson was pleased with my paper and offered me the opportunity of serving as his assistant in Western History for the coming year. Had I accepted his offer, there is a strong likelihood that this book might have been written a good many years earlier. However, I did not feel financially able to continue my graduate studies at that time, so I declined his helpful offer and began using my knowledge trying to earn enough at college teaching to pay off the cost of having acquired it. When I returned to Wisconsin some years later, Professor John Donald Hicks agreeably allowed me to write a dissertation upon a subject of my own choosing, perhaps demonstrating thereby the truth of Professor Paxson's dictum.

Another of Professor Paxson's beliefs was that the author of a book ought always to say something good about his work in his preface because reviewers invariably would pick it up and repeat it in their reviews. This may have been true forty years ago but, on the other hand, reviewers may have changed their habits since that remote and unsophisticated era. There is an infallible way to find out and I propose to take it. From this point on, this preface will consist entirely of the good things that the author is not too modest to say about his own work.

The primary obligation of a historian is to set the record straight. Devotion to truth and accuracy must be his guiding principle. Accounts of Kit Carson's life have been clouded by so much untruth and inaccuracy as to make a reliable work about him a badly needed book. Within the framework of fact, however, a biographer does well to maintain a genuine sympathy and respect for his subject. I maintain that Carson's life was sufficiently exciting and adventurous in reality that to paint the rose beyond its natural color would be not only unhistorical but also supererogatory. While remaining strictly within the bounds of factual knowledge, I have had no intention or desire deliberately to debunk Carson's life or character.

In this book, therefore, I have been at pains to write the truth insofar as it can be ascertained, and to expose such untruth as has been given currency over the years. There are a number of things which I have been able to establish that are presented here for the first time in any book on Carson. The pseudo-Carson material of Oliver P. Wiggins has been repudiated as completely false and without foundation. The confused chronology of Carson's memoirs for the years 1835–40 has been systematically corrected insofar as the present state of our knowledge will allow. The actual writer of the Carson memoirs, as dictated by him, is shown to have been neither Dr. Peters nor Jesse Turley, as hitherto has been assumed. Instead, it finally has been established that the scribe was John Mostin, who served as Carson's interpreter or secretary during the years 1854–59. Every person mentioned in the Carson memoirs has been identified, without exception. That Carson helped to construct Bent's Fort has been shown to have been an impossibility. That he had a band of hunters and trappers under his own command for several years has been shown to have no basis in fact. A somewhat different route for the crossing of the Continental Divide by Frémont's third expedition has been worked out in place of the one that usually has been accepted.

There are a good many other points that could be made here, but I have a strong conviction that a preface should not be very long, and also an abiding belief that some things should be left for interested readers to discover for themselves.

I cannot lay claim to having followed Carson all over the American West. However, I have driven my Dodge over a great many of the trails he once traversed on muleback or horseback. I have visited a large number of the sites that are associated with his eventful career. I have sought to entice the wary and elusive trout in many of the streams where he formerly trapped the industrious beaver. Such activities have been both pleasures in themselves and useful supplements to my pursuit of anything on Carson to be found in books.

Kit Carson was straightforward and honest beyond most men, and I like to think that he would be pleased with my efforts to set forth the facts concerning his life, insofar as they can be determined as the centennial anniversary of his death approaches. May his memory be ever green among us as the finest symbol of the early days of the American West.

Harvey L. Carter

*Colorado Springs, Colorado*
*August 25, 1967*

# Acknowledgments

Public recognition is due Mr. Lawrence F. Towner, librarian and director of the Newberry Library, Chicago, Illinois, for granting permission to produce my edition of the Carson memoirs.

And, to the various staff members of the Bancroft Library, Berkeley, California; of the Tutt Memorial Library, Colorado College, Colorado Springs, Colorado; of the Huntington Library, San Marino, California; and of the Missouri Historical Society Library, St. Louis, Missouri, for the courtesies extended to me in response to requests for materials, either by correspondence or in person.

And, to Mr. Jack K. Boyer, director of the Kit Carson House and Museum, Taos, New Mexico; to Mrs. Alys Freeze, head of the Western History Department of the Denver Public Library, Denver, Colorado; and to Miss Maxine Benson, state historian of Colorado, The State Historical Society Library, Denver, Colorado; and to various staff members of these institutions, for expert assistance in the matter of illustrations.

And, to Mrs. Ruth Weber and Mrs. Derrie Frost, of the secretarial staff, Colorado College, Colorado Springs, Colorado, for their cheerful services in the typing of my manuscript.

And, to the following persons, for prompt response to various requests that will not be enumerated here: Mr. W. B. Metcalf, supervisor of the Routt National Forest, Steamboat Springs, Colorado; Mr. Jonas Olsoff, assistant librarian, The New York State Library, Albany, New York; Miss Jane F. Smith, director, Social and Economic Records Division, The National Archives, Washington, D. C.; Mrs. Dortha M. Bradley, assistant archivist, the State Records Center and Archives, Santa Fe, New Mexico; Professor Norma L. Peterson, Adams State College, Alamosa, Colorado; Professor Morris F. Taylor, Trinidad Junior College, Trinidad, Colorado; Miss

Quantrille D. McClung, Denver, Colorado; Professor John Roberts and Professor Richard Beidleman, Colorado College, Colorado Springs, Colorado; Mrs. Betty Mahaffy, Colorado College, Colorado Springs, Colorado; Mrs. Margaret Reid, librarian, The Pikes Peak Regional Library, Colorado Springs, Colorado; Mr. Fred Rosenstock, Denver, Colorado; and Dr. James V. Carris, Colorado Springs, Colorado.

To all of these my grateful thanks are hereby cordially extended.

To four individuals, I owe a somewhat more personal debt which I wish to acknowledge here.

Professor LeRoy R. Hafen, Brigham Young University, Provo, Utah, has given me encouragement and advice in the matter of untangling the sequence of events inaccurately given by Carson in his memoirs, for which I am most grateful.

Mrs. Janet Shaw Lecompte, Colorado Springs, Colorado, has been most generous in talking over some of my Carson problems with me, providing information from her detailed knowledge of the early history of the Southwest that frequently led to a solution. For this I am most deeply appreciative.

My colleague, Professor James Trissel, Colorado College, has supplied, upon very short notice, ten line drawings illustrative of familiar, everyday things in the life of Carson, and for his fine work I am deeply pleased as well as obligated.

My daughter, Mrs. Cherry Carter Kinney, Hartwick College, Oneonta, New York, has been extremely helpful, typing revisions and additions and going over my manuscript for errors. For her performance of these tedious tasks, I am very thankful indeed.

For all errors of commission or omission that remain, I am to be held responsible. I have written the kind of book about Carson that I wanted to write. On certain points, Carson experts will disagree with my views. My mind is open to convincing evidence on any point. Meanwhile, I hope that most of my conclusions will be received as sound contributions to knowledge of Christopher Carson, his life, and his times.

H. L. C.

# ‘DEAR OLD KIT’

*The Historical Christopher Carson*

# I. The Carson of History and Legend

At the height of the fur trade in the Far West, about the year 1835, it is probable that there were nearly three thousand men associated in one way or another with the business of gathering beaver pelts, either by trapping or by trading for them with the Indians. The names of more than four hundred of these men are known, but of all those familiar to students of the subject, only one name is commonly recognized by the average American living in the latter half of the twentieth century. That name is Kit Carson. Carson became a living legend in his own lifetime, and the passing of a century since his death has not noticeably obscured his renown, although it has all but obliterated any knowledge that the public may have possessed of the events upon which his fame was founded.

Fame has its own *modus operandi*; its ways are beyond the powers of logical analysis. To some, as to Kit Carson, it comes unsought. There are others who seek it unremittingly, only to be passed by unnoticed. There are still others who achieve some temporary measure of fame by their ambitious pursuit of it, but are overshadowed by those who achieve more permanent renown through what seems to be merely a combination of fortuitous circumstances.

American Beaver
(Castor Canadensis)

There can be little question that fortune smiled upon Kit Carson. Yet it is the thesis of this book that fortune has seldom smiled upon so deserving a person. A fair-sized list could be compiled of those whose names are of more historical significance in the development of the fur trade than Carson. Yet not one name on such a list would be that of a more thoroughly likeable man than he, and not one name would be that of a man as free from unadmirable characteristics. Honesty, simplicity, devotion to duty, and loyalty are traits that he had beyond most men of his time—or of any time—and these traits admittedly should be rewarded, but all too often are not. That is why one cannot help feeling that Carson deserved his good fortune.

In 1835, he was only one of many men in the Rocky Mountains, leading a rough, hard, and materially unrewarding life—but a life that was active, free, and filled with adventure. He was not one of the leaders of his kind. He had been to California and back, it is true, but by way of a route far to the south of the old Oregon country in which he now found himself, and therefore somewhat outside the comprehension of most of his fellow trappers. He was only twenty-five, and small and prosaic in appearance. Yet at the rendezvous of that year, the second he attended, Carson did something that lifted him a little way above the common run of his fellows. He fought a duel with a Frenchman whom he disliked and considered a bully. He painfully wounded his adversary and escaped unscathed. Rev. Samuel Parker, a missionary on his way to Oregon that year, reported the incident, its provocation, its outcome, and the names of the participants in a book that he published in the East three years later.[1] Thus was Kit Carson launched on his way to fame.

It is not to be supposed that this first appearance of his name in print had much effect on the

1 Rev. Samuel Parker, *Journal of an Exploring Tour beyond the Rocky Mountains* (Ithaca, 1838), 79–80.

general public. The book was not widely read and the incident received but a few lines of print. Undoubtedly the effect among the Mountain Men themselves was somewhat greater, as the story of the duel was repeated around the campfires. Carson had raised himself a notch in the estimation of his fellows—but only a notch.

He continued to trap until it was no longer possible to make a living in that way, but he was not singled out for any advancement; the fur trade was declining too fast for any possibility of that. He had no business experience as a bourgeois or partisan. He was just a free trapper, who managed to scrape up a living for himself and his squaw and two small children until 1841. About that time his squaw died, and since things had gone to pot in the mountains anyhow, he made his way to Bent's Fort.

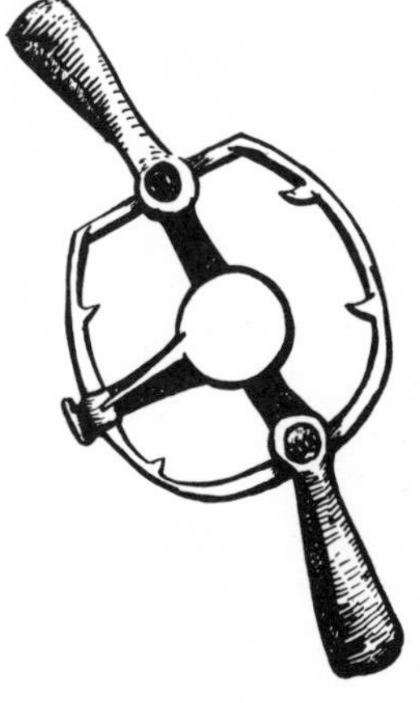

Beaver Trap

The next year, 1842, Carson went home to Missouri for the first time since he had run away in 1826. Aboard a Missouri River steamboat, entirely by accident he had a conversation with John C. Frémont that changed the course of his life. Frémont was looking for a guide for an authorized government expedition along the Oregon Trail and into the Rocky Mountains. Carson said he reckoned he knew that country pretty well. Frémont was convinced, liked Carson, and hired him. Next year, in 1843, Frémont went out again—this time all the way to California and back—and Carson was his guide. Frémont wrote up the reports of both expeditions, and through the influence of his father-in-law, Senator Thomas Hart Benton of Missouri, 10,000 copies of the *Reports* were printed and distributed at government expense in 1845.

The reports appeared at an opportune time. "Manifest Destiny" was in the air. The "Young America" movement was booming. Thousands of Americans were in the process of adopting the very satisfying belief that a wise Providence had decreed that the United States would naturally extend its boundaries in all directions. Acceptance of this doctrine awakened many people to the realization that a few hundred Americans had been serving as the advance agents of our Manifest Destiny for some time. These were the Mountain Men, of whom Carson was one. They were not conscious of playing such a role, but the public, in its enthusiasm, ignored that fact.

The role enacted by Frémont was a different matter altogether. He was perfectly conscious of the part he played. Frémont was a romantic whose ability, though considerable, was never quite equal to the task of placing him upon the pinnacle of greatness that he was sure he deserved to occupy. Although something of a scholar, he liked a life of outdoor adventure. Born out of wedlock to a French father and a Virginian mother, he seemed determined to win public acclaim sufficient to erase the disapproval clouding his birth and early years.

Frémont's *Reports* told the story of his first two expeditions well. No government reports, before or since, have been as readable as his. Francis Parkman read them, decided to make a western trip himself, and wrote *The Oregon Trail*. Lewis Hector Garrard read them, at a younger age than Parkman, and was impelled to go at once to the West. His *Wah-to-yah and the Taos Trail* was the result. Brigham Young read them and led his Mormon followers to Salt Lake. Farmers read them, sold their farms, and began the long journey by wagon to the Willamette Valley.

That was not all. Publishing houses reprinted the government reports for at least the next ten years.[2] How many thousands of copies were sold is impossible of estimate, but they were on the best-seller list until the outbreak of the Civil War.

Frémont was deliberately advancing his own career by this well-chosen means. His was the

2
In these editions, the word *Report* in the title was usually changed to *Narrative*, and I have so cited the work in editing the Carson memoirs. The following editions have been noted, and there were probably others. Chronologically listed they are: D. Appleton and Company, New York, 1846 and 1849; Wiley and Putnam, London, 1846; Hall and Dickson, Syracuse, 1848; A. Weichart, Leipsic, 1848; G. H. Derby and Company, Buffalo, 1850; Derby and Miller, Auburn, 1854; and Miller, Orton, and Mulligan, New York, 1856.

greatest acclaim, but a portion of the public's adoration also went to Kit Carson. Frémont was not niggardly with praise of his men. Although he did not make Carson the central figure of his story—that was reserved for himself—still, he gave him good billing. But he also did this for others in his employment, and not for Carson alone. He spoke very favorably of the knowledge and experience of Thomas Fitzpatrick and Joseph R. Walker, who were considerably older men than Carson, and more distinguished in the fur trade than Carson had been. The difference in age made it hard for Frémont to warm up to them. He always referred to them as Mr. Fitzpatrick and Mr. Walker, but he seldom referred to Mr. Carson. It was just plain Carson or, more often, Kit. The more firmly established place that the older men had held in the fur trade also made them less adaptable than Carson. Fitzpatrick and Walker had been leaders and found it difficult to follow a younger man. Carson had not been a leader and was only three years older than Frémont.

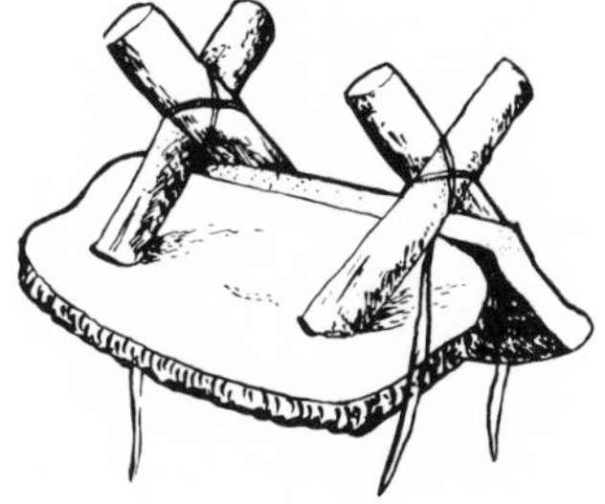

Pack Saddle

In addition, there was Basil Lajeunesse, whom Frémont described as his "favorite man." Readers could sense, however, that he was a little too much Frémont's man. He does not come through to the reader as an individual who can stand on his own. Finally, there was Alexis Godey. Frémont admired Godey as he admired Carson, and in one quality, that of coolness under fire, he was Carson's superior. He won somewhat the larger share of credit in the famous exploit wherein he and Carson recovered for two Mexicans the horses stolen by Indians and took two scalps in the process. The Indian that Carson had "killed" had to be killed a second time by Godey, so he got both the scalps. Godey, like Lajeunesse, was a Creole. This was all right with Frémont—he preferred Frenchmen, being half French himself and speaking French as

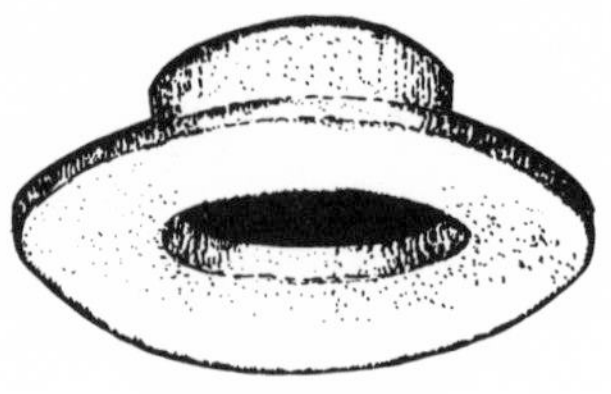

Beaver Hat

easily as English. His American reading public, however, was not going to take a Frenchman to its heart if it could find a more genuinely American hero, and this it found in Kit Carson.

How much the alliteration of the name helped is impossible to say, but it certainly did nothing to detract. When Frémont made it clear that Carson was a skillful horseman, a good buffalo hunter, a fearless Indian fighter, and a man who knew his way over the vast expanse of the Great West—a man who could actually guide "the Pathfinder," as Frémont had come to be known —his reading public selected Carson as the man who most deserved its admiration.

Let us add to the power of Frémont's pen the power of Senator Benton's tongue. Thomas Hart Benton was the Colossus of the Jacksonian Democrats in the United States Senate. Those other Colossi, Daniel Webster, Henry Clay, and John C. Calhoun, were all anti-Jackson Senators. Benton was Senator from Missouri for thirty consecutive years. He was a man who walked along the streets of St. Louis with his nose elevated at an angle, looking neither right nor left and speaking to nobody; who told his constituents that the way he voted was his business, not theirs. Yet he was elected five times as Senator. Obviously his ego was enormous, yet not only was he a good senator for his state, but also he had the most consistent record of adhering to his avowed beliefs of any man in the Senate. He was a champion of the West and of Western Expansion long before the country caught up with him on the wave of Manifest Destiny. Benton was an orator in public and a talker in private of no slight ability. When his son-in-law brought Carson to his home, Benton took a liking to him, as most people did. Thereafter, he became Carson's champion and recounted his adventures in public and in private. Not even Senator Everett Dirksen extolling the beauties of the neglected marigold could wax more eloquent than Senator Benton describing the latest exploit of his favorite frontiersman.[3]

Finally, there was the Senator's daughter, Jessie Benton Frémont. Forced to try to support her family by writing after the Frémont fortunes had waned and after Carson was dead, she wrote a number of newspaper pieces and stories paying tribute to Carson, whom she genuinely liked and respected. Thus she contributed her bit toward keeping his memory alive at a time when it might otherwise have faded.

Carson, therefore, had the benefit of publicity not only from his employer and leader, Frémont, but also from the latter's wife and father-in-law. It was a powerful trio, which had its political enemies, to be sure; but there is no evidence that this ever resulted in detriment to Carson, unless an instance may be found in the failure of the Senate to confirm President Polk's nomination of him for a lieutenant's commission in the regular army. Although he was fortunate in attracting the favorable attention of these three publicity minded people, it must be said that Carson merited their praise. Much of the success of Frémont's expeditions must be attributed to his ability and his willingness to cope with the most arduous tasks the Pathfinder set for himself to accomplish. Many Mountain Men were less co-operative and less reliable as guides than Carson, even under more favorable circumstances. He always entered fully into the spirit of Frémont's enterprises, even though he may not have seen the necessity or understood the purpose of some of them.

Carson himself may have contributed slightly to the growth of his own literary reputation. He was interviewed by a reporter for the *Washington Union*, which published an abbreviated story of his life in its issue of June 16, 1847. This was on the occasion of his first trip to Washington

3
Senator Benton was especially important in keeping Carson in the public eye during the events of Frémont's third expedition and the subsequent controversy between Frémont and Kearny. Frémont's *Memoirs of My Life* (New York, Chicago, 1887) dealt fully with the third expedition and were responsible for keeping interest in Carson from waning, but the *Memoirs* were by no means as widely read as the *Reports.*

as a dispatch bearer and the story concentrated chiefly on his recent adventures in California, especially the Klamath Lake fight. But he also indicated that he had been to California earlier, as a trapper, and he told the story of his duel with Shunar, the Frenchman, without mentioning him by name.[4]

Frémont's *Reports* not only gave Carson his first push up the ladder of fame, but also they have remained a reliable source of factual information concerning him. The Carson presented by Frémont is not a complete picture, but it is an important component of the historical Carson. Although highly favorable, that picture is not exaggerated.

The Carson of fact, as presented by Frémont, had captured the imagination of the upper stratum of the reading public. The Carson of fiction soon made his appearance, and it was the fictional Carson who took by storm the lower and larger strata of readers. The earliest appearance of Carson as a fictional character seems to have been in *Holden's Dollar Magazine* for April, 1848. This was followed by two novels in book form published in 1849. One of these, published in Boston, was *Kit Carson, Prince of the Gold Hunters*, by Charles Averill, who may also have written the story for the magazine already mentioned.[5] Averill depicted Carson as young, handsome, and of Herculean stature. He is an Indian fighter, of course, killing redskins, whom he calls "critters" and "varmints," by the dozen, and he is also said to be the discoverer of gold in California and a successful defender of his riches against the evil intent of would-be despoilers. It is easy to see that this fictional Carson, although doubtless inspired by the real Carson of Frémont's *Reports*, was a vastly different person both in physical appearance and in achievements. Carson had no connection with the discovery of gold other than bearing the earliest announce-

4 This short sketch was reprinted in the *Supplement to the Connecticut Courant* (Hartford, July 3, 1847), and from this source it is reproduced in Appendix B in order to facilitate comparison with Carson's memoirs of 1856. It will be found that Carson tells a consistent story, often in almost the same words.

5 See Kent Ladd Steckmesser, *The Western Hero in History and Legend* (Norman, 1965), 36; also Henry Nash Smith, *Virgin Land* (New York, 1950), 94–96.

ments of it to Washington among the dispatches he carried. He was never a gold seeker.

The second novel of 1849 in which Carson appeared as a prominent character was Emerson Bennett's *The Prairie Flower or Adventures in the Far West*, published in Cincinnati. This was neither Bennett's first nor his last book, for he was a prolific producer of thrillers teeming with romantic adventure. It differs from his other works mainly in that Sidney W. Moss, a settler in Oregon, claimed to have written it, read it to an admiring literary society in Oregon City during the winter of 1842–43, and sent the manuscript to Indiana with Overton Johnson, one of a pair of itinerant former Wabash College students, in 1844.[6] Johnson and his partner, William Winter, published an interesting account of their own travels in 1846. Somehow, Moss charged, Bennett got hold of his story and published it as his own work. The truth or falsity of this charge cannot be ascertained, but it should be pointed out that in 1850 Bennett wrote a sequel using the same characters, including Carson, in further adventures.[7]

Bennett's Carson is chiefly an Indian fighter, noted equally for his ubiquity and his ambidexterity. When hostile Indians in large numbers appear, Carson is asked what he would propose doing. He replies, "Why, sir, to arm and mount on good horses a dozen or fifteen of us, dash into them and fight our way out." Bennett has Carson show contempt for Indians as fighters, but when his absurd plan is about to be put into execution, the fictional Carson is said to whisper solemnly, "Forward! Each man for himself and God for us all." It turns out that the Indians surprise them rather than the reverse, whereupon Carson shouts "Riddle them, tear out their hearts, scalp and send them to h - - l," and the author compares him to Napoleon at the bridge of Lodi.

6
See Henry R. Wagner, *The Plains and the Rockies: A Bibliography of Original Narratives of Travel and Adventure, 1800–1865*, revised by Charles L. Camp (Columbus, 1953), No. 162.

7
The sequel was entitled *Lenni-Leoti or Adventures in the Far West.* In it, Carson again miraculously appears to save the heroes and heroines of the book from Indians. Other more villainous trappers are introduced under the improbable designations of Black George, Rash Will, Fiery Ned, and Daring Tom! Prairie Flower turns out to be white after all; she is none other than Evaline Mortimer, the long-lost daughter of the Marquis of Lombardy!

The fictional Carson is a marvelous creature, as will be apparent from the following description of his actions as the fight develops.

> Two powerful Indians, hard abreast, weapons in hand, and well mounted, rushed upon him at once, and involuntarily I uttered a cry of horror, for I thought him lost. But no! With an intrepidity equalled only by his activity, a weapon in either hand, he rushed his horse between the two, and dodging by some unaccountable means the blows aimed at his life, buried his knife in the breast of one, and at the same moment, his tomahawk in the brain of the other. One frightful yell of rage and despair and two riderless steeds went dashing by.
> ... before I could re-gain my feet, I saw another [blow] aimed at my head by a powerful Indian, who was standing over me. At this moment, when I thought my time had come and "God have mercy on my soul" was trembling on my lips, Kit Carson, like an imbodied spirit of battle, thundered past me on his powerful charger, and bending forward in his saddle, with a motion as quick as lightning itself, seized the scalp lock of my antagonist in one hand and with the other completely severed his head from his body, which he bore triumphantly away.[8]

With this picture of Kit, riding off with the head of an Indian—or was it the body?—in one hand, we may take leave of Carson, as he appears in *The Prairie Flower*, regardless of authorship. Nor need we take notice of the large number of similar novels by various other authors which continued to be available for the next fifty years. Sufficient to remark that they sold for not more than twenty-five cents (usually ten cents) and were eagerly read, especially by growing boys. Obviously, despite all that can be said in criticism of the literary and historical shortcomings of such books, they had a powerful effect in fixing the name of Kit Carson permanently in the folk memories of the American people.[9]

8 Emerson Bennett, *The Prairie Flower* (Cincinnati, 1849), 62–68.

9 There were fictional representations of Carson in the works of two Englishmen that were based upon some first hand knowledge of him and of other trappers but which, nevertheless, are fictional. One was in George Frederick Ruxton, *Life in the Far West* (London, 1851; New York, 1855), 193–4, 199. The citation is to the American edition. The other was in Sir William Drummond Stewart, *Edward Warren* (London, 1854), 248–250. Ruxton's work was widely read but that of Stewart was very little known.

*The fictional Carson*. (From Johannsen, *The House of Beadle and Adams*) See page 231.

On Carson's second overland transcontinental journey as a dispatch bearer in 1849, he had the good fortune to be attended as far as Santa Fe by an admirer of good literary ability, Lieutenant George D. Brewerton, who published a detailed factual account of the trip some four years later.[10] This very interesting and truthful account is one of the best delineations of Kit Carson ever written. It was done, of course, from life and in action. He had the advantage of observing Kit in his natural element.

10 George D. Brewerton, "A Ride with Kit Carson," *Harper's Magazine*, Vol. VII (August, 1853), 307–45.

The party numbered twenty-eight in all and was well armed but very scantily supplied with food. Brewerton says that Carson's "keen eye was continually examining the country and his whole manner was that of a man deeply impressed with a sense of responsibility." His extreme caution extended to the campfire in whose light he would never linger, and to his sleeping arrangements with half-cocked pistols and rifle conveniently laid out. We are told how he conducted conversations with a party of Digger Indians, passing around his own pipe for the ceremonial smoke; how he related the story of Tabeau's death five years earlier and pointed out the spot as they passed; how he explained the numerous bones of horses by telling the story of Old Bill Williams and the great horse stealing raid on California in 1840 (in which Carson was not a participant).

Later we read about his supervision of the party's efforts to cross a swollen river and about his masterly handling of a large band of hostile Jicarilla Apaches, where he faced them down by drawing a line on the ground and daring them to cross it. Although Brewerton greatly admired Carson, he did not represent him to the reader as perfect. He told how Carson missed a shot at a fleeing Indian who was stopped by another member of the party. Brewerton's sketch was a notable addition to our knowledge of Carson, all the more important because Kit himself devoted so little space to this particular journey while dictating his memoirs, dealing with it in about 250 words.

The next contribution to the development of both the historical and the legendary Kit Carson was made by Dr. DeWitt Clinton Peters, an army surgeon, who had been stationed at Taos during the years 1854–56, while Carson was Indian Agent. Both men had taken part in Colonel T. T. Fauntleroy's campaign against the Utes in San Luis Valley in 1855 and had participated in the battle of Saguache.

Sometime during the last two months of 1858, a biography of Carson was published in New York, consisting of 534 pages, with Dr. Peters as the author of record, although he mentioned a friend, C. Hatch Smith of Brooklyn, as having given "valuable assistance in revising, correcting and arranging the manuscript."[11] In the preface, Dr. Peters stated that the "facts narrated" by Carson, upon which the biography was based, had been dictated by Carson "at the urgent solicitation of many personal friends" and later put at his disposal. He made no claim to having written down the "facts narrated" himself. In the 1874 edition, Peters repeated this explanation except for the fact that no collaborator was mentioned. The first edition contained some internal evidence revealing that Dr. Peters added a few details not based on the Carson memoirs which had been put at his disposal.[12] These were in the nature of stories that Peters had heard Carson tell in Taos. The later edition contained a very poor account of the years from 1856, when the memoirs end, to Carson's death in 1868. Even the original edition is more than five times the length of Carson's memoirs. Obviously a great deal of padding had been done.

Dr. Peters was in Europe from 1856 to 1858 at least, and possibly from 1856 to 1860.[13] In either

11
The work was entitled *The Life and Adventures of Kit Carson, the Nestor of the Rocky Mountains, from Facts Narrated by Himself.* Most copies bore the date 1859 rather than 1858.

12
The discovery of the Carson memoirs and problems pertaining to them will be discussed later. See also Note 322 (Page 148, below) of my edition of the *Memoirs* in this book.

13
See Christopher Carson, *Kit Carson's Autobiography*, edited and with an introduction by Milo M. Quaife (Lincoln, 1965), xviii.

case, in view of his absence it seems probable that a very large part of the padding of the biography was done by his collaborator, C. Hatch Smith. It is reasonable to assume that the excessive panegyrics and tiresome moralizing that characterize the book were provided by Smith rather than by Peters, who does not seem to have been inclined so strongly in this direction, judging by his letters and by the fact that, as an army surgeon, he undoubtedly was acquainted with some of the more unpleasant realities of life.

It is fair to point out that the manuscript of Carson's memoirs shows evidence of a very thorough job of editing in the handwriting of Dr. Peters. It is regrettable that he did not publish the manuscript as he had corrected it. But we owe him a debt of enormous proportions on two counts as it stands. First, we must be grateful for his (and Smith's) biography, with all its shortcomings, because it served as the basis for all the lives of Carson written until 1926, when the first edition of the *Memoirs* was published. Second, we owe him still more thanks for having preserved the manuscript of the *Memoirs* itself.

The Peters biography provided the materials and set the tone for several Carson biographies that appeared from 1860 to 1889. That of Charles Burdett, a writer of no particular distinction, was the first on the scene.[14] Burdett did no research beyond Peters and he did not scruple to introduce a few flights of fancy here and there. He took less space to tell his story than Peters, and he presented Carson as an exemplary person while at the same time stressing his adventures.

In the following year, Edward E. Ellis produced a somewhat more skillfully written biography.[15] Ellis was primarily a writer of fiction (often under a pseudonym). For example, under the name of J. F. C. Adams he wrote *The Fighting Trapper or Kit Carson to the Rescue*, a lurid piece of work.[16] But even though he wrote both

14
Charles Burdett, *The Life of Kit Carson, the Great Western Hunter* (Philadelphia, 1860).

15
Edward S. Ellis, *The Life and Times of Christopher Carson, the Rocky Mountain Scout and Guide* (New York, 1861).

16
Adams, J. F. C. [Edward S. Ellis] *The Fighting Trapper or Kit Carson to the Rescue* (Beadle's Dime Library No. 68) (New York, 1879).

fact and fiction he did not combine them or attempt to pass the fiction off as fact. In 1889 a new edition of the Ellis biography of Carson appeared which contained letters that he had solicited from General Rusling and General Sherman, telling of their acquaintance with Carson. This was his sole contribution to any real knowledge of Carson.

John S. C. Abbott was a prolific writer of biographies ranging from ancient to modern history, some of them in collaboration with his brother, Jacob Abbott, the author of the *Rollo* books. In 1873, he published a life of Carson which outstripped all others in its aim to make Kit a strong moral example for readers.[17] Abbott filled a pulpit for fourteen years and everything he wrote was didactic of the Christian virtues. His Carson does not drink or swear, and always resists temptation of every kind. Abbott himself was not so scrupulous in one respect. Noticing that Peters had told how Carson stayed with an "old mountaineer, Kinkead," during his first winter in Taos, Abbott made Kinkead into a venerable and decrepit character who taught Carson to live a virtuous life, and then killed him off, having no further use for him! Abbott's only real contribution was a letter from Dr. Tilton telling of Carson's death and some things Carson had told him during his attendance on the aging scout as a physician.

Burdett, Ellis, and Abbott all had one thing in common. They all presented a rehash of Peters' biography, without taking quite so long to tell it. They all repeated Peters' error of saying that Carson was a hunter for Bent's Fort for eight years. This was to have unfortunate consequences, as we shall see. There were two subsequent editions of Abbott's work, and all of these biographies seem to have sold well. Their combined effect was to make Kit Carson into a paragon of all the virtues and, at the same time,

17
John S. C. Abbott, *Christopher Carson, Known as Kit Carson* (New York, 1873).

to represent him as the greatest single factor in reducing the Indian population of Western America. Meanwhile, that flamboyant and bibulous embodiment of the later frontier, William F. Cody, known to all as Buffalo Bill, had a whack at writing his own version of western expansion.[18] His idea was that this phenomenon was chiefly the work of four men of heroic mold, Daniel Boone, Davy Crockett, Kit Carson, and himself. Although Cody sincerely admired Carson, there can be little doubt that his primary aim was to establish himself in better company than he habitually kept in actual life. In this he was not entirely successful, since Emerson Hough later wrote a book on the first three frontiersmen and left Cody out of it.[19]

A most interesting feature of the accumulation of legendary material around the figure of Kit Carson is to be found in the fact that certain individuals made a practice of claiming to have been closely associated with Kit over a period of years, supplying a wealth of detail designed to convince people that they really had done so. Two instances of this practice are deserving of special notice. In both cases, what was narrated as fact by these men was actually a tissue of lies. The claims of both men have been exposed as false. In the first case, that of William F. Drannan, the exposure has been generally accepted. In the second case, that of Oliver Perry Wiggins, it has not yet been generally recognized that his pretensions were completely fraudulent.

William F. Drannan published two books in which he claimed to have had a close connection with Carson over a period of twelve years, from 1847 to 1859.[20] These books were actually written by his wife, for he was not highly literate himself. The books formed the means of livelihood for the couple and were sold by Drannan personally to a considerable extent, but they were also sold in some cities through regular outlets,

18 William F. Cody, *The Story of the Wild West....* (Philadelphia, 1888).

19 Emerson Hough, *The Way to the West, and the Lives of Three Early Americans—Boone—Crockett—Carson* (Indianapolis, 1903).

20 William F. Drannan, *Thirty-one Years on the Plains and in the Mountains* (Chicago, 1899) and *Capt. William F. Drannan, Chief of Scouts* (Chicago, 1910). Actually, the second book conflicts with the first one in its account of the years 1856–59.

*The legendary Carson.* (Courtesy of Denver Public Library)
*See page 231.*

and newsboys sold them widely to travelers on railroad trains. Drannan claimed to have met Carson in St. Louis in 1847 and to have been befriended by him. Carson was in St. Louis in that year, but he went on to California, whereas Drannan said he was engaged in other activities in other places. Drannan also claimed to have been at Carson's wedding in Taos. This event occurred in 1843, before Drannan claimed to have met Carson and when Drannan was but eleven years old. He also said that he was present at Carson's duel with Shunar (whom he called Shewman) in 1852. The date of this duel was 1835. These instances will suffice to demonstrate the falseness of his story.[21] He seems never to have been taken seriously by any writer on Carson, so his false information did a minimum of damage.

Oliver Perry Wiggins never wrote or published anything himself. He contented himself with telling tales of Kit Carson to anyone in Colorado who would listen to him. The result was that although some people considered him a faker, most people believed him, including Francis W. Cragin of Colorado Springs, who gathered a great mass of material on the early history of Colorado and adjacent states by interviews between the years of 1903–1908. Cragin had some doubts about the authenticity of Wiggins' information, but he had succeeded in getting such a complete story from him that he clung to the belief that it was true. However, he did not finish writing the history he intended and his material has not been used to any great extent until recently.[22] Wiggins' great triumph was persuading Edwin L. Sabin, a really competent researcher into the life and times of Carson (except for this one grand aberration), to accept everything he said as gospel truth. Wiggins spent his later years in Denver and it was there that Sabin first talked with him, in 1910, when Wig-

21 For a more complete exposure of Drannan see W. N. Bate, *Frontier Legend: Texas Finale of Capt. Wm. F. Drannan, Pseudo-Frontier Comrade of Kit Carson* (New Bern, 1954). Drannan died in Mineral Wells, Texas, in 1913.

22 Mr. Cragin's degree was in geology, not in history. He gathered a great deal of valuable material but it must be used with caution and only by persons who know early Far Western history fairly well. His papers, (hereafter referred to as F. W. Cragin Papers), are in The Pioneer's Museum, Colorado Springs, Colorado. See Dorothy Price Shaw, "The Cragin Collection," *Colorado Magazine*, Vol. XXV (July, 1948), 166–78. Mrs. Shaw's daughter, Mrs. Janet S. Lecompte, has made extensive and extremely competent use of the Cragin Papers in her valuable contributions to our knowledge of the fur trade.

gins was eighty-seven years old.[23] He had been telling his preposterous yarns for quite a while and probably believed them himself by that time. At any rate, Sabin took the bait (and hook, line, and sinker along with it), and since his work on Carson is reliable in other respects he has been accepted by subsequent writers in respect to the authenticity of the Wiggins material as well.[24]

Wiggins claimed to have come west with a wagon train in 1838 and to have been practically adopted by Kit Carson, who rode up somewhere along the trail with a large band of men and protected the train from the Kiowa Indians. In the spring of 1838 Carson actually was fighting Blackfeet on the Madison River; in the summer he was at the rendezvous on the Popo Agie; in the fall he went from Brown's Hole with Thompson and Sinclair to trade with the Navahos; and in the winter he was at Fort Davy Crockett. Wiggins said they proceeded to Taos, a town he credited Kit Carson with having founded, and wintered there. Wiggins' description of Taos is convincing proof that he had never seen the place.

The next year, 1839, Wiggins said he was with Carson at a great Indian powwow at the Soda Springs, at the foot of Pikes Peak. Actually, Carson was trapping with Dick Owens in the Laramie Mountains that spring, was at the Green River rendezvous that summer, and went to Brown's Hole that fall.

Wiggins claimed that his association with Carson covered the twelve years from 1838 to 1850. It was Peters' statement that Carson had been a hunter for Bent's Fort for eight years that gave Wiggins an opportunity. He asserted that Carson only killed buffalo twice a year for the fort—an absurdity to anyone familiar with hunting and the preservation of meat—and that during the rest of the time he was the leader of his own

23
Oliver Perry Wiggins was probably born on Grand Island in the Niagara River on July 23, 1823, and died in Denver, November 30, 1913. I say probably because he himself at various times gave various birth dates to various people. He claimed to have been wounded at the battle of Monterrey, Mexico, but also claimed to have guided a party of Mormons to Salt Lake during the same time. Both claims were false, so it was not only the relations with Carson that Wiggins invented; the truth simply was not in him. Yet he must have been a most plausible talker to get people like Cragin and Sabin to credit his adventures despite the fact that he contradicted himself even while talking to the same person.

24
Wiggins has been exposed as a complete charlatan by Lorene and Kenny Englert, "Oliver Perry Wiggins; Fantastic Bombastic Frontiersman," *The Denver Westerners Roundup* Vol. XX (February, 1964), 3–14, a very able and entertaining article.

band of hunters and trappers, consisting of Oliver Wiggins, Ike Chamberlain, Sol Silver, Bob Dempsey, and a number of other wholly fictitious characters. This also can be traced to Peters, for he treated Carson always as the leader of any group of trappers with whom he happened to be. As a matter of fact, Carson never stated in his *Memoirs* that he was the leader of any party, large or small. Of course the names of the men in this band of Carson's were supplied by Wiggins. They had no existence except in his remarkable imagination, for he was shrewd enough to know that if he supplied the names of real persons his story could be checked, with the inevitable result that he would be exposed for what he was. He also said that Carson's first wife, the Arapaho girl, Waa-nibe, was named Alice, although he confessed that he could not remember her very distinctly.

Wiggins was aware of the fact that Carson accompanied Frémont as a guide, so he stated that Carson took his band along with him when he worked for Frémont's first two expeditions, but that only Carson was employed. The others ranged ahead of the expedition or fell behind it, hunting and trapping as they went. According to Wiggins, this continued only across Idaho on the second expedition, and not into California. The fictitious band then returned to Colorado. The preposterous nature of this assertion has not prevented its acceptance by many writers. Frémont, far from having additional men attached to his party, allowed eleven of his employees to return from Fort Hall. Wiggins was aware of this, too, and represented them to be deserters, which they were not. Apart from the fact that neither Frémont nor Carson mentioned any such band of trappers, the story is discredited by the known scarcity of game in the Snake River region and the short rations that Frémont's men endured while traveling there.[25]

25
In my analysis of Wiggins, I have not only depended upon the work of the Englerts, already cited, but I have also personally checked the Wiggins life story in F. W. Cragin Papers, Notebooks XVIII, XIX, XXII, XXIII, XXIV, XXV, and XXVI, which Cragin took down during the year 1903. As a result, I am prepared to state that nothing Wiggins said of his relations with Carson was true, and that while there may be some truth in what he tells of his own life from 1850 to 1870, it is highly doubtful that it can be separated from the falsehoods. It is reasonably certain that Wiggins did not come West before 1850, and only as far as Scott's Bluff, Nebraska, at that time. He may have done a little trapping, but his assertion that a trapper carried twenty traps is completely wrong. Five traps per man was the rule during the time that Carson was a trapper. A gun Wiggins gave to the Colorado State Museum in Denver, purported to have been Carson's, is also a fake as far as Carson's ownership is concerned.

26
Captain James Hobbs, *Wild Life in the Far West . . . .* (Hartford, 1872).

27
Dr. LeRoy R. Hafen knew Rutledge in Denver and has told me some things about him.

28
Edwin L. Sabin, *Kit Carson Days* (New York, 1914). Hereafter referred to as Sabin, *Kit Carson* (1914).

*Among the buffalo* (From Frémont, *Memoirs of My Life*) See page 232.

Another man who claimed to have known Carson in the area around Bent's Fort was James Hobbs.[26] His book has been quoted by some writers on Carson, but it is of extremely dubious worth. Still another impostor was Dick Rutledge, who flourished in Denver as late as the 1920's, wearing his hair and beard *à la* Buffalo Bill and calling himself the "Last of the Scouts." He pushed the date of his birth back ten years in order to claim to have known Carson. He wrote nothing and was not taken very seriously by anyone.[27]

Edwin L. Sabin was a fiction writer, but he was highly interested in Carson's life and did extremely valuable research on that subject. His book was the standard work on Carson for many years and deservedly so, for despite his reliance on Wiggins, he contributed a great deal to our knowledge of Carson.[28] He worked at a time when it was still possible to learn something by interviews with elderly people and he followed up his leads with skill, turning up an amazing amount of fugitive material. He was aware of some discrepancies in chronology, but made only slight progress in correcting them. The collection of photographs that appeared in his first edition is remarkably complete. His depiction of Carson within the historic setting of his time is excellent, except for his credence of Wiggins. His work on Carson's later years, heavily buttressed by government documents, has been of great value to all writers on Carson since his time.

The second edition of Sabin's book contained a great deal of revision but unfortunately the valuable photographs were replaced by drawings.[29] Also unfortunately, he did not eliminate the Wiggins material in this revision. He reduced the eight years Carson supposedly spent at Bent's Fort to four years (1838–42) and omitted some of Wiggins' more obvious misstatements, but he still clung to the idea that the Wiggins story was genuine. By the time Sabin revised his work, Stanley Vestal had published his impressionistic study of Carson, so Sabin reinforced his dubious Wiggins material by citing Vestal, who had got his Wiggins material from Sabin's first book, who had got it from Wiggins himself! It is almost enough to shake one's faith in recorded history.

Stanley Vestal was the pen name of Walter S. Campbell, an English professor in the University of Oklahoma, who was an early Rhodes Scholar. Concerning his life of Carson, nothing good can be said from the point of view of the historian except that it has a felicitous title.[30] Given a choice between fact and folklore, Vestal was a man who would choose the folklore every time. He said that he regarded his book as an epic. There is an epic quality about the men of the early Far West and their deeds, therefore it is not necessary to ignore the known facts of history in order to produce an epic of the Far

29 Edwin L. Sabin, *Kit Carson Days*. 2 vols. (New York, 1935). Hereafter referred to as Sabin, *Kit Carson*, (1935)

30 Stanley Vestal, *Kit Carson, the Happy Warrior of the Old West* (Boston, 1928).

West. Yet this is what Vestal did, whenever it suited him. Regrettably, his book has been taken as straight biography by the uninformed and by some writers who should have known better.

A couple of pertinent examples will not be amiss at this point. Bernard De Voto's *Across the Wide Missouri*, a widely acclaimed book that made a genuine contribution to knowledge of the fur trade, is unreliable in its information covering Kit Carson. The author has this to say about Carson, after conferring on him the rank of Brigadier-General in the United States Army (Kit was Brevet Brigadier-General in the New Mexico Volunteers) and marrying him off to a Mexican heiress (Josefa inherited one or two small pieces of land of no great value, near Taos):

> He maintained a group of veterans for miscellaneous purposes, hunting, trading, trailing, guard duty, but also trapping. The Carson men went into the mountains for beaver and sometimes Kit went with them. They were a specialist and expert group and Kit was bright, he kept them equipped with the newest armament and possibles and he learned business as few mountain men ever did.[31]

There is not a word of truth in this. It is pure Oliver Wiggins and pure balderdash. It was taken (though not acknowledged) from Stanley Vestal, who took it from Edwin L. Sabin (also unacknowledged), who got it from Oliver P. Wiggins. That old fabricator drew a long bow in more ways than one.

Another example is found in David Lavender's *Bent's Fort*, another book that made a solid contribution to the history of the fur trade but also perpetuated the pernicious influence of Wiggins as it had been popularized by Stanley Vestal. Lavender wrote about Kit Carson joining Frémont for his first expedition in these words:

> His plans jumping ahead, Kit sent two Delaware Indians from Kansas Landing to Taos. They

31
Bernard De Voto, *Across the Wide Missouri* (Boston, 1947), 374–75.

carried word for Sol Silver, Oliver Wiggins, and others of Kit's crew of rollicking free trappers to meet him near South Pass. When Fremont's expedition turned homeward in the fall, Kit would leave it and trap south with his men through the high meadows of the Colorado Rockies.[32]

The same comment applies to this passage as to the one above, and need not be repeated. Neither Frémont nor Carson ever said anything about such arrangements. The immediate source is Vestal (unacknowledged) and the ultimate source is Wiggins. An interesting thing transpired in Lavender's book, in that Sol Silver, whom Wiggins invented, became more important than his inventor. He is mentioned first in the passage just quoted and there are four listings of his name in the index, where the name of Wiggins does not appear at all.

The measure of Vestal's book is found on the opening page. Carson was born on December 24, 1809. That day was not satisfactory to the author, so he changed it to December 25. The year, since it was the year in which Abraham Lincoln also was born, was allowed to stand unchanged. Vestal also insisted upon having Carson kill Shunar in their celebrated duel. He cited the oral tradition of the Arapaho Indians as his authority for introducing this refinement. The only other testimony that ever supported this view was that of Smith H. Simpson, who told Sabin that he had heard Carson tell it that way. But Carson did not tell it that way in the two written accounts that have come directly from his mouth, both of which were available to Vestal.

Vestal seized upon a fictional scene from Ruxton's *Life in the Far West*, in which Carson turns a Mexican fandango in Taos into a free-for-all fight and enlarged upon it in such a way as to make it appear as fact. He stated that Ruxton had said in his preface that everything in his

32 David Lavender, *Bent's Fort* (New York, 1954), 212. If either Lavender or DeVoto had examined the life story of Wiggins in the Cragin Papers, as I have done, I am confident they would have concluded, as I did, that it is completely spurious. I shall regard with benign satisfaction all future writers who, when they encounter any reference to Kit Carson's band and his lieutenant, Oliver Wiggins, and his sub-lieutenants, Ike Chamberlain and Sol Silver, will dismiss it as a farrago of imagination, created by Oliver P. Wiggins and now relegated to the never-never land of its origin.

book was true and that Ruxton, as an English gentleman, was worthy of belief. Nevertheless, much of Ruxton's book is demonstrably fictional.

The greatest error of the book, however, is perpetuation of Wiggins' band of Carson men. Vestal accepted Wiggins, Sol Silver, and Ike Chamberlain as members of a Carson's band, and added a number of real trappers who had associated with Carson, but not necessarily in the area of Bent's Fort and not necessarily at the same time. Vestal had them all sit around a Kiowa campfire and exchange bragging with the Kiowas about the number of coups they had counted.

Throughout the book, he omitted such Carson material as had no appeal to him for use in an epic. Vestal contributed nothing to our factual knowledge of Carson. To the Carson legend, now reaching enormous proportions, he contributed a great deal. That such a book could have been published after the first edition of Carson's long-lost memoirs had appeared is almost incredible, yet such was the case.

In 1926, Blanche Grant edited and published *Kit Carson's Own Story of his Life*, which was the basis for Peters' biography but which had long been lost.[33] It was discovered among the effects of William Theodore Peters, a son of Dr. Peters, upon his death in Paris in 1905. Clinton Peters, another son, sold the manuscript a few years later and eventually it was acquired by Edward E. Ayer and passed on to the Newberry Library in Chicago, where it remains, docketed as Number 139 of the Ayer Collection. But two typewritten copies of it had been made, and it was from one of these that Miss Grant worked. She had acquired her copy from Charles L. Camp, who had used it as the basis for a very scholarly article in 1921.

Clinton Peters believed that the manuscript was in the handwriting of his mother and so

33
Christopher Carson, *Kit Carson's Own Story of His Life as dictated to Col. and Mrs. D. C. Peters about 1856–57, and never before published*, edited by Blanche C. Grant (Taos, 1926).

stated to Professor Camp, who passed the information on to Miss Grant. This is now known to be erroneous. Miss Grant was no scholar, but she was an interested collector of Carsoniana. Her edition contained very little in the way of editorial identification and comment. It was, however, a fairly close presentation of the original manuscript, and she performed a valuable service to historical scholars by making it available in print.

In 1935, the same year that Sabin revised his monumental work, Dr. Milo M. Quaife issued a second edition of Carson's memoirs as Number 33 of his famous series of *Lakeside Classics.*[34] Unlike Miss Grant, Quaife worked from the original manuscript, although he decided not to follow it literally but to render it into clearer and more correct English. He argued that since it was dictated to begin with, there was no way to tell whether the words were Carson's or those of his amanuensis. Therefore, he felt that it was not important to preserve the exact language of the original manuscript. Dr. Quaife was a well-known historical scholar and one of the great editors of historical materials.[35] He produced a readable version of Carson's memoirs and there were only a few instances where the changes he made in the text produced a change in the meaning. Nevertheless, the total effect is to convey the impression that Carson was somewhat more gifted in expression than was actually the case.

Quaife's annotation was also considerably fuller and more authoritative than that of Miss Grant. He had edited so many western narratives, however, that he fell into the habit of occasionally citing them when some other reference would have been more to the point. One particular statement made by Carson mystified him completely. He could find no explanation for the 111 forts built by the Blackfeet in one of their fights. Yet Joe Meek explained it very clear-

34 Christopher Carson, *Kit Carson's Autobiography*, edited with an introduction by Milo M. Quaife (Chicago, 1935). A paper-bound photoprint edition was issued by the University of Nebraska Press (Lincoln, 1965).

35 Milo M. Quaife is the only writer on Carson with whom I ever had more than a passing acquaintance. I used to enjoy long talks with him at historical meetings. Few people are willing to do that nowadays, unless they have some ulterior motive. I regard such individuals as a vanishing breed. Quaife's rough appearance belied his polished editorial talents. He judged historians not by their reputations but by whether or not they would submit a manuscript in decent shape.

ly to Mrs. Victor, and Quaife, of course, was familiar with her *River of the West.* Perhaps he was rushed for time, since he always got his *Lakeside Classics* out in time for distribution as Christmas presents.[36]

The introduction that Quaife wrote for his edition measurably advanced the knowledge of the circumstances under which Carson dictated his memoirs. Quaife was able to prove that the manuscript was not in the handwriting of Dr. Peters, and that the editorial corrections of the manuscript, in a different ink, were by his hand. He further proved that Mrs. Peters could not have written it for two reasons. First, Dr. Peters was unmarried when he was stationed at Taos in 1854–56, and second, it was not in the handwriting of Mrs. Peters. He then made the reasonable but erroneous assumption that because Carson had transferred the manuscript to "Mr. Jesse B. Turly to be used as he may deem proper for our Joint Benefit," it had been written by Turley. The conclusion was untenable because the manuscript was not in Turley's handwriting either, as will presently appear.[37]

With the publication by Henry Nash Smith of an article entitled "Kit Carson in Books," in 1943, there began a new type of literature on Carson.[38] Writers of this school were interested in the Mountain Man as a literary type and in Carson as a typical Mountain Man. They were not concerned with Carson as a historical figure or with facts of his life. Their interest lay in Carson as a symbolical figure, that is, as a symbol of the American frontiersman, whether portrayed in fact or in fiction—but chiefly in the American public's opinion of him, which they regarded as largely a product of his fictional portrayal. To Smith and to others who followed him, Carson was the literary heir and descendant of Leatherstocking, Cooper's famous frontier character.

Others who developed this line of analysis

36
They were published by the Lakeside Press of R. R. Donnelley's and Sons Company and sent out to favored individuals "with the compliments of the season" from Thomas E. Donnelley, president.

37
Quaife's introduction is well worth reading, in spite of its unwarranted conclusion. He was also the first to call attention to the part played by C. Hatch Smith as a collaborator of Dr. Peters.

38
Henry Nash Smith, "Kit Carson in Books," *Southwest Review*, Vol. XXVIII (Winter, 1943), 164–90. Smith's views on Carson as a literary type are more or less summarized in his book *Virgin Land* (New York. 1950), 88–98.

were Marshall W. Fishwick in his *American Heroes: Myth and Reality* and Kent Ladd Steckmesser, *The Western Hero in History and Legend*. The former was concerned with the whole galaxy of American heroes and made no particular contribution regarding Carson other than to point out that the best comparison with his character and career is to be found in the life of Daniel Boone.[39] Steckmesser was concerned with four Western characters, Kit Carson, Billy the Kid, Wild Bill Hickok, and George A. Custer. He was interested in separating the historical fact from the legendary tradition that had accumulated around these men. He discerned two legendary Carson types which, oddly enough, are sometimes combined. The first is the genteel hero, carefully built up to be a model for youth to follow. The second is the blood and thunder hero, who is the more natural model for youth to admire. He concluded that there is less of a gap between the real Carson and the legendary Carson than between history and legend in the other cases he had examined. In other words, Carson *was* a pretty decent chap and he *did* have some rather exciting adventures. On one point Steckmesser is definitely mistaken. Following Vestal, he credited the real Carson with having his own group, known as the Carson men, from 1834 onward. He rejected the "mule fort" incident of Carson and Meek, however, which was Vestal's starting point for the mythical Carson band. The "mule fort" incident could have occurred and probably did occur in 1833. It could not have occurred in 1834. But Carson's own band of men was entirely mythical. The author must also have been mistaken when he stated that Carson renounced the Catholic church. He gave neither evidence nor authority for the statement and it is probable that none exists.

The year 1962, for some unknown reason or possibly for no reason at all, was the *annus*

39 Marshall W. Fishwick, *American Heroes: Myth and Reality* (Washington, 1954), 13, 111, 205. Strangely enough, the pioneer work on this subject, Dixon Wecter, *The Hero in America* (New York, 1941), made no mention at all of Kit Carson. It is an unaccountable omission.

*mirabilis* of Carsoniana. Three works were published that require notice in any survey of Carson literature. Two are biographies; one is a genealogy; all were written by women.[40]

The genealogy, compiled by Quantrille D. McClung, is a most useful work of reference. It was her happy inspiration to include the Bent and Boggs families as well, certain members of which were so closely connected with Kit Carson that the useful quality of the compilation is greatly enhanced. The author also made frequent citations to authorities and brief quotations from them. Where contradictory records existed, all were given and, where possible, a preference was indicated. Slips were few, and this reliable reference work, rounded out by a complete index, is a welcome addition to Carson literature.

The two biographies were written by Bernice Blackwelder and M. Marion Estergreen. Both are the product of a good many years of investigation by the authors. Both are very readable works, marked by genuine admiration for the subject, and both make some original contributions on small points, even beyond the exhaustive researches of Sabin. Although the Blackwelder book is about 20 per cent longer, the Estergreen book is somewhat more explicit in its factual details—but the more swiftly moving style of the Blackwelder biography probably has more appeal for most readers. Estergreen is more informative on the period before 1842; Blackwelder is fuller on the period after 1848; the treatment of the years 1842–48 is approximately equal.

The shortcomings of both books are of a similar nature, for both authors perpetuated some of the legendary material about Carson that ought to have been swept away. Both continued to be convinced, against rather overwhelming evidence to the contrary, that he was literate; both

40
Bernice Blackwelder, *Great Westerner: The Story of Kit Carson* (Caldwell, 1962); M. Marion Estergreen, *Kit Carson: A Portrait in Courage* (Norman, 1962); Quantrille D. McClung, *Carson-Bent-Boggs Genealogy* (Denver, 1962).

insisted that he helped to build Bent's Fort, which can be shown to have been impossible; both firmly believed that Carson had his own band of men, including Wiggins and his imaginary helpers Chamberlain and Silver, without having examined Wiggins' story as dictated to Cragin; and even though both were aware of certain chronological difficulties in the period 1835–41, they made only slight progress in resolving them.

Beyond this point, Blackwelder made a number of minor errors such as killing off Matthew Kinkead, who lived into the 1850's, putting Carson in the company of Dick Wootton in 1832, when Wootton did not come West until 1836, having Carson kill Shunar in their duel, and killing off Governor Meriwether in 1857, when he lived until 1892.[41]

Despite such criticisms, these biographies represent a great advance over previous lives of Carson in their literary qualities, and some advance in scholarship, as well. The latter would have been greater if a more precise and extensive system of annotation had been used. In general, although these authors tended to rely too heavily on oral and family tradition at points where documentary evidence was against it, readers will get a reasonably accurate view of Carson from either of these commendable and, in many ways, admirable books.

By way of anticlimax, there appeared, two years later, still another biography, which deserves at least one superlative—it is the worst book on Carson I have ever read.[42] The author, Noel Gerson, had written eighteen works of fiction and it seems a pity that his life of Carson was not also given that classification. It was written, not only without taking into account the very recent and praiseworthy efforts of the two works just reviewed, but also without recourse to either the Grant or the Quaife version of Car-

41 Blackwelder, *Great Westerner*, 26, 51, 63, 288

42 Noel Gerson, *Kit Carson: Folk Hero and Man* (New York, 1964).

*Carson and Godey returning from Indian fight.* (From Frémont, *Memoirs of My Life*) See page 232.

son's memoirs or to the firsthand account of Brewerton that was valuable for so many years. Obviously intended as a popular work, Gerson's book is entirely devoid of any annotation and would be ignored here, except for the fact that it is clearly intended for adult rather than juvenile readers.[43]

Gerson's account of Carson's family, both in boyhood and as a man, is hopelessly garbled and his handling of dates, geography, and personal names is frequently highly inaccurate.[44] Moreover, the author made a number of errors of greater consequence, a few of which will be mentioned here.

He quoted a long passage, descriptive of Carson, which is purported to have come from the memoirs of Sir William Stuart [*sic*]. Sir William Drummond Stewart composed no memoirs. He said that Ewing Young lived a retired life in Taos, where Carson often visited him in the 1840's and 1850's. Young died in Oregon in 1841. He said that Carson led a large trapping expedition to the Pacific in the summer of 1838. Carson was at the rendezvous on the Popo Agie that summer. He said that beaver from Young's first California expedition was sold in Taos for $12.00 per pound. This is at least double the price received. He stated that Eastern land speculators came to the rendezvous of 1837 and because of Carson's national fame, offered him lucrative employment, which he declined. Carson was not nationally known until 1845. He stated that Frémont crossed the Sierras with sixty-five men. The second expedition had forty-one men to Fort Hall and thirty men thereafter. He stated that Carson superintended the Kiowas, Comanches, Apaches, Cheyennes, and Utes from his Agency at Rayado. Carson had charge of only the Southern Utes and the Jicarilla Apaches, and his Agency was located at Taos.

The author presumed to correct Frémont's

43 There are many lives of Carson written expressly for younger readers, all of which have been excluded from consideration in this survey, although one or two are very good examples of their kind.

44 I must confess that I have not read Gerson's work word for word beyond the first chapter. Beyond that point, I merely scanned the pages, noting the errors. This procedure resulted in a compilation of more than a hundred errors, of which I have chosen to mention only those of some magnitude.

eyewitness account of a buffalo hunt. He also explained that of course Carson knew that bears could climb trees. But Carson knew, as the author did not, that grizzly bears could not climb trees, and this knowledge was the reason for Carson's hurried ascent of an aspen tree. Gerson apparently believed that the annual rendezvous continued to be held after the Civil War and that in those later years women were often present. The last rendezvous was held in 1840. In short, the author's amazing ignorance of his subject is equalled only by that of the publisher in issuing such a work as nonfiction. Perhaps the most astounding thing in the book is the expression of the author's conviction that Kit Carson was the inspiration for Owen Wister's character "the Virginian," a cowboy of a later era. It is a thoroughly bad book and one can only hope that readers will not take it seriously. Certainly no student of Western history should be deceived by it.

In 1968, my short sketch of Kit Carson made its appearance.[45] In it, a reasoned and systematic effort was made to straighten out the confused chronology of the period 1835–40, as given in Carson's memoirs. Correction also was made of a number of other legendary or mythical ideas that have been commonly accepted since Sabin's time, including the imaginary tales of Oliver P. Wiggins.

In the course of preparing this sketch, I became convinced that a new edition of Carson's memoirs was badly needed. If, in addition, the remaining years of his life were to be dealt with, and a survey of the growth of information and misinformation about Carson were to be made, it seemed to me that a reliable reference work on Carson would be the result. It would be a book in which Carson would be allowed to tell his own story, insofar as possible, but supplemented by annotation on a more comprehensive scale

45
Harvey L. Carter, "Kit Carson," *Mountain Men and the Fur Trade of the Far West*, VI (edited by LeRoy R. Hafen) (Glendale, 1968).

than in any existing work, so that an adequate historical background would be provided.

Beyond this, it occurred to me that after making the research necessary for such a work, I might possibly have a sufficiently solid understanding of Carson to be able to write a character sketch of him that would better explain the sort of man he was, and that this sketch would round out the study in a useful way.[46]

In summary it may be said that interest in Carson as a historical character has been high and bids fair to remain so. He has been fortunate in attracting the attention of some extremely devoted admirers and assiduous researchers. So many details concerning his life have been brought to light that it is unlikely a great deal more will be discovered. The historical Carson has been well established and is able to stand without artificial aid of any kind.

The legendary Carson, also, has continued to flourish, through the conscious intention of some writers, the inadvertence of others, and the desire of still others to gratify a hero-worshipping public. The Carson of history and the Carson of legend will always remain intermingled for those who prefer to see him in that way. Beneath all the "fooforaw," to use a Mountain Man's term for fuss and feathers, the true Kit Carson can still be found. When the tinsel trappings are stripped away, the Carson who stands revealed is a real man and well worth knowing.

46 I believe that it is allowable for me to set forth what I have attempted to do in the present work, as a part of my survey of the literature on Kit Carson. Any evaluation of the success of my attempt will have to be left to others.

# II. The Kit Carson Memoirs, 1809-1856

[EDITORIAL FOREWORD: In preparing this edition of Carson's memoirs, it has been my object to reproduce with a minimum of change the narrative dictated by Carson in 1856 and written for him, as is now known, by John Mostin. The corrections introduced into the manuscript by Dr. DeWitt C. Peters have been excluded. The manuscript contains almost no paragraphing, however, and very little in the way of punctuation. These have been supplied by the editor at his discretion. The capitalization of the original manuscript has been retained nearly always, but capitalization has been supplied wherever it is missing at the beginning of sentences. Original spellings have been retained. Anything in parentheses in the original narrative has been retained in that form. Anything appearing in brackets in the present edition is not a part of the original narrative but has been supplied for the purpose of clarity. Usually the clarifications are taken from the corrections of Dr. Peters, but some are supplied by the editor, including all bracketed dates. Only a small fraction of the changes intended by Dr. Peters have been employed at all. The editor has not thought it necessary to call attention to points where his rendition of the original narrative differs from the Grant and the Quaife editions, except in two or three instances. However, a comparison will reveal that differences exist, and where this is the case the present edition is faithful to the original manuscript.]

Hawkens Flintlock Rifle

I WAS BORN on the 24 Decr. 1809 in Madison County, Kentucky.[1] My parents moved to Missouri when I was one year old. They settled in what is now Howard County.[2] For two or three years after our arrival, we had to remain forted and it was necessary to have men stationed at the extremities of the fields for the protection of those that were laboring.

For fifteen years I remained in Missouri. During that time I remained in Howard County. I was apprenticed to David Workman to learn the saddler trade.[3] I remained with him two years. The business did not suit me and, having heard so many tales of life in the Mountains of the West, I concluded to leave him.[4] He was a good man, and I often recall to my mind the kind treatment I received from his hands. But taking into consideration that if I remained with him and served my apprenticeship I would have to pass my life in labor that was distasteful to me, and being anxious to travel for the purpose of seeing different countries, I concluded to join the first party for the Rocky Mts.

In August, 1826, I had the fortune to hear of a party bound for that country to which I desired to go. I made application to join this party and, without any difficulty, I was permitted to join them.[5] On the road, one of the party, Andrew Broadus, met with a serious accident. He was taking his rifle out of a wagon for the purpose of shooting a wolf and, in drawing it out, [it] was accidentally discharged, [he] receiving the contents in the right arm. He suffered greatly from the effects of the wound. We had no medical man in the party. His arm began to mortify and all were aware that amputation was necessary. One of the party stated that he could do it. The man was prepared for any experiment to be tried that was considered of service to him. The doctor set to work and cut the flesh with a razor and sawed the bone with an old saw. The

1
William Carson, grandfather of Kit Carson, is thought to have been born in the north of Ireland about 1720, and to have emigrated to Pennsylvania between 1738 and 1748. He was of Scottish extraction. He settled in Rowan County, North Carolina, before 1761, where he received a grant of land and married Eleanor McDuff. The date of his death is uncertain but it was prior to 1776. His eldest son, Lindsey Carson, father of Kit, was born in 1754, saw irregular service in the American Revolution and, soon after it ended, married Lucy Bradley. They lived in Iredell County, North Carolina, until 1792, when they moved to Madison County, Kentucky. Lucy Carson died in 1793 and, in 1796, Lindsey married Rebecca Robinson. Kit Carson's half-brothers and sisters by his father's first marriage were William (1786), Sarah (1788), Andrew (1790), Moses Bradley (1792), and Sophia (1793). His full brothers and sisters were Elizabeth (1798), Nancy (1799), Robert (1801), Matilda (1803), Hamilton (1805), Hampton (1812), Mary (1814), Sarshall (1816) and Lindsey (1818), born after the death of his father. Birth dates are in several cases problematical. See the very thorough compilation of genealogical data in McClung, *Carson-Bent-Boggs*, 10–39.

2
Lindsey Carson had settled at Boon's Lick, Howard County, Missouri, probably in 1811. During the War of 1812, he and his sons, Andrew and Moses, rendered militia service at Fort Kinkead. The family may have "forted up" there or at Fort Hempstead or Fort Cooper, and apparently they farmed their land while keeping

a close watch against hostile Indians. Lindsey Carson died in 1818 from the effects of having been struck by a falling tree. His widow married Joseph Martin in 1821. The names of Kit's half-brothers and a half-sister by this second marriage of his mother are unknown. Such details of his background and early life as are known may be found in Estergreen, *Kit Carson*, 3–22, and in Blackwelder, *Great Westerner*, 13–20. Some statements about his early years must be weighed carefully and accepted with caution or, in some cases, rejected. It is clear, however, that he was known as Kit from a very early age.

3
David Workman lived in Old Franklin, which was the outfitting point for caravans going West in the 1820's. Workman had this advertisement inserted in the *Missouri Intelligencer*, October 6, 1826, after Carson had run away. "Notice is hereby given to all persons, that Christopher Carson, a boy about 16 years old, small of his age, but thick-set; light hair, ran away from the subscriber, living in Franklin, Howard County, Missouri, to whom he had been bound to learn the saddler's trade, on or about the first of September last. He is supposed to have made his way to the upper part of the state. All persons are notified not to harbor, support, or assist said boy under penalty of the law. One cent reward will be given to any person who will bring back the said boy." David Workman himself went out to Santa Fe in company with Captain Ezekiel Williams less than a year later. They left Franklin in May, 1827, with 105 men and 53 wagons. See Louise Barry, "Kansas before 1854: A Revised Annals," *Kansas Historical Quarterly*, Vol. XXVIII (Spring, 1962), 35. David Workman died on the La Puente ranch of his brother, William Workman, in California, in 1855.

4
Kit's half-brother, Andrew, and his brother, Robert, had both been to Santa Fe with George Champlin Sibley's surveying expedition in 1825. See Kate L. Gregg, *The Road to Santa Fe* (Albuquerque, 1952), 246. His half-brother, Moses, had been a trapper on the Missouri River from 1819 to 1825 and may have traded in Santa Fe as early as 1826. See Harvey L. Carter, "Moses Carson," *Mountain Men and the Fur Trade of the Far West*, II (edited by LeRoy R. Hafen) (Glendale, 1965), 75–79. Hereafter referred to as *Mountain Men* (ed. by Hafen), II. It was doubtless from these members of his own family that young Kit heard enticing tales of the adventurous West.

5
In August, 1826, a company left Ft. Osage, Missouri, bound for Santa Fe. William Wolfskill, Andrew Broadus, and probably George Yount were members of it. The fact that Broadus was along makes it almost certain that this was the wagon train with which Kit traveled. Barry, "Kansas before 1854 . . . ," *Kansas Historical Quarterly*, Vol. XXVIII (Spring, 1962) 29.

Certainly the oft-repeated assertion that he traveled with Charles Bent is untrue because Bent first went to Santa Fe in 1829. Barry, "Kansas before 1854 . . . ," *Kansas Historical Quarterly*, Vol. XXVIII, 53.

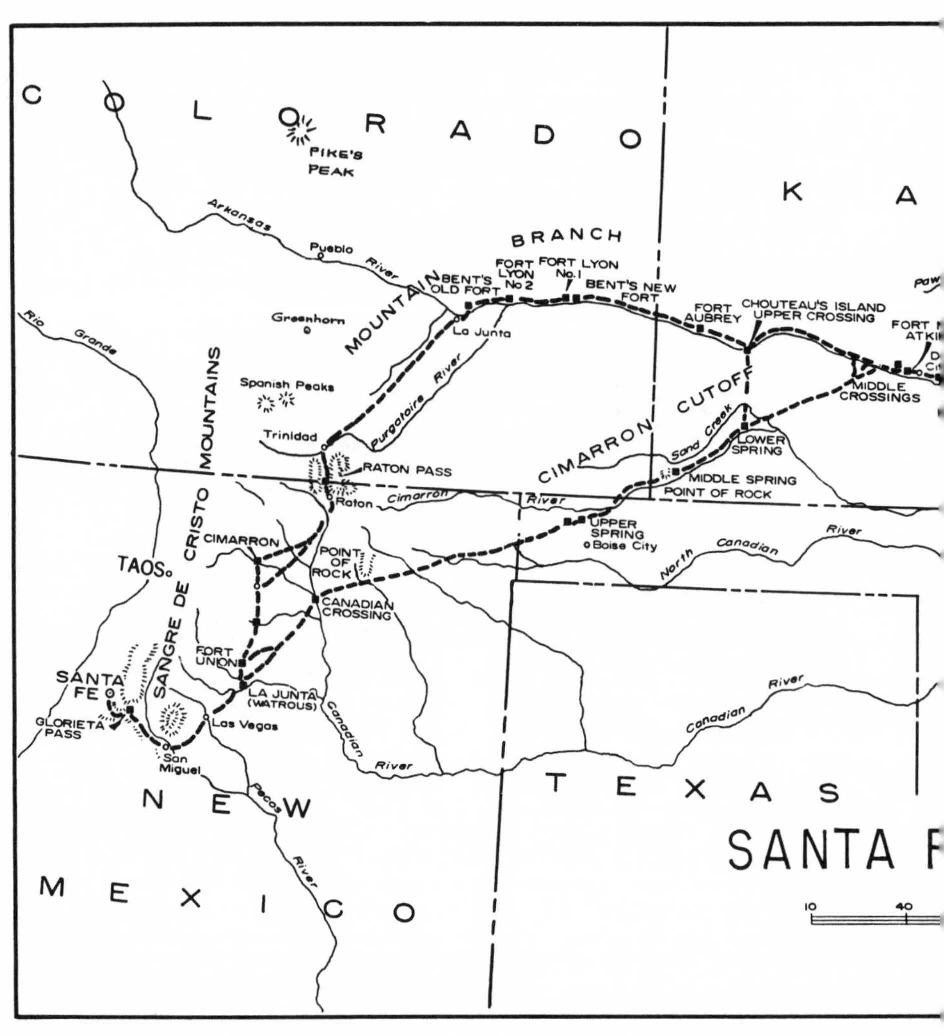

COLORADO
PIKE'S PEAK
Arkansas River
Pueblo
BRANCH
MOUNTAIN
BENT'S OLD FORT
FORT LYON No 2
FORT LYON No.1
BENT'S NEW FORT
FORT AUBREY
CHOUTEAU'S ISLAND UPPER CROSSING
MIDDLE CROSSINGS
K A
Greenhorn
La Junta
Rio Grande
Spanish Peaks
Purgatoire River
Trinidad
CIMARRON CUTOFF
Sand Creek
LOWER SPRING
MIDDLE SPRING
POINT OF ROCK
RATON PASS
Raton
Cimarron River
UPPER SPRING
Boise City
North Canadian River
SANGRE DE CRISTO MOUNTAINS
TAOS
CIMARRON
POINT OF ROCK
CANADIAN CROSSING
FORT UNION
SANTA FE
LA JUNTA (WATROUS)
GLORIETA PASS
Las Vegas
San Miguel
Canadian River
Canadian River
NEW MEXICO
Pecos River
TEXAS
SANTA F
10
40

The Santa Fe Trail

arteries being cut, to stop the bleeding he heated a king bolt of one of the wagons and burned the affected parts, and then applied a plaster of the tar taken from off the wheel of a wagon. The man became perfectly well before our arrival in New Mexico.[6]

We arrived in Santa Fe in November, and I proceeded to Fernandez de Taos,[7] my present place of residence, the same month, and remained during the winter with an old mountaineer by the name of Kincade.[8]

In the spring [1827] I started for the States but, on the Arkansas River, I met a party en route for New Mexico and I joined them and remained with them till their arrival in Santa Fe. I then hired with a man—his name I have forgotten—to drive team, my wages being one dollar per day. I remained in his employ till our arrival in El Paso. I took my discharge and returned to Santa Fe.

I left Santa Fe for Taos shortly after my arrival from El Paso and got employment of Mr. Ewing Young, to do his cooking, my board being the remuneration.[9] In the spring [1828], I once more departed for the States, met a party on the Arkansas, and again returned to Santa Fe. I then was employed by Col. Tramell, a merchant, as Interpreter.[10] I accompanied him to Chihuahua and then hired with Robert McKnight to go to the copper mines near Rio Gila.[11] I remained at the mines a few months, driving team. I was not satisfied with this employment, took my discharge, and departed for Taos, and arrived in August, 1828.

Some time before my arrival, Mr. Ewing Young had sent a party of trappers to the Colorado of the West. They, in a fight with the Indians, were defeated, having fought all of one day, and gaining no advantage, they considered it prudent to return.[12] Young then raised a party of forty men, consisting of Americans, Cana-

6
Andrew Broadus had been a member of Sibley's expedition in 1825. It is unreasonable to believe that Kit Carson performed the amputation, as stated by Blanche C. Grant in *Kit Carson's Own Story* (Taos, 1926), 10. As the narrative will attest, Carson himself made no such claim. The story of the amputation was repeated by Josiah Gregg in his *Commerce of the Prairies* (New York and London, 1844), 59–60.

7
A census of New Mexico compiled by order of the government gives the 1827 population of Santa Fe as 5,757 and that of Taos as 3,606 in that year. Santa Fe was the capital of New Mexico but the largest city was Santa Cruz de la Cañada, located between Santa Fe and Taos, with a population of 6,508. Taos enjoyed popularity with the trappers because it was nearer to good beaver country and because it was not under the direct scrutiny of governmental authorities.

8
Matthew Kinkead was born in Madison County, Kentucky, in 1795, and later moved to Boon's Lick, Howard County, Missouri, which may account for his befriending of Kit Carson, a boy of the same background. He served, along with the older Carson boys, in Captain Sarshall Cooper's Missouri Rangers during the War of 1812. He first came to New Mexico in 1824. Although, at thirty-one, he was about twice the age of Kit when they wintered together in 1826–27, he was not the old man that Carson made him out to be. He lived for a time at Mora, New Mexico, with Teresita Suaso, by whom he had a son, Andres, and a

daughter, Rafaela. From 1842 to 1847 he lived on the Arkansas, first at Pueblo and then above Hardscrabble. He was encountered on the Oregon Trail in 1848 and soon afterward went to California, where he spent his last years. He was a pioneer farmer and cattleman of the Arkansas Valley. See Janet S. Lecompte, " Matthew Kinkead," *Mountain Men* (ed. by Hafen), II, 187–99.

9

In historical significance, Ewing Young ranks among the most important of the fur traders and trappers of the Far West. He was born in Washington County, Tennessee, probably in 1792. He came to Santa Fe in 1822 and pioneered the trapping of the Arizona streams in the years prior to the 1829–31 expedition described by Carson. Carson learned a great deal from Young but he was an apt pupil and Young came to depend on him as one he could trust. Young went again to California in 1832, and thence guided Hall J. Kelley to Oregon in 1834. Despite unmerited suspicion by Dr. John McLoughlin, he succeeded in becoming a prosperous wheat farmer, cattle raiser, and pioneer lumberman in Oregon. He died there in 1841. A son, Joaquin, came from Taos to Oregon to successfully claim his estate. See Harvey L. Carter, "Ewing Young," *Mountain Men* (ed. by Hafen), II, 379–401.

10

This was Philip Trammell, a merchant of Franklin, Missouri, whose trading permit, or *guia,* was granted December 14, 1827. See David Weber, *The Extranjeros* (Santa Fe, 1976), 31, 43.

Carson's early facility with spoken Spanish is indicated by his having served as an interpreter.

11

Robert McKnight was born in Augusta County, Virginia, about 1789. Stimulated by the publication of the *Journals* of Zebulon Montgomery Pike, he formed a partnership with James Baird for exploitation of the Santa Fe trade in 1812. The entire party of ten men was imprisoned by the Spanish authorities. Finally released in 1821, after Mexican independence, they returned to St. Louis. Not liking the ineffective efforts of the Federal Government to secure compensation for his confiscated goods, McKnight returned to Santa Fe and became a Mexican citizen. He operated the Santa Rita del Cobra Copper Mine in present Grant County, New Mexico, until 1846, the year he died. See *A Message From the President of the United States Relative to the Arrest and Imprisonment of Certain American Citizens at Santa Fe . . . April 15, 1818* (Washington, 1818), 15 Cong. 1 sess., *H.R. Doc. 197*, Serial 12.

12

Carson refers here to the fact that Young had sent, not led, a party of trappers to the Gila River in 1828,

diams and Frenchmen, and took command. I joined the party. We left Taos in August, 1829.

In those days licenses were not granted to citizens of the United States to trap within the limits of the Mexican territory.[13] To avoid all mistrust on the part of the Government officers, we travelled in a northern direction for fifty miles, and then changed our course to southwest, travelled through the country occupied by the Navajo Indians, passed the village of Zuni, and on to the head of the Salt River, one of the tributaries of Rio Gila.[14]

We, on the headwaters of the Salt River, met the same Indians that had defeated the former party.[15] Young directed the greater part of his men to hide themselves, which was done, the men concealing themselves under blankets, pack saddles, and as best they could. The hills were covered with Indians and seeing so few, they came to the conclusion to make an attack and drive us from our position. Our commander allowed them to enter the camp and then directed the party to fire on them, which was done, the Indians losing in killed fifteen or twenty warriors and great number in wounded. The Indians were routed, and we continued our march and trapped down the Salt River to the mouth of San Francisco River, and up to the head of the latter stream.[16] We were nightly harassed by the Indians. They would frequently of nights crawl into our camp, steal a trap or so, kill a mule or horse, and endeavor to do what damage they could.

The party was divided on the head of San Francisco River; one party to proceed to the Valley of Sacramento in California, of which I was a member, and the other party to return to Taos for the purpose of procuring traps to replace those stolen, and to dispose of the Beaver we had caught. Young took charge of the party for California, consisting of eighteen men.

but they soon returned because of trouble with the Apaches. They did not reach the Colorado River.

13
Governor Armijo had reversed the policy of granting licenses to trap, instituted by his predecessor Governor Narbona. In the summer of 1827, Ewing Young had been imprisoned, had his furs confiscated, and his license revoked. In order to avoid trouble in 1829 he pretended to be heading for American territory and then doubled back to reach the streams of Arizona.

14
The Salt or Salido River rises near the Arizona-New Mexico border and flows westward through present Phoenix to its junction with the Gila River, which, in turn, empties into the Colorado River near Yuma.

15
They were Apache Indians, probably Coyotero Apaches.

16
What Carson calls the San Francisco River is today called the Verde River. Its junction with the Salt River is a few miles east of present Phoenix. Both Salt River and Verde River were good beaver streams.

We remained a few days after the departure of the party for Taos, for the purpose of procuring meat and making the necessary arrangement for a trip over a country never explored.[17] Game was very scarce. After remaining three days continually on the hunt to procure the necessaries, we had only killed three deer, the skins of which we took off in such a manner as to make tanks for the purpose of carrying water. We then started on our expedition in the best of spirits, having heard from the Indians that the streams of the valley to which we were going were full of Beaver, but the country over which we were to travel was very barren, and that we would suffer very much for want of water, the truth of which we very soon knew.

The first four days march was over a country sandy, burned up, and not a drop of water. We received at night a small quantity of water from the tanks which we had been fortunate to have along. A guard was then placed over the tanks to prohibit anyone from making use of more than his due allowance.

After four days travel we found water. Before we reached the water the pack mules were strung along the road for several miles. They having smelt the water long before we had any hopes of finding any, and then each animal made the best use of the strength left them after their severe sufferings to reach the water as soon as they could. We remained two days. It would have been impracticable to have continued the march without giving the men and animals rest they so much required.

After remaining two days encamped we started on our expedition and for four days travelled over country similar to that which we travelled over before our arrival to the last water. There was not any water to be found during this time, and we suffered extremely on account of it. On the fourth day we arrived on the Colo-

17
From the headwaters of the Verde River, their route lay northwest to the Colorado River just below the Grand Canyon. A spring near present Truxton, Arizona, was formerly known as Young's Spring. See Charles L. Camp, "Kit Carson in California," *California Historical Society Quarterly*, Vol. I (October, 1922), 117–18.

18
They were near present Topock, Arizona, where the Santa Fe railroad crosses the river.

19
This stream was the Mojave River of Southern California. On leaving it, they traveled over the Old Spanish Trail pioneered by Padre Francisco Garcés in 1776.

20
Jedediah Smith had visited San Gabriel Mission for several days in the late fall of 1826, and James Ohio Pattie had innoculated 960 people there against smallpox only a few months prior to Young's arrival. Padre José Bernardo Sanchez was in charge of the mission during the

rado of the West, below the Great Cañon.[18] It can better be imagined, our joy, than described, when we discovered the stream.

We had suffered greatly for want of food. We met a party of the Mohavi Indians and purchased of them a mare, heavy with foal. The animal was killed and eaten by the party with great gusto; even the foal was devoured. We [encamped] on the banks of the Colorado three days, recruiting our animals and trading for provisions with the Indians. We procured of them a few beans and corn. [Then] we took a southwestern course and in three days' march, struck the bed of a stream which rises in the coast range, has a northeast course, and is lost in the sands of the Great Basin.[19] We proceeded up the stream for six days. In two days after our arrival on the stream, we found water. We then left the stream and travelled in a westerly direction and in four days, arrived at the Mission of San Gabriel.[20]

At the Mission there was one priest, fifteen soldiers, and about one thousand Indians. They had about eighty thousand head of stock, fine fields and vineyards—in fact, it was paradise on earth. We remained one day at the Mission, received good treatment of the inhabitants, and purchased of them what beef we required. We had nothing but butcher knives to trade, and for four they would give a beef.

In one day's travel from this Mission, we reached the mission of San Fernando[21] having about the same number of inhabitants, but not carried on as large as the one of San Gabriel. We then took a northwest course and passed the mountains to the valley of the Sacramento. We had plenty to eat and found grass in abundance for our animals. We found signs of trappers on the San Joaquin. We followed their trail and, in a few days, overtook the party and found them to be of the Hudson Bay Company.[22] They were sixty men strong, commanded by Peter Ogden.[23]

period of these first three American visits. San Gabriel Mission was founded in 1771, by Padre Junipero Serra. Only the church is still standing today. Young and Carson did not visit the pueblo of Los Angeles, ten miles to the west of San Gabriel. See Dale L. Morgan, *Jedediah Smith and the Opening of the West* (Indianapolis and New York, 1953), 201–204; James O. Pattie, *The Personal Narrative of James O. Pattie of Kentucky*, edited by Timothy Flint, with historical introduction and footnotes by Milo M. Quaife (Chicago, 1930), 348–49.

21 Founded in 1797, the Mission of San Fernando stood twenty miles north of Los Angeles in the San Fernando Valley. It was abandoned, in 1847, at the time of the American conquest of California. The Young party passed into the valley of the San Joaquin rather than into the Sacramento Valley, as Carson states.

22 The Hudson's Bay Company was founded in England in 1670, as a result of the efforts of Radisson and Groseillers, French-Canadian explorers who were unable to interest the French government in their plans for a fur-trading company. It is still in existence.

23 In historical significance, Peter Skene Ogden, like Ewing Young, was one of the most important fur traders. He was born in Quebec in 1794, of Tory parents who had migrated there from New Jersey at the close of the American Revolution. He made his first appearance west of the Rockies in 1818. From 1821, when the North-

We trapped down the San Joaquin and its tributaries and found but little beaver, but game plenty, elk, deer, and antelope in thousands. We travelled near each other until we came to the Sacramento; then we separated, Ogden taking up the Sacramento for Columbia river.[24] We remained during the summer. [It] not being the season for trapping, we passed our time in hunting.

During our stay on the Sacramento a party of Indians of the Mission of San Rafael ran away and took refuge at a village of Indians that were not friendly with those of the Mission.[25] The priest of San Rafael sent a party of fifteen Indians in pursuit. They applied for assistance from a village that was friendly and were furnished with the number they required. They then moved towards the village where the runaways were concealed and demanded them to be given up, which was refused. They attacked the village and after a severe struggle they were compelled to retreat. They came to us and requested assistance. Mr. Young directed me and eleven men to join. We turned to the village and made an attack, fought for one entire day. The Indians were routed; [they] lost a great number of men. We entered the village in triumph, set fire to it, and burned it to the ground.

The next day we demanded the runaways and informed them that if not immediately given up we would not leave one of them alive. They complied with our demands. We turned over the Indians to those from whom they had deserted and we returned to our camp. Mr. Young and four of us proceeded with the Indians to San Rafael. We took with us the Beaver we had on hand. We were well received by the missionaries.

At the Mission we found a trading schooner, the Captain of which was ashore.[26] We traded with him our furs and for the money, purchased

west Company merged with the Hudson's Bay Company, until his death in 1854, he was the most active and far-ranging trader and trapper in the employ of the company. His journal of the trip mentioned by Carson was lost when his boat upset at the Dalles of the Columbia River on July 3, 1830. See John Scaglione, "Ogden's Report of his 1829–1830 Expedition," *California Historical Society Quarterly*, Vol. XXVIII (June, 1949), 117–24; and Ted J. Warner, "Peter Skene Ogden," *Mountain Men and the Fur Trade of the Far West*, III (edited by LeRoy R. Hafen) (Glendale, 1966), 213–38. Hereafter referred to as *Mountain Men* (ed. by Hafen), III.

24
Actually, the Young and Ogden parties seem to have traveled up the Sacramento River to the Pit River before they separated. The summer referred to was that of 1830.

25
The Mission of San Rafael, north of San Francisco, was established in 1817 and had more than eleven hundred Indians attached to it. Joseph J. Hill, "Ewing Young in the Fur Trade of the Southwest, 1822–1834," *Oregon Historical Society Quarterly*, Vol. XXIV (March, 1923), 25, following H. H. Bancroft, attributes this incident of the runaway Indians to the Mission of San José, established in 1797. It appears that Carson confused the two missions in his memory of this incident.

26
Hill, "Ewing Young," *Oregon Historical Society Quarterly*, Vol. XXIV (March, 1923), identifies the ship captain as Don José Asero.

horse[s] of those at the Mission. After having purchased all we required, [we] returned to our camp. Shortly after, a party of Indians during the night came to our camp, frightened our animals and ran off some sixty head. Fourteen were discovered in the morning. Twelve of us saddled and took the trail of the lost animals, pursued them upwards of one hundred miles into the Sierra Nevada. We surprised the Indians when feasting of[f] some of our animals they had killed. We charged their camp, killed eight Indians, took three children prisoners and recovered all our animals, with the exception of six that were eaten, and returned to our camp.

On the first Septr. we struck camp and, returning by the same route which we had come, passing through San Fernando. We traveled to the Pueblo of Los Angeles, where the Mexican authorities demanded our passports.[27] We had none. They wished to arrest us but fear deterred them. They then commenced selling liquor to the men, no doubt for the purpose of getting the men drunk so that they would have but little difficulty in making the arrest. Mr. Young discovered their intentions, directed me to take three men, all the loose animals, packs, etc. and go in advance. He would remain with the balance of the party and endeavor to get them along. If he did not arrive at my camp by next morning I was directed to move on as best I could and, on my return to report the party killed, for Young would not leave them. They were followed by the Mexicans, furnishing them all the liquor they could pay for. All got drunk except Young. The Mexicans would have continued with them till they arrived at the Mission of San Gabriel, then, being re-inforced, arrest the party, only for a man by the name of Jas. Higgins dismounting from his horse and deliberately shooting Jas. Lawrence. Such conduct frightened the Mexicans, and they departed in

27
Spanish policy had always been to exclude foreigners from the colonies and to imprison interlopers who ignored regulations. The policy was considerably relaxed, both in New Mexico and California, after Mexican independence. Nevertheless, foreigners were still regarded with suspicion by the authorities. Carson does not mention the names of the officials, but the governor was José Maria de Echeandia, who had imprisoned the Pattie party three years earlier. Young's experience in 1830 prompted him to obtain both an American and a New Mexican passport prior to his second expedition to California.

28
Doubtless Carson's conclusion is correct. However, he was not completely informed about the cause of all the trouble. Three of Young's men, Francois Turcote, Jean Vaillant, and Anastase Carier, decided to return to New Mexico and went to Monterey to request passports for that purpose. The would-be deserters were apprehended by Young and forced to remain with the party. Their action had brought to the attention of the Mexican officials the fact that Young's party had entered California and traveled about as it pleased without permission. From Carson, we know the names of James Higgins and James Lawrence; from the Mexican records, we know the names of these three Frenchmen; adding the names of Carson and Young, we know the names of seven of Young's party of nineteen. Francisco Turcot, aged sixty, born in Canada, was living north of Taos, according to the U.S. Census of 1850 for Taos County, New Mexico.

There is a slight discrepancy beall haste, fearing that if men, without provocation, would shoot one another, it would require but little to cause them to murder them.[28]

About dark Young and party found me. The next day we departed and pursued nearly the same route by which we came, and in nine days we arrived on the Colorado. Two days after our arrival on the Colorado, at least five hundred Indian warriors came to our camp. They pretended friendship, but a such large number coming, we mistrusted them and closely watched their manoeuvers. We discovered where they had their weapons concealed, and then it became apparent to us that their design was to murder the party. There were but few of us in camp, the greater number being out visiting their traps. I considered the safest way to act was not to let the Indians know of our mistrust and to act in a fearless manner. One of the Indians could speak Spanish. I directed him to state to the Indians that they must leave our camp inside of ten minutes. If one should be found after the expiration of that time, he would be shot. Before the expiration of the ten minutes, everyone had left.

We trapped down the south side of Colorado River to tide water without any further molestation, and up the north side to the mouth of the Gila, then up the Gila to near the mouth of San Pedro.[29] Near the mouth of the San Pedro, we saw a large herd of animals, horses, etc. We knew that Indians were near, and not having forgot the damage those same Indians done, we concluded to deprive them of their stock. We charged their camp. They fled, and we took possession of the animals. The same evening we heard a noise, something like the sound of distant thunder. We sprung for our arms and sallied out to reconnoiter. We discovered a party of Indians driving some two hundred horses. We charged them, firing a few shots. The Indians run, leaving us sole possessors of the horses.

tween the number of the party as recalled by Carson and that stated by Young, who told the California authorities that he had twenty-two men, all but one of whom had come with him from New Mexico. James J. Hill, "Ewing Young in the Fur Trade of the Far Southwest," *Oregon Historical Quarterly*, Vol. XXIV (March, 1923), 23–25.

29
The San Pedro River enters the Gila from the south about forty miles east of Florence, Arizona.

30
The Gila River rises about forty miles due north of the Santa Rita del Cobra mines. They left the river in the vicinity of present Gila, New Mexico, and went eastward to the mines.

31
The fact that only Carson remained behind with Young is an indication that Young considered him the most reliable member of the party, despite his relative youth and inexperience. It is probable that beaver was worth at least $4.00 per pound in Santa Fe, and perhaps as much as $5.00 per pound.

32
Carson has furnished us with a good description of the carefree life of the trappers when they had money. This was the way they rewarded themselves for the privations and exertions of their lonely and strenuous life when they were actively engaged in getting furs. The same pattern was followed by the cowboys of the later frontier.

Those horses had been stolen by the Indians from Mexicans in Sonora. Having now more animals than we could take care of, we concluded to dispose of them to best advantage. We chose out as many as we required for riding and packing purposes, killed ten, dried the meat to take with us, and left the balance loose. I presume the Indians got them.

We continued up the Gila to opposite the copper mines.[30] We went to the mines, found Robert McKnight, then left our beaver with him. We could not bring it to the settlements to dispose of on account of not having license to trap in Mexican Territory. We concealed our beaver in one of the deep holes dug by the miners. Young and I remained a few days at the mines, the balance of the party had started for Taos.[31] Young and I went to Santa Fe. He procured a license to trade with Indians on the Gila. He sent a few men to the mines to get the beaver he had concealed. They got it and returned to Santa Fe. Every one considered we had made a fine trade in so short a period. They were not aware that we had been months trapping. The Beaver was disposed of to advantage at Santa Fe, some two thousand pounds in all.

In April, 1830 [1831], we had all safely arrived at Taos. The amount due us was paid and each of us having several hundred dollars, we passed the time gloriously, spending our money freely—never thinking that our lives were risked in gaining it. Our only idea was to get rid of the dross as soon as possible but, at the same time, have as much pleasure and enjoyment as the country would afford. Trappers and sailors are similar in regard to the money that they earn so dearly, daily being in danger of losing their lives. But when the voyage has been made [and they have] received their pay, they think not of the hardships and danger through which they have passed, spend all they have and are ready for

33 Thomas Fitzpatrick was at this time a partner in the Rocky Mountain Fur Company, formed at the rendezvous of 1830 when he and James Bridger, Milton Sublette, Henry Fraeb, and Jean Baptiste Gervais bought out the firm of Jedediah Smith, David Jackson, and William Sublette. Fitzpatrick had been forced to accompany Smith, Jackson, and Sublette on their expedition to Santa Fe (in the course of which Smith had been killed by Indians) in order to secure trade goods to take to his partners in the Rocky Mountains. Fitzpatrick, born in Ireland in 1798, died in Washington, D.C., in 1854. Known to the Indians as Broken Hand, he was in later life, like Carson, a guide for Frémont and an Indian Agent. See LeRoy R. Hafen and William J. Ghent, *Broken Hand: The Life of Thomas Fitzpatrick, Chief of the Mountain Men* (Denver, 1931), for an able full-length biography.

34 Carson refers to the North Platte River. They traveled on the main north-and-south trail, used by the Indians and trappers, which skirted the eastern edge of the Front Range of the Rocky Mountains.

35 Jackson's Hole, an extensive mountain meadow, lies between the Tetons and the Wind River Mountains some forty miles south of Yellowstone Park. The Snake River runs through it. It took its name from David Jackson, of Smith, Jackson, and Sublette, in 1829, although it had been explored by John Colter as early as 1807–1808 and by Andrew Henry's trappers in 1810. See DeVoto, *Across the Wide Missouri*, 387, 389.

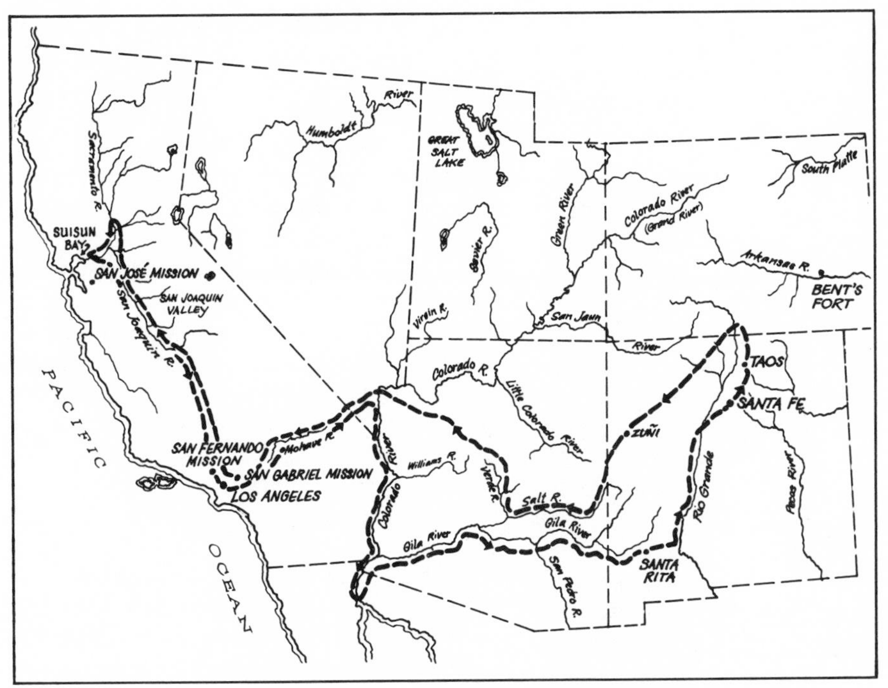


Ewing Young's California Expedition, 1829–31

another trip. In all probability [they] have to be furnished with all that is necessary for their outfit.[32]

In the fall of 1830 [1831] I joined the party under Fitzpatrick, for the Rocky Mountains on a trapping expedition.[33] We traveled north till we struck the Platte River and then took up the Sweetwater, a branch of the Platte.[34] We trapped to the head of the Sweetwater and then on to Green River, and then to Jackson's Hole,[35] a fork of the Columbia River; and from there on to the head of Salmon River.[36] Then we came to the camp of a part of our band that we had been hunting, then we went into winter quarters on the head of Salmon River. During winter we lost some four or five men when out hunting Buffalo. They have been killed by the Blackfeet Indians.[37]

In April 1831, [1832] we commenced our hunt again. We trapped back on to Bear River, the principal stream that empties into the Great Salt Lake, then on to Green River. We there found a party of trapper[s] under charge of Mr. Sinclair.[38] They [had] left Taos shortly after we had. They had wintered on little Bear River, a branch of Green.[39] They told me that Capt. Gaunt was in the New Park, that he and party had wintered near the Laramie. I wished to join his party.[40] Four of us left the party and struck out in search of Gaunt. In ten days, we found him and party at the New Park.[41]

We remained trapping in the Park for some time, and then through the plains of Laramie and on to the south fork of the Platte, then to the Arkansas.[42] On our arrival on the Arkansas, Gaunt took the Beaver we had caught to Taos. The party remained on the Arkansas, trapping. The Beaver was disposed of, the necessaries for our camp were purchased, and in the course of two months Gaunt joined [us]. We trapped on the waters of the Arkansas until the river began

36
The Salmon River heads in the mountains of east central Idaho, two-hundred miles west of Jackson's Hole.

37
Prior to the smallpox epidemic of 1837, trapping companies in the northern Rocky Mountains were constantly beset by the Blackfeet. Their home territory extended from the Yellowstone River northward into Canada and from the Continental Divide eastward to the lands of the Sioux. There were four subtribes commonly classed as Blackfeet. They were the Blackfoot proper, the Piegans, the Bloods, and the Gros Ventres, who were really northern Arapahoes who had assimilated the customs of the Blackfeet. Actually, the Bloods were most frequently encountered by the trappers.

38
Alexander Sinclair was one of forty-two trappers recruited in Arkansas and led to the Rocky Mountains in 1830 under the captaincy of Robert Bean. Bean "showed the white feather" in the first skirmish with Indians and returned to Arkansas. The company broke up in Taos during the winter of 1830–31, but Alexander Sinclair led fifteen of them north to trap and they wintered in Brown's Hole in 1831–32. The death of Alexander Sinclair at the battle of Pierre's Hole, in July, 1832, caused the final dissolution of his band of trappers. See LeRoy R. Hafen, "The Bean-Sinclair Party of Trappers, 1830–1832," *Colorado Magazine* Vol. XXXI (July, 1954), 161–71; and George Nidiver, *The Life and Adventures of George Nidiver, 1802–1883*, edited by William H. Ellison (Berkeley, 1937), 6–27.

to freeze, and then went into winter quarters on the main stream.[43] During the winter we passed a pleasant time. The snow was very deep and we had no difficulty in procuring as much buffalo meat as we required.

In January [1833] a party of men had been out hunting and returned about dark. Their horses were very poor, having been fed during the winter on cottonwood bark; they turned them out to gather such nourishment as they could. That night a party of about fifty Crow Indians came to our camp and stole nine of the horses that were loose.[44] In the morning we discovered sign of the Indians and twelve of us took the trail of the Indians and horses. We travelled some forty miles. It was getting late. Our animals were fatigued for [on] the course over which we came, the snow was deep, and many herds of buffaloes having passed during the day was the cause of our having a great deal of difficulty in keeping the trail.

We saw, at a distance of two or three miles, a grove of timber. Taking into consideration the condition of our animals, we concluded to make for the timber and camp for the night. On our arrival, we saw fires some four miles ahead of us. We tied our animals to trees and, as soon as it became dark, we took a circuitous route for the Indian Camp.

We were to come on the Indians from the direction in which they were traveling. It took us some time to get close enough to the camp to discover their strength. We had to crawl, and used all means that we were aware of, to elude detection. After considerable crawling etc., we came within about one hundred yards of their camp. The Indians were in two forts of about equal strength. They were dancing and singing, and passing the night jovially in honor of the robbery committed by them on the whites. We saw four horses. They were tied at the entrance

39
The Yampa River, a tributary of Green River in northwestern Colorado, was called the Little Bear River by the trappers of this time.

40
Captain John Gantt was born in Queen Anne, Maryland, in 1790. He was an officer in the U.S. Army from 1817 to 1829, serving on the Missouri River frontier. When he was discharged from the Army as a result of court-martial proceedings, he formed a partnership with Jefferson Blackwell, of St. Louis, and entered the fur trade, in which he was active from 1831 to 1834. In the latter year he built Fort Cass on the Arkansas River six miles east of present Pueblo, Colorado, and initiated trade with the Cheyennes and Arapahoes. Plagued by unfounded rumors that his firm was insolvent, circulated by Thomas Fitzpatrick in 1832, and out-traded by William Bent on the Arkansas, Gantt abandoned the fur trade in late 1834. He guided Colonel Henry Dodge's Dragoons to the Rockies in 1835 and later guided overland parties to California, where he died in 1849. See Harvey L. Carter, "John Gantt," *Mountain Men and the Fur Trade of the Far West*, V (edited by LeRoy R. Hafen) (Glendale, 1968), 101–16. Hereafter referred to as *Mountain Men* (ed. by Hafen), V, and Zenas Leonard, *The Adventures of Zenas Leonard*, edited by John C. Ewers (Norman, 1959), 3–42; and Janet S. Lecompte, "Gantt's Fort and Bent's Picket Post," *Colorado Magazine*, Vol. XLI (Spring, 1964), 111–25, a most important article.

41
The New Park, also called North Park, was sometimes referred to as

of the fort. Let come what would [we] were bound to get our horses. We remained concealed in the brush until they laid down to sleep, [we] suffering severely from the cold.

When we thought they were all asleep, six of us crawled towards the animals. The remainder was to remain where they were as a reserve for us to fall back on in case of not meeting with success. By hiding behind logs and crawling silently towards the fort, the snow being of great service to us for when crawling we were not liable to make any noise, we finally reached the horses, cut the ropes and, by throwing snow balls at them, drove them to where was stationed our reserve. We then held council taking the views of each in regard to what had best be done. Some were in favor of retiring; having recovered their property and received no damage, they would be willing to return to camp. Not so with those that had lost no animals. They wanted satisfaction for the trouble and hardships they had gone through while in pursuit of the thieves. Myself and two more were the ones that had not lost horses and we were determined to have satisfaction, let the consequence be ever so fatal.[45] The peace party could not get a convert to their [side]. Seeing us so determined for a fight (there is always a brotherly affection existing among the trappers and the side of danger always being their choice) we were not long before all agreed to join us in our perilous enterprise.[46]

We started the horses that were retaken to the place where we tied our other animals, with three men as escort. We then marched direct for the fort from which we got our horses. When within a few paces of the fort, a dog discovered us and commenced barking. The Indians were alarmed and commenced getting up. We opened a deadly fire, each ball taking its victim. We killed nearly every Indian in the fort. The few that remained were wounded and made their

Park Kyack or the Bull Pen, because of the buffalo herds there. It is located on the headwaters of the North Platte, just east of the Continental Divide and between the Park Range and the Medicine Bow Range of the Rocky Mountains. It comprises most of Jackson County, Colorado.

42
The Laramie Plains is the name given to the high, level country around present Laramie, Wyoming, across which the Laramie River flows before cutting through the Laramie Mountains to join the North Platte River near the site of Old Fort Laramie.

43
Gantt's winter quarters were in the vicinity of present Pueblo, Colorado.

44
The home range of the Crows was between the Yellowstone and North Platte Rivers and east of the Wind River Range. They were considered to be the most accomplished horse thieves of all the Western Indians, generally content to rob the whites rather than kill them and end the opportunities for stealing from them in the future.

45
The determination to fight, simply for the excitement and adventure involved in doing so, is of considerable interest. That the young Kit Carson had such determination was a fact of which the mature Carson, noted for his caution, would certainly have disapproved. Yet it is obvious, from the space devoted to this incident, that Carson enjoyed re-living the experience in telling about it.

escape to the other fort, the Indians of which commenced firing on us; but without any effect, we keeping concealed behind trees and only firing when we were sure of our object. It was now near day, the Indians could see our force, and it being so weak, they concluded to charge on us. We received them and when very close, fired on them, killing five and the balance returned to their fort. After some deliberation among the Indians, they finally made another attempt which met with greater success to them. We had to retreat but, there being much timber in the vicinity, we had but little difficulty in making our camp, and then, being reinforced by the three men with the horses, we awaited the approach of the enemy. They did not attack us. We started for our main camp and arrived in the evening. During our pursuit for the lost animals we suffered considerably but, in the success of having recovered our horses and sending many a redskin to his long home, our sufferings were soon forgotten.[47] We remained in our camp without any further molestation until Spring [1833]. We then started for Laramie on another trapping expedition.

Before our departure we cached what Beaver we had on hand, some four hundred pounds. When we arrived on the south fork of the Platte, two men of the party deserted, taking with them three of our best animals. We suspected their design, and Gaunt sent myself and another man in pursuit. They had a day the start and we could not overtake them. When we arrived at our old camp, we discovered that they had raised the Beaver and taken it down the Arkansas in a canoe which we had made during the winter for the purpose of crossing the river. The men and beaver we never heard of. I presume they were killed by Indians. Such a fate they should receive for their dishonesty. The animals we recovered and contented ourselves happy; they be-

46
Carson's insistence of the brotherly affection of trappers is in marked contrast to Joe Meek's insistence that every man looked out for himself and disregarded the welfare of his fellow trappers. It is chiefly a measure of the psychological differences between Carson and Meek, for numerous instances supporting each man's point view are to be found in the literature of the fur trade. For Meek's view, see Frances Fuller Victor, *River of the West* (Hartford, 1870), 250.

47
Curiously enough, the story of this fight seems to have survived among the Cheyenne Indians. Black Whiteman, one of two Cheyennes who accompanied Gantt's men, told the story to George Bird Grinnell. He claimed that the white trappers killed only two of the Crows, the two Cheyennes accounting for the other deaths. See Stanley Vestal, *Kit Carson, Happy Warrior of the Old West* (Boston and New York, 1928), 67–71. The scene of this fight was just south of present Colorado Springs, Colorado.

48
Joe Meek, however, related that he and Carson and Levin Mitchell, together with three Delaware Indians, Manhead, Jonas, and Tom Hill, made an excursion into the Comanche country in the spring of 1834. That he was in error as to the date we know from his reference to the death of a trapper named Guthrie by a stroke of lightning in the Bayou Salade soon afterward. This definitely occurred in 1833. The only year that Carson could possibly have made such a trip is 1833, while he was at Gantt's houses on the Arkansas. They could have encountered Co-

ing of much more service to us than men that we could never more trust.

We took possession of one of the buildings that were built during the winter and made the necessary preparations for our defense, not having the remotest idea how long we should have to remain. Being by ourselves we never ventured very far from our fort unless for the purpose of procuring meat. We kept our horses picketed near and at night slept in the house, always keeping a good lookout so that we might not be surprised when unprepared.[48] We remained about a month and Mr. Blackwell, Gaunt's partner, arrived from the States.[49] He had with him some ten or fifteen men. Shortly after their arrival four trappers of Gaunt's party arrived. They were sent to find us to see whether we were dead or alive, the former being the general belief.

We remained only a few days after the arrival of the trappers. They stated that Gaunt's camp was in the Balla Salado [Bayou Salade], the head waters of the south fork of the Platte.[50] When four days on the march, we were encamped, all sitting eating of our breakfast, we discovered a party of Indians trying to steal our horses. We suspected no danger and had turned our horses out to graze, some hobbled and some [loose]. As soon as we perceived the Indians, we made for them. They run off. One Indian was killed. They only stole from us one horse; one of the Indians having been lucky enough to have mounted one of the loose horses and made his escape.

We then traveled that day about fifty miles and thought that we had got clear of the Indians. We camped on a beautiful stream, one of the tributaries of the Arkansas.[51] During the night we had our best animals staked. We had with us a very watchful dog and during the night he kept continually barking. We were aware of Indians being close and kept good watch. In the morning, myself and three others proposed go-

manches anywhere south of that river, so they may not have gone far. As Meek tells it, they cut the throats of their mules and forted up behind them to hold off two hundred Comanches, of whom they shot forty-two. The Indians' horses shied off at the scent of the mule blood and would not approach near enough for the Indians to overwhelm the trappers. Under cover of night, the six trappers made their way back to the Arkansas on foot. See Victor, *River*, 154–158. Fitzpatrick's letter of November 13, 1833, which fixes the date of Guthrie's death and consequently the date of the mule fort incident, is in the Sublette Papers, Missouri Historical Society, St. Louis, Missouri.

49 Beyond the fact that he was Gantt's partner, very little is known of Jefferson Blackwell. His job was to bring out the trading goods while his partner conducted the trapping operations. Blackwell was known among the Cheyennes as Tall Crane. He is said to have fathered a child among the Cheyennes. See George Bird Grinnell, "Bent's Old Fort and Its Builders," *Kansas Historical Society Collections* (1919–22), XV, 18.

50 Balla Salado is Carson's rendering into Spanish of the French term, Bayou Salade, otherwise known as South Park. Smaller high mountain meadows were known to the trappers as holes, but the more extensive ones were designated parks. South Park was first explored by Captain Zebulon Montgomery Pike in December, 1806. The sources of the South Platte rise in the mountains on its western and northwestern borders. Buffalo entered it from the east by way of

ing to a fork that we knew of, it not being far, and we wished to visit [it] to see for Beaver sign. If good we intended to trap it; if not, to proceed on our journey.

About an hour after we left, a large party of Indians charged the camp running off all the loose animals. Four men immediately mounted four of the best animals and followed and in a short time overtook the Indians and recaptured all of the animals. One of the four was severely wounded in the affray. One Indian was killed.

The route which we had to go to reach the fork was over a mountain that was difficult to pass. After some trouble, we crossed, and arrived at our destination but found no Beaver sign. On our return we took a different route from that which we had come. As we got around the mountain and were near our former trail, I saw in the distance four Indians. I proposed to charge them.[52] All were willing. We started for them, but when near we found we had caught a tartar. There were upwards of sixty Indians. They had surrounded us and our only chance to save our lives was a good run. We done so, the Indians firing on us from all directions. We run the gauntlet for about two hundred yards, the Indians were often as near as twenty yards of us. We durst not fire, not knowing what moment our horses might be shot from under us and the idea of being left afoot, your gun unloaded, was enough for to make any man retain the shot which his gun contained. We finally made our escape and joined the party at the camp. One of the men was severely wounded, it being the only damage we received.

On our arrival at camp we were informed of what had transpired during our absence. It was then easy enough to account for the Indians having followed us. They saw us leave camp and, as they had the misfortune to lose the animals they had stolen, they intended to have our scalps.

Kenosha Pass at its northeastern extremity. It comprises about half of the area of Park County, Colorado, and has an elevation of from 8,000 to 9,500 feet.

51
Chalk Creek or Cottonwood Creek is indicated, depending on whether they went south or north after reaching the Arkansas River by way of Trout Creek Pass.

52
An error in judgment by Carson, which demonstrates that his habitual caution in later years was acquired. His inclination was toward action.

53
Old Park was the name used by the trappers for what is now called Middle Park. Lying on the upper waters of the Grand River, now called the Colorado River, it is less well-defined and less level than North Park or South Park. It is the only one of the three parks on the western slope of the Continental Divide. Its elevation is from 8,000 to 9,000 feet and it comprises the southern half of Grand County, Colorado.

54
Carson and his two unnamed companions became free trappers with no obligation to sell their furs to any particular company. Up to this time, he had been employed either at a set seasonal wage or as a free trapper, who had agreed to sell his furs to his successive employers, Young, Fitzpatrick, and Gantt.

55
It was long assumed that this was Stephen Louis Lee, who came to Santa Fe in 1824 and was killed in the Taos Revolt of January, 1847.

This asumption was erroneous. Carson's employer was Captain Richard Bland Lee, a career Army officer stationed at St. Louis during this period but sent to Santa Fe by the War Department on some unknown mission. Lee's explanation of his long stay abroad is found in his letter to the Adjutant General, dated at Washington, D.C., November 4, 1834, the original of which is in the National Archives.

Lee says that he left Abiquiu with twelve men (among whom was Carson, though unmentioned) on November 19, 1833, and arrived at the junction of White and Green Rivers after a march of forty-three days, remaining there till February 22, 1834. On this date he began a march of twenty days which took him to [Little] Snake River. He then returned by a mountain route to Santa Fe, arriving there on June 12, 1834. On August 5, he returned to Missouri with a caravan, reaching Independence on October 3, 1834. The *Missouri Republican*, October 14, 1834, reported that "A small company of traders arrived in this city [St. Louis] last week from Santa Fe . . . among the number who have returned is Capt. R. B. Lee, U. S. Army. The present company brought with them eleven wagons, with the contents, belonging to Messers. Bent, St. Vrain and Co." See Sabin, *Kit Carson Days*, II (1935), Note 199, p. 928.

Richard Bland Lee was of the famous Lee family of Virginia and was a first cousin of Robert E. Lee. He was at West Point in 1814 and, after a long army career, fought for the South in the Civil War. He died in 1875. See Francis B. Heitman, *Historical Register and Dictionary of the United States Army*, I (Washington-1903), 625. Although Lee promised

They made a very good attempt, but thank God, failed.

We made a fort and remained encamped for the night—could not move until the wounded men were properly cared for. In the morning we made a litter to carry one of the wounded—the other could ride horseback—and then pursued our course and in four days march we found Gaunt, remained at camp until our wounded men recovered, then started for the Old Park.[53] We found Beaver scarce, there having been so many trappers before us.

I and two others concluded to leave the party and go make a hunt on our own hook.[54] We trapped nearly all the streams within the mountains, keeping from the plains from fear of danger. We had very good luck; having caught a great amount of Beaver, we started for Taos to dispose of it and then have the pleasure of spending the money that caused us so much danger and hardship to earn. We arrived at Taos in October, 1832 [1833], disposed of our beaver for a good sum, and everything of mountain life was forgotten for the time present.

In Taos, I found Captain Lee[55] of the U.S.A., a partner of Bent and St. Vrain.[56] He purchased goods to trade with the trappers. I joined him and in the latter part of the month of October [1833] we started for the mountains to find the trappers. We followed the Spanish trail,[57] that leads to California, till we struck White River, took down the White River till we struck Green River, crossed Green to the Winty [Uinta], one of its tributaries.[58] There we found Mr. Robidoux.[59] He had a party of some twenty men that were trapping and trading.

The snow was now commencing to fall and we concluded to go into winter quarters. We found a place that answered every purpose on the mouth of the Winty. We passed a very pleasant winter. During the winter a California In-

*"Lieutenant" Carson, 1848.* (From 1914 edition of *Kit Carson Days,* by Sabin; courtesy of State Historical Society of Colorado) *See page 232.*

dian of the party of Mr. Robidoux run off with six animals, some of them being worth two hundred dollars per head. Robidoux came to me and requested that I should pursue him. I spoke to Captain Lee and he informed me that I might use my pleasure. There was a Utah village close by; I got one of the Indians to accompany me. We were furnished with two fine animals and then took the trail of the runaway. He had taken down the river, his object being to make California.

When travelling about one hundred miles, the animal of the Indian gave out. He would not accompany me any further. But I was deter-

a further report on his mountain journeys, apparently it was never made. His dates agree closely with those recollected by Carson, so there is no doubt of the identity, despite the fact that Lee mentions none of the fur traders or trappers with whom he had dealings. It seems reasonably certain that he took advantage of his army mission to engage in private trading ventures of his own.

56
Bent Brothers and St. Vrain was the dominant trading company of the early southwest. Charles Bent was born on November 11, 1799, in Charleston, West Virginia, and came to St. Louis with his parents at an early age. He engaged in the fur trade on the Missouri River before coming to New Mexico in 1829. From 1835, he lived with Maria Ignacia Jaramillo (whose younger sister married Kit Carson) and had children by her, but there is no record of their marriage, although she is commonly referred to as Mrs. Charles Bent. In 1846, he was appointed the first civil governor of New Mexico, by General Stephen Watts Kearny. While on a visit to Taos, January 19, 1847, he was killed in the presence of his family by rebellious Indians and Mexicans of Taos, who sought to overthrow American rule. See Harold H. Dunham, "Charles Bent," *Mountain Men* (ed. by Hafen), II, 27–48. Bent's Fort, William Bent, and Céran St. Vrain are noticed separately in Notes 125 and 307, below.

57
The Spanish Trail, usually called the Old Spanish Trail, ran northwest from Taos to Grand Junction, Colorado, thence westward to Green River and across the Wasatch Moun-

mined not to give up the chase. I continued in pursuit and, in thirty miles, I overtook the Indian with the horses. Seeing me by myself [he] showed fight. I was under the necessity of killing him, recovered the horses, and returned on my way to our camp and arrived in a few days without any trouble.[60]

Some trappers came to our camp and informed us that Fitzpatrick and Bridger[61] were on Snake River encamped.[62] In March [1834] we struck out for the purpose of finding their camp. In fifteen days, we found their camp. Then Captain Lee sold his goods to Fitzpatrick to be paid in Beaver. When paid, Lee started for Taos. I joined Fitzpatrick and remained with him one month. He had a great many men in his employ, and I thought it best to get three men and go hunt by our selves.[63] I done so. We passed the summer trapping on the head of Laramie and its tributaries, keeping [to] the mountains, our party being too weak to venture on the plains.

One evening, when we were on the route to join Bridger's party, after I had selected the camp for the night, I gave my horse to one of the men and started on foot for the purpose of killing something for supper, not having a particle of anything eatable on hand. I had gone about a mile and discovered some elk. I was on the side of a ridge. I shot one, and immediately after the discharge of my gun I heard in my rear a noise. I turned around and saw two very large grizzly bears making for me. My gun was unloaded and I could not possibly reload it in time to fire. There were some trees at a short distance. I made for them, the bears after me. As I got to one of the trees, I had to drop my gun—the bears rushing for me, I had to make all haste to ascend the tree. I got up some ten or fifteen feet and then had to remain till the bears would find it convenient to leave. One remained but a short time,

tains of central Utah, thence southwest to the Mojave River, and thence across the Mojave Desert to San Bernardino and on to Los Angeles, California. The eastern portion was pioneered by Padres Domínguez and Escalante, in 1776; the western portion, by Padre Garcés, in the same year. The two were linked by Jedediah Smith's expedition in 1826, and, from that time, it was increasingly used for commerce between New Mexico and southern California by both Mexicans and Americans. LeRoy R. Hafen and Ann W. Hafen, *The Old Spanish Trail* (Glendale, 1954) deals thoroughly with all phases of its history.

58
The Uinta River, of northeastern Utah, was pronounced by the trappers as it is spelled here.

59
Antoine Robidoux was the most important member of a St. Louis family, most of whom were engaged in the fur trade of the Southwest. He was born in St. Louis on September 22, 1794. After trading in Taos, where he married Carmel Benavides, he established Fort Uncompahgre, at the site of present Delta, Colorado, and Fort Uintah (called Winty by the trappers), near present White Rocks, Utah. Both forts were sometimes called Fort Robidoux. Fort Uncompahgre was short-lived, but Fort Uintah lasted till 1844, when it was destroyed by hostile Indians. Mosca Pass, over the Sangre de Cristo Range, was sometimes called Robidoux Pass. Robidoux served as guide and interpreter for General S. W. Kearny in New Mexico and California and was severely wounded at the battle of San Pasqual. He died on

the other remained for some time and with his paws would nearly unroot the small aspen trees that were around the one which I had ascended. He made several attempts at the one in which I was, but could do no damage. He finally concluded to leave, of which I was heartily pleased, never having been so scared in my life. I remained in the tree for some time and when I considered the bears far enough off, I descended and made for my camp in as great haste as possible.[64] It was dark when I arrived and [I] could not send for the elk which I had killed, so we had to pass the night without anything to eat. During the night we caught Beaver, so we had something for breakfast.

We remained in this place [head of the Laramie] some ten or fifteen days, when Bridger came, making his way for summer rende[z]vous.[65] We joined him and went to Green River, the place of rende[z]vous. Here was two camps of us. I think that there was two hundred trappers encamped. Then, till our supplies came from St. Louis, we disposed of our beaver to procure supplies. Coffee and sugar [were] two dollars a pint, powder the same, lead one dollar a bar, and common blankets from fifteen to twenty five dollars apiece.[66]

We remained in rende[z]vous during August and in September camp was broken up and we divided into parties of convenient size and started on our fall hunt. In the party of which I was a member there were fifty men.[67] We started for the country of the Blackfeet Indians, on the head waters of the Missouri. We made a very poor hunt as the Indians were very bad. We had five men killed. A trapper could hardly go a mile without being fired upon. We found that we could do but little in their country, so we started for winter quarters.

In November [1834] we got to Big Snake River, where we camped. We remained here till

August 29, 1860, at St. Joseph, Missouri, a town founded by his brother, Joseph Robidoux. See William S. Wallace, *Antoine Robidoux, 1794–1860* (Los Angeles, 1953); and also Albert B. Reagan, "Forts Robidoux and Kit Carson" in *New Mexico Historical Review*, Vol. X (April, 1935), 121–32.

60
This incident illustrates one of Carson's characteristics, that of dogged persistence in achieving an objective, all the more remarkable because he was alone.

61
James Bridger, one of the most famous of the Mountain Men, was born in Richmond, Virginia, on March 17, 1804, and moved with his family to St. Louis in 1812. He was one of the youngest men to respond to General William H. Ashley's advertisement for trappers in 1822. At the time Carson first met him, he was a partner in the Rocky Mountain Fur Company. After that company succumbed to competition, he worked for the American Fur Company for a time and then built Fort Bridger, on the Oregon Trail in southwestern Wyoming, where he had Louis Vasquez for a partner for several years. During his later years he was a scout and guide for various army officers and railroad surveyors. He died on July 17, 1881, at his farm, located in what is now Kansas City, Missouri. For a full biography see J. Cecil Alter, *Jim Bridger* (Norman, 1962).

62
When Carson refers to the Snake River he invariably means the Little Snake River, of northwestern Colorado and southern Wyoming. When

February 1833 [1835]. Nothing of moment having transpired till February, [when] the Blackfeet came and stole eighteen horses.[68] Twelve of us followed them and caught up in about fifty miles. They had travelled as far as they could on account of the snow. We endeavored to get the horses (some shots had been fired) but could not approach near enough to the Indians to do any damage. They had snow shoes, we had none; they could travel over the snow without any difficulty, we would sink in the snow to our waists.

The horses were on the side of a hill where there was but little snow. [Our] only object now was to get the horses. We wished a parley. The Indians agreed. One man from each [side] was to proceed halfway the distance between us and have a talk. It was done. [We] talked some time the Indians saying that they thought we were Snake Indians, [that] they did not wish to steal from the whites. We informed them that, if they were friendly, why did they not lay down their arms and have friendly talk and smoke. They agreed and laid down their arms. We done the same. Each party left one man to guard the arms. We then met at the place where the two first were talking [and] talked and smoked.

The Indians were thirty strong. They sent for the horses, [but] only returned with five of the worst. They said [they] would not give more. We broke for our arms, they for theirs. Then the fight commenced. I and Markhead was in the advance, approaching two Indians that were remaining in the rear, concealed behind two trees; I approaching one and Markhead the other.[69] Markhead was not paying sufficient attention to the Indian. I noticed him raise his gun to fire. I forgot entirely the danger in which I was myself and neglected my Indian for the one of Markhead. As the Indian was ready to fire on Markhead, I raised my gun and took sight. The

he means the Snake River of Idaho, he always calls it the Big Snake River.

63
Again Carson became a free trapper, but this time with the understanding that he would deal with the Rocky Mountain Fur Company.

64
Almost every trapper had dangerous encounters with grizzly bears. According to Carson's niece, Teresina Bent Scheurich, Carson referred to this adventure as his "worst difficult experience."

65
The first rendezvous was held in 1825 and the last one in 1840. This was the rendezvous of 1834, on Ham's Fork of Green River. It was Carson's first attendance at such a gathering. They were usually held in July or August, but this one was in late June. The shifting of camps was because of the need for forage. It was at this rendezvous that Nathaniel Wyeth made his second appearance in the West and also that Jason Lee, the Methodist missionary bound for Oregon, was present. Fraeb and Gervais dropped out of the Rocky Mountain Fur Company and Fitzpatrick, Bridger, and Milton Sublette endeavored to carry on. See LeRoy R. Hafen, "A Brief History of the Fur Trade of the Far West," *Mountain Men* (ed. by Hafen), I, 140–45.

66
The fur trading companies had two schedules of prices for goods sold. One was for whites, on which prices were high; the other was for Indians, on which prices were higher.

67
Because of hostile Indians, some men

Indian saw it, endeavored to conceal himself. I fired and he fell. The moment I fired I thought of the Indian that I was after. I noticed him. He was sighting for my breast. I could not load in time so I commenced dodging as well as I could. He fired; the ball grazed my neck and passed through my shoulder.

We then drew off for about a mile and encamped for the night. It was very cold [and we] could not make any fires for fear the Indians might approach and fire on us. We had no covering but our saddle blankets. I passed a miserable night from the pain of the wound, it having bled freely, which was frozen. In the morning the Indians were in the same place. We were not strong enough to attack, so we started for camp. Bridger with thirty men then started for the place where we left the Indians but, when he arrived, the Indians had gone to the plains and, of the stolen animals, we had only recovered the five which they had given us.

In a few days we started on our spring hunt,[70] trapped the waters of Snake and Green Rivers, made a very good hunt and then went into Summer quarters on Green River[71] [1835]. Shortly after making rendezvous our equipment arrived, then we disposed of our beaver to the traders that came up with our equipment. We remained in summer quarters till September.

There was in the party of Captain Drips[72] a large Frenchman, one of those overbearing kind and very strong.[73] He made a practice of whipping every man that he was displeased with, and that was nearly all. One day, after he had beaten two or three men, he said that for the Frenchmen, he had no trouble to flog, and as for the Americans, he would take a switch and switch them.[74] I did not like such talk from any man, so I told him that I was the worst American in camp. Many could t[h]rash him, only [they did not] on account of being afraid, and that if he

in each party were camp keepers and others were active trappers. Carson was always of the latter group.

68
Joe Meek also tells the story of this encounter with the Blackfeet, adding the detail that one of the stolen horses was Bridger's race horse Grohean. His account differs in some details from that of Carson and he is less precise in dating the event. Since he says that there were thirty in the white party, where Carson says there were twelve, it is possible that Meek was in the second party led by Bridger, which arrived after the Indians had gone. In that case, he was telling from hearsay the story of Carson's being wounded. See Victor, *River*, 141.

69
Mark Head was a trapper who was noted for his reckless daring, both as an Indian fighter and as a hunter of grizzly bears. He came from Virginia. Like Carson, he spent some time on the Arkansas in the 1840's and was killed at the Red River settlement north of Taos in 1847, where the inhabitants had risen in support of the Taos rebellion. Many writers wrote the name as Markhead, but it was almost certainly Mark Head. See Harvey L. Carter, "Mark Head" in *Mountain Men* (ed. by Hafen), I, 287–93.

70
The fur companies made a hunt in both spring and fall. It was the spring hunt that greatly reduced the number of beaver by trapping many of the mothers before the young were able to care for themselves.

71
The valley of Green River in southwestern Wyoming was the favorite location for a rendezvous. Six were held at the mouth of Horse Creek, a tributary of Green River, as was this one in 1835. The Green River was called the Siskeedee by the Indians. There are variant spellings of the name. Hunting knives of the Hudson's Bay Company bore the initials GR, which stood for George, Rex, but the American trappers supposed they stood for Green River. Hence, a knife was called a Green River in the parlance of the trappers.

72
Andrew S. Drips was well known as a field captain for the American Fur Company, which dominated the fur trade of the Missouri River and had now invaded the territory formerly monopolized by the Rocky Mountain Fur Company and its predecessors. He was born in Ireland, in 1789. In 1842 he was appointed Indian agent for the tribes on the Upper Missouri. Frémont had hoped to engage him as guide in that year but, failing to find him, hired Carson instead. Drips died in Kansas City, Missouri, in 1860. There is no complete account of his life but he figures prominently in DeVoto, *Across the Wide Missouri.*

73
The description of strong and overbearing applies to the Frenchman in Drips' company, not to Drips himself. The Frenchman was called Shunar (no doubt an Americanized spelling of Chouinard or Chinard or some similar French name) and it was he with whom Carson fought the duel. Beginning with Dr. De Witt Clinton Peters, *The Life and Adventures of Kit Carson, the Nestor of the Rocky Mountains* (New York, 1858), many writers have referrred to the Frenchman as Shunan and have conferred upon him the undeserved title of captain, which properly belonged to Andrew S. Drips. Some have altered the name to Shuman. Carson does not refer to his antagonist by name, but the Reverend Samuel Parker gives it as Shunar in his contemporary account of the duel, and Dr. Peters has written it into the manuscript.

74
Shunar was "making his brag," as it was called. It was a common custom on the frontier—and not exclusively confined to the frontier—in early nineteenth-century America for certain men who enjoyed brawling to make a brag concerning their prowess as fighters and offer to take on all comers. Nearly always such men were impelled to do this by having downed several drinks of hard liquor. However, Captain Smith H. Simpson, who knew and served under Carson in later years, said that Carson told him that he and Shunar were rivals for the favor of a young squaw and that he understood it was the Arapaho girl that Carson married soon afterward. See Sabin, *Kit Carson Days* (1914). Vestal, *Kit Carson, Happy Warrior*, 114–22, embroiders this into a very fancy story, based on conversations with Arapahoes of two or three generations later. It is a plausible conjecture, which would appear believable if it could be shown that any Arapahoes were camped near the rendezvous site in 1835. Available evidence affords no indication of their presence, but the possibility that a woman was involved cannot be completely rejected.

made use of any more such expressions, I would rip his guts.

He said nothing but started for his rifle, mounted his horse, and made his appearance in front of the camp. As soon as I saw him, I mounted my horse and took the first arms I could get ahold of, which was a pistol, galloped up to him and demanded if I was the one which he intended to shoot. Our horses were touching. He said no, but at the same time drawing his gun so he could have a fair shot. I was prepared and allowed him to draw his gun. We both fired at the same time; all present said but one report was heard. I shot him through the arm and his ball passed my head, cutting my hair and the powder burning my eye, the muzzle of his gun being near my head when he fired. During our stay in camp we had no more bother with this bully Frenchman.[75]

On the first [of] September [1835] we departed on our Fall hunt, trapping the Yellowstone and Big Horn Rivers, and crossed over to the Three Forks of the Missouri, and up the North Fork, and wintered on Big Snake River and its tributaries.[76] There we found Thomas McCoy, one of the Hudson Bay traders.[77] Antoine Godey,[78] four more, and myself joined McCoy, having heard of Mary's River, now called the Humboldt, and beaver on it was plenty.[79] Trapped down Mary's River near where [it] loses itself in the great basin, and found but few beaver. Then we went up it some eighty miles, then struck across to the waters of Big Snake River. There we separated; McCoy going to Fort Walla Walla[80] and we for Fort Hall.[81] On our march we found no game; the country was barren. For many days the only food we [had] was roots and we would bleed our horses and cook the blood. About four days travel before we got to the fort, we met a party of Indians. I traded with them for a fat horse, which we killed. [We]

75
Rev. Samuel Parker, *Journal of an Exploring Tour Beyond the Rocky Mountains* (Ithaca, 1838), 79–80, provides the earliest account of this duel and the first appearance of Kit Carson's name in print after the advertisement for him as a runaway apprentice. Parker was present at the rendezvous but he does not specifically state that he witnessed the fight. He concludes his account, which conforms closely to that of Carson, by saying that Kit "went for another pistol" but "Shunar begged that his life might be spared." The implication is that Carson spared him, and this is certainly the implication of Carson's own story. Sabin, relying on the statement of Smith H. Simpson, says that Carson killed Shunar. If Carson told the story that way to Simpson in later years, the wish was probably father to the thought. Vestal, *Kit Carson, Happy Warrior*, 123–28, giving his authority (in a letter to Milo M. Quaife) as Watan, an Arapaho, who was not present, also insists that Carson killed Shunar. Had he done so, under the circumstances, it would have been plain murder. Parker makes the explanation, after his account of the fight, that the Mountain Men "would see 'fair play' and would 'spare the last eye'; and would not tolerate murder, unless drunkenness or great provocation could be pleaded in extenuation of guilt." This seems to settle it, for there is no indication that Carson was drunk and Shunar was giving no provocation when begging for life. Jessie Benton and others have testified that Carson could never tell the story without showing marked resentment for Shunar. From a psychological viewpoint, this is convincing proof that Kit did not kill him; his death would

have removed the cause for anger, while his continued life would have served to make Kit wish that he had killed him.

76
The Yellowstone flows across southern Montana to join the Missouri, of which it is the largest tributary. The Big Horn is the lower and northward-flowing portion of a Wyoming river which joins the Yellowstone in Montana; the upper and southeastward-flowing portion is called Wind River. The Three Forks of the Missouri designate the spot in Gallatin County, Montana, where the Jefferson, Madison, and Gallatin Rivers combine to form the Missouri within the space of about a quarter of a mile. The North Fork would be the Jefferson River.

The Big Snake flows across Idaho and turns north to join the Columbia. It is longer than the Columbia, measuring from their junction to their sources, just as the Green is longer than the Colorado; but long usage confers on the Columbia and the Colorado the status of principal streams and on the Green and the Snake the status of tributaries.

The itinerary Carson describes here does not seem to fit any known fall hunt. Clearly, he did spend the winter of 1835–36 on the Big Snake, but between two seasons of trapping for the Hudson's Bay Company. Probably the early portion of this itinerary should be ascribed to the fall of 1836, when Bridger is known to have been in the Crow country; the later portion could apply to any one of several spring hunts. The fact that Carson cites no specific incidents connected with this itinerary makes it impossible to be definite about the date.

Up to this point, with the exception of having fallen one year behind in dating events from 1831 to 1834, Carson has been correct in his chronology. Beginning here, however, and continuing for several years—1835–39—his chronology is considerably confused. Events are related which he ascribes to 1839 but which belong to 1835. Since he could not tell the story of his fight with Shunar without getting very angry all over again, a reasonable explanation of his errors at this point would be that his hot-headed recollection of his duel beclouded his memory as he dictated his memoirs.

77
Thomas McKay was the quarter-blood son of Alexander McKay, one of the Astorian partners, and the step-son of Dr. John McLoughlin, Hudson's Bay Company factor at Fort Vancouver. He had trapped the Snake River country in 1826–27 under Peter Skene Ogden, who recommended him highly to his superiors. In 1834, he established Fort Boise. He attended the rendezvous of 1836 and afterward conducted the missionaries, Marcus Whitman and Henry Spalding and their wives, from Fort Bonneville to Fort Boise. Carson's period of service with him was in the spring of 1836. McKay died in 1849. There is no connected account of Thomas McKay, but see the many references to him in the *Index to Oregon Historical Quarterly*, Vols. I–XL.

78
Alexis Godey, called Alexander by Frémont and Antoine here, by Carson, was in his first season as a trapper. Later he was with Frémont on his second and third expeditions, be-

feasted for a couple of days and then started for the Fort, where we safely arrived.

We were received kindly by the people, treated well and remained a few days, then started to hunt Buffalo, they not being more than a days travel from the fort. We killed a good many buffalo and returned to the Fort. The Blackfeet Indians must have seen us when hunting, for that night they came to the Fort and stole every animal we had.

We were encamped outside of the Fort, but our animals [were] in one of the corrals belonging to it. During the night the sentinel saw two men approach and let down the bars and drive out the animals, thinking that it was one of us, turning out the animals to graze. We were now afoot and had to remain [at the fort]. In about a month McCoy came and we joined him and started for the Rendezvous on Green River [1836]. He had plenty of animals and we purchased [mounts] of him.

In six days travel, we reached the rendezvous at the mouth of Horse Creek on Green River, remaining in rendezvous some twenty days.[82] McCoy went back to Fort Hall. I joined Fontenelle's party and we started for the Yellowstone.[83] Our party was one hundred strong, fifty trappers and fifty camp keepers. We had met with so much difficulty from the Blackfeet that this time, as we were in force, we determined to trap wherever we pleased, even if we had to fight for the right.

We trapped the Yellow Stone, Otter, and Muscle Shell Rivers and then up the Big Horn and on to Powder River, where we wintered. During our hunt we had no fights with the Blackfeet—we could not know the cause. Near our encampment was the Crow Indian village. They were friendly and [we] remained together during the winter. They informed us of the reason of us not being harrassed by the Blackfeet

came a lieutenant in the California Battalion in 1846, and was captured at San Pasqual. He was the hero of Frémont's disastrous fourth expedition in 1849, in which year he returned to California. He married Maria Antonia Coronel and became a rancher and sheepherder near Bakersfield. From 1863 to 1883 he was employed by Edward Fitzgerald Beale on his extensive ranch system. Godey was born in St. Louis in 1818, died in Los Angeles on January 19, 1889, and was buried in Bakersfield. Frémont admired his coolness and daring and classed him with Carson and Owens as a man of action. See *Los Angeles Times*, January 21, 1889.

79
Mary's River was the early name for the Nevada stream that had its name changed to Humboldt by John C. Frémont. It took the earlier name from Peter Skene Ogden's squaw and was sometimes called Ogden's River. Ogden was first to explore it.

80
Donald McKenzie established Fort Walla Walla for the Hudson's Bay Company in 1818, at the junction of the Walla Walla River with the Columbia. At first it was called Fort Nez Percé. The Whitman Mission was about fifteen miles east of it. See Alexander Ross, *Fur Hunters of the Far West*, edited by Milo M. Quaife (Chicago, 1924), 204–208.

81
Fort Hall was built by Nathaniel Wyeth in 1834, and sold by him to the Hudson's Bay Company two years later, after which it was maintained as a trading post until 1856. It was a stopping place for overland travelers on the Oregon Trail during

these years. It was located about eight miles north of present Pocatello, Idaho. See Frank C. Robertson, *Fort Hall: Gateway to the Oregon Country* (New York, 1963).

82
At the rendezvous of 1836 were Narcissa Whitman and Eliza Spalding, the first white women to make the overland transcontinental journey. Meek, in Victor, *River*, 199–200, says that he, Carson, Newell, and a Flathead chief named Victor made an excursion to the Sweetwater with Captain Drips during the rendezvous of 1836, and that all lost their horses except Carson and himself, who kept their mounts saddled and roped to themselves while they slept. Sooner or later they all returned to the rendezvous on Horse Creek.

83
Lucien Fontenelle was born in New Orleans about 1807. He was orphaned in youth and made his way to St. Louis, where he was employed by the American Fur Company, working usually in close association with Andrew Drips. In 1834 he and Drips worked out a merger with Fitzpatrick, Bridger, and Milton Sublette. The new group was called Fontenelle, Fitzpatrick, and Company, but had financial backing from the American Fur Company, which took it over in 1836, at the rendezvous. Carson was not with Fontenelle for the fall hunt, however, because Fontenelle was not in the mountains that winter. He returned for the rendezvous of 1837 and conducted the hunt of 1837–38, which Carson here ascribes to 1836–37 by an error of memory. Reports of Fontenelle's suicide at Fort Laramie in 1837 are erroneous for his letter to P. A. Sarpy, dated August 5, 1838, is in the Missouri Historical Library files. See Sabin, *Kit Carson Days* (1914), 116; also Alter, Jim Bridger, 162; and LeRoy R. Hafen, "A Brief History of the Fur Trade of the Far West" in *Mountain Men* (ed. by Hafen), I, 145–63; and also Alan C. Trottman, "Lucien Fontenelle," *Mountain Men* (ed. by Hafen), V, 81–100.

84
The great smallpox epidemic began among the Blackfeet in the spring of 1837; the infection was brought up the Missouri River by an American Fur Company steamboat; it wiped out the Mandans as a tribe and killed off about two-thirds of the Blackfeet before its course was run. Carson continues to recount the events of the 1837–38 season, while ascribing them to 1836–37.

85
The date should be April 1, 1838, since Carson's recollection of events places them one year too early. Fontenelle did not establish the winter camp on Powder River until December, 1837. Because of the hard winter, they were late breaking camp in the spring. Osborne Russell, *Journal of a Trapper*, edited by Aubrey L. Haines (Portland, 1955), 35–36, says they broke camp on March 25; Robert Newell, *Memoranda*, edited by Dorothy Johansen (Portland, 1959) says March 29; Joe Meek, in Victor, *River*, says March 1. It is possible that different parties moved out at different times. Russell and Newell kept contemporary records and they agree that the year was 1838.

Powder River rises in central Wyoming and flows north to meet the Yellowstone. The camp was near the "Portugee Houses" of a former Bon-

during our hunt. It was that the small-pox was among them and they had gone north of the Missouri, there having none remained on our hunting ground.[84]

We remained in camp on Powder River till the first of April.[85] We passed in camp a pleasant time. Only it was one of the coldest winters I ever experienced. For fear of danger, we had to keep our animals in a corral. The feed furnished them was cottonwood bark, which we would pull from the trees and then throw it by the fire.

The buffalo we had to keep from our camp by building large fires in the bottoms. They came in such large droves that our horses were in danger of being killed by them when we turned them out to eat of the branches of trees which we had cut down. When [we] broke up camp [we] started two men for Fort Laramie where the American Fur Company had established a trading post. They never reached there. I presume they were killed by the Sioux Indians.[86]

We then commenced our hunt, trapping the streams we had in the Fall to the Yellowstone and up Twenty Five Yard River[87] to the three forks of the Missouri and then up the North Fork of the Missouri.[88] There we found that the small-pox had not killed all the Blackfeet, for there was a large village of them in advance of us. We cautiously travelled on their trail till we found they were only one day ahead. Six of us then left the main party to pursue the Indians [to] find out their strength; the balance of the party continuing its march in our rear. We discovered them. They were driving in their animals and making preparations to move their camp. We joined the main party and gave the information of the movements of the Indian village.

We had come within four miles of their village and, as we were determined to try our

neville trader, Antonio Montero. These were located a few miles west of present Sussex, Wyoming. The site was farther east than the usual winter quarters and was chosen in order to be near a large herd of buffalo. In Victor, *River*, 249–50, Joe Meek tells a story about hunting buffalo here with Carson and a Frenchman, Marteau. Marteau was injured, but Carson insisted on caring for him and getting him safely to camp. Meek said the camp numbered three hundred men.

86
Fort Laramie was constructed in 1834 by William Sublette and Robert Campbell, near the junction of the Laramie and North Platte Rivers. It was sometimes referred to as Fort William, Fort John, or Fort Lucien. It became a United States Army post in 1849 and was a way station on the Oregon Trail. See William Marshall Anderson, "Narrative of a Ride to the Rocky Mountains in 1834," edited by Albert J. Partoll, *Frontier and Midland*, Vol. XIX (Fall, 1938), 54–63; also LeRoy R. Hafen and Francis M. Young, *Fort Laramie and the Pageant of the West, 1834–1890* (Glendale, 1938).

87
The Twenty-Five Yard River is the Shield's River, which enters the Yellowstone from the north about five miles below Livingston, Montana. Thus, they crossed the mountains considerably north of Bozeman Pass.

88
Russell, *Journal*, 85–86, says they ascended the Gallatin River (the South Fork) and then crossed to the Madison River (the Middle Fork).

strength to discover who had right to the country, I with forty men started for the village—sixty men being left to guard the camp—and we soon reached the village, attacked it, and killed ten Indians. The fight commenced and we continued advancing, they retreating, for about three hours. Our ammunition began to give out; the Indians were soon aware of the fact. They then knowing that they had advantage of us, turned on us. We fought them as well as we could, considering the scarcity of our ammunition. We run retreating for our camp. The Indians would often charge among us. We would turn and give fire. They would retreat, then we would continue our course.

As we were passing a point of rocks the horse of Cotton fell.[89] He was held to the ground by the weight of his horse. Six Indians made for him for the purpose of taking his scalp. I dismounted, fired, and killed one Indian. The balance run. By this time Cotton had got released from the pressure on him, his horse had arose, and he mounted and made the camp. When I fired, my horse got frightened and broke away from me and joined the party in advance. I noticed White—he was not far from me—called him, and as soon as he saw the predicament I was in he came to me.[90] I mounted his horse [behind him] and we continued our retreat and soon reached our camp. The Indians took position in a pile of rocks about one hundred and fifty yards from us. They commenced firing on us. We returned [their fire], but finding that no execution could be done, we concluded to charge them; done so. It was the prettiest fight I ever saw. The Indians stood for some time. I would often see a white man on one side and an Indian on the other [side] of a rock, not ten feet apart, each dodging and trying to get the first shot. We finally routed them, took several scalps, having several of our men slightly wounded. This

Since Russell's contemporary account is more reliable than Carson's reminiscence, it is probable that Carson errs in saying they ascended the Jefferson (the North Fork). The ensuing fight took place, therefore, on the Madison River. Russell's description of it, Russell, *Journal*, 87–88, differs materially from Carson's, but they may not have been near one another.

89
The trapper rescued by Carson was Cotton Mansfield, a crony of Bridger's. Meek in Victor, *River*, 230–31, reports that Mansfield called out, "tell Old Gabe [Bridger] that Old Cotton is gone!"

90
The trapper who rescued Carson was probably David White, who stole a horse and went over to the Hudson's Bay Company a few days later. See Newell, *Memoranda*, 37.

91
This was the rendezvous of 1838, held at the junction of the Popo Agie with Wind River, the site of present Riverton, Wyoming. Their route was from the Madison to Henry's Fork, thence via Pierre's Hole and across the Teton Range; thence via Jackson's Hole and across the Wind River Range; thence down Wind River to the rendezvous. See Russell, *Journal*, 89–90.

92
The missionary party consisted of Cushing and Myra Eels, William and Mary Gray, Asa and Sarah Smith, Elkanah and Mary Walker, and Cornelius Rogers. They arrived on June 21, 1838. See *First White Women Over the Rockies*, edited by Clif-

ended our difficulties with the Blackfeet for the present hunt.

We continued up the north fork to the head of Green River, where an express overtook us, saying that the rendezvous would be on Wind River.[91] We then started for rendezvous; arrived in eight days. Our equipment had come up, also some missionaries for the Columbia,[92] also an English nobleman, Sir William Stuart, a man that will be forever remembered by the mountaineers that had the honor of his acquaintance for his liberality to them and for his many good qualities.[93]

Among the missionaries was old father de Smitt—now he is at the Catholic University of St. Louis.[94] I can say of him that if ever there was a man that wished to do good, he is one. He never feared danger when duty required his presence among the savages and if good works on this earth are rewarded hereafter I am confident that his share of glory and happiness in the next world will be great.

In twenty days the rendezvous broke up, and I and seven men went to Brown's Hole, a trading post.[95] I there joined Thompson and Sinclair's[96] party on a trading expedition to the Navajo Indians.[97] We traded for thirty mules. We returned to Brown's Hole. After our arrival, Thompson took the mules to the South Fork of the Platte, disposed of them to Sublett and Vasques, and returned with goods that would answer for trading with Indians.[98] I was now employed as the hunter for the Fort and continued as such during the winter. I had to keep twenty men in venison.

In the Spring,[99] I joined Bridger. In the party there was myself, Dick Owens, and three Canadians.[100] We five started for the Black Hills to hunt.[101] We trapped the streams in the vicinity of the hills. We separated; Owens and myself taking one course, and the Canadians another.

ford M. Drury (Glendale, 1966), III, 79ff, 89ff.

The Swiss adventurer, Captain J. A. Sutter, whom Carson was to know a few years later in California, was present at the rendezvous of 1838, although Carson does not mention him as being among his acquaintances there. Sabin, *Kit Carson Days*, II, Note 159, p. 920, quotes from a manuscript of Sutter's Personal Reminiscences in the Bancroft Library, Berkeley, California, the following statement, which indicates that the two men met at the rendezvous of 1838. "I took with me only one of my men, a German, also an Indian boy whom I had bought from Kit Carson at the Rendezvous for a hundred dollar beaver order on the Hudson's Bay Company worth at Rendezvous $130."

93
Sir William Drummond Stewart was born at Murthly Castle, Perthshire, Scotland, on December 26, 1795. He fought under Wellington at Waterloo, subsequently became a world traveler, and developed a passion for hunting in the American Far West. He attended every rendezvous from that of 1833 to that of 1838, so Carson probably had become acquainted with him some years earlier. Stewart made his farewell trip to the Rockies in 1843. Commissioned by Stewart, and traveling with him, artist Alfred Jacob Miller has preserved the life of the trappers and Indians in his sketches and paintings. See Alfred Jacob Miller, *The West of Alfred Jacob Miller,* (edited by Marvin C. Ross) (Norman, 1951). Stewart wrote two novels based on the American West. He died, on April 28, 1871, in Scotland. See Mae Reed Porter and Odessa Davenport, *Scotsman in*

*Buckskin* (New York, 1963), 156–72, for his attendance at the rendezvous of 1838.

94
Father Pierre Jean De Smet, after earlier work among the Pottawatomies, became famous as the missionary to the Flatheads. He raised funds for his work by going personally to Europe and, in 1853, estimated that he had traveled 125,000 miles. He was born in Belgium on January 30, 1801, and died in St. Louis on May 23, 1873. He first came west in 1840, with Andrew Dripps, and attended the rendezvous of that year on Green River. The fact that Carson knew him is substantial evidence that Kit attended the rendezvous in 1840, because he could not have met De Smet at any earlier time. See H. M. Chittenden and A. T. Richardson, *The Life, Letters, and Travels of Father Pierre Jean De Smet, S. J.* (New York, 1905), 201.

95
Brown's Hole is located in the extreme northwestern corner of Colorado, in Moffat County. About thirty miles long and six miles wide, it is traversed by Green River, which enters through Red Canyon from the northwest and exits to the southeast by a sudden plunge into Lodore Canyon. It was found by William H. Ashley and his trappers in 1825, while they were trying to navigate Green River.

The trading post in Brown's Hole, located just above the confluence of Vermillion Creek with Green River, was called Fort Davy Crockett. It was built and operated by Philip Thompson, William Craig, and Prewitt Sinclair. The date of its construction was probably 1836 and it was abandoned in 1840.

96
Philip Thompson was born in Tennessee in 1810 or 1811 and died in Oregon in 1854. Craig was born in Virginia in 1807, first entered the fur trade in 1829, and died in Idaho Territory in 1869. Prewitt Sinclair was the brother of Alexander Sinclair, who was killed at Pierre's Hole in 1832. All were squaw men, as was Carson, whose wife, an Arapaho named Waa-nibe, meaning Singing Grass, was undoubtedly with him at Fort Davy Crockett at this time, in the fall of 1838, which is one possible date for the birth of their daughter, Adaline. See LeRoy R. Hafen, "Fort Davy Crockett, Its Fur Men and Visitors" in *Colorado Magazine,* Vol. XXIX (January, 1952), 17–33; also Frederick A. Mark, "William Craig," in *Mountain Men* (ed. by Hafen), II, 99–116; also LeRoy R. Hafen, "Philip F. Thompson," *Mountain Men* (ed. by Hafen), III, 339–47. For material on Adaline, see McClung, *Carson-Bent-Boggs*, 69ff.

97
The Navaho, or Navajo, Indians occupied northwestern New Mexico and northeastern Arizona.

98
Andrew Sublette and Louis Vasquez established an adobe fort on the South Platte about thirty miles north of present Denver, Colorado, in the fall of 1835. Here they operated, despite competition from three other forts in the vicinity, until 1840 or 1841, when they sold it to Lock and Randolph, who abandoned it in 1842.

Andrew Sublette was born in Kentucky, in 1808 or 1809, and died in

We trapped for three months, made a good hunt, and then started to find the main camp. We found it on a tributary of Green River. We remained with the main party till the month of July, and then went into rendezvous on the Popoaghi, a tributary of Wind River.[102] About the 20th of August, we started for Yellowstone, trapped all the streams within the vicinity of Yellowstone and on it went into Winter quarters.

About the 1st of January, a few men were out hunting not far from camp, and discovered a party of Blackfeet.[103] As soon as information was brought us of the nearness of our old enemies, a party of forty men started to meet them and we drove them on an island in the Yellow Stone, where they strongly fortified themselves. It was late when we commenced the attack. We continued the fight till sunset, and then had to retire.[104] We lost one man in killed, a Delaware Indian, a brave man, and one wounded.[105]

In the morning we started for the Indians, arrived at the place where they had fortified themselves, but they had left. On examination of the fort we discovered that during the attack of the previous evening that they had lost several. There was a great quantity of blood in the fort and, there being a hole in the ice of the stream, we found where they had disposed of their dead, there being a large trail made from the fort to the hole in the ice. We now knew that the main village of the Blackfeet was not far. Bridger, an old experienced mountaineer, said, "Now, boys, the Indians are close. There will in a short time [be] a party of five or six hundred return to avenge the death of those we had slain and it was necessary for us to be on the look-out." In the course of fifteen days his words were verified.

At the distance of one mile from camp there was a large Butte on which, during the day, on its summit we posted a sentinel. He could command a view of the surrounding country.[106] On

California in 1852. He was the third of five brothers who engaged in the fur trade of the Rocky Mountains. Louis Vasquez was born in St. Louis, of a Spanish father and a French mother, on October 3, 1798. He was the youngest brother of Baroney Vasquez, interpreter for the Pike expedition of 1806–1807. From 1842 to 1855 he was Jim Bridger's partner at Fort Bridger. He died in Westport, Missouri, in September, 1868. See Doyce B. Nunis, *Andrew Sublette, Rocky Mountain Prince* (Los Angeles, 1960); and LeRoy R. Hafen, "Louis Vasquez," *Mountain Men* (ed. by Hafen), II, 321–38.

99
The date was the spring of 1839, Carson's recollection being in error by one year.

100
Richard Owens may have come to the mountains with Nathaniel Wyeth's second expedition. His origins and his final years are both obscure. He later followed Carson to the Arkansas and lived for a time at the Greenhorn settlement, twenty-five miles south of El Pueblo. Through Carson's efforts, he became a member of Frémont's third expedition and then became Captain of Company A of the California Battalion of Mounted Riflemen. He was present at Frémont's court-martial in Washington, D.C., but was not called upon to testify. He returned to Taos and is certainly identified for the last time guiding a company of forty-niners to the gold fields of California. See Harvey L. Carter, "Richard Owens," *Mountain Men* (ed. by Hafen), V, 283–90.

the fifteenth day he discovered the Blackfeet marching towards us. They encamped on a large island and immediately commenced making fortifications. They were coming for three days. There were at least 1500 warriors. We commenced fortifying our positions as soon as we knew of their approach. We were confident that they would come in force. Our forts were built strong. Nothing but artillery would be able to do it any damage. We were prepared to receive them. The Indians had constructed one hundred and eleven forts on the evening of the arrival of the last of their reinforcements. They had a war dance. We could hear their songs and we well knew that in the morning they would make the attack. We were prepared. They came, saw the strength and invicibility of our position. They fired a few shots, but done no execution, and finding that they could not do us any damage only by charging our breast works, which they declined, they commenced retiring.[107]

We desired them to make the attack. We were only sixty strong, the Indians 1500, but there was not one of our band but felt anxious for the fight. Nothing could persuade them to attack us. They departed, went about one mile [away]. All sat in council. In a short time they arose, one half going in the direction of the Crow Indian country, and the other taking the course they had come. We remained at our fort till Spring without any further molestation.

We kept our animals in [during] the nights, feeding them on cottonwood, and in the day allowed them to graze, but well guarded. On the return of Spring we commenced our hunt, trapped the tributaries of the Missouri to the head of Lewis Fork,[108] and then started for rendezvous on Green River, near the mouth of Horse Creek, there [we] remained till August, and then myself and five others went to Fort Hall and joined a party of the Northwest Fur

101
The Black Hills are the Laramie Mountains, invariably so called by the trappers. There is no indication that the Black Hills of South Dakota are meant, although some Carson biographers have so stated.

102
The rendezvous on the Popo Agie was that of 1838, already noticed. Whether this statement can be taken to mean that he and Owens attended the rendezvous of 1839 on Green River is problematical, but they probably did so. They did not go to the Yellowstone in 1839 after the rendezvous. Newell, *Memoranda*, 38, says that he met Carson and Owens on Black's Fork of Green River on August 23, 1839, and that they all went on to Brown's Hole, where they arrived September 1, 1839. There is other evidence that Carson was at Fort Davy Crockett in the fall and winter of 1839. E. W. Smith, en route to Oregon, saw and talked to him there on October 2, 1839. Carson told Smith of a fight on the Little Snake River a few days earlier, in which Carson and six other trappers drove off twenty Sioux by killing their chief. See "The E. Willard Smith Journal" in *To the Rockies and Oregon*, edited by LeRoy R. Hafen and Ann W. Hafen (Glendale, 1955), 174–75. Joe Meek in Victor, *River*, 261, lists Owens among the horse thieves in a well-known episode later that fall, and Carson among a group of twenty-five who endeavored to return the horses to the Shoshones, from whom they had been taken unjustifiably.

103
The events which Carson now recounts belong to the 1836–37 season

Company.[109] Trapped to head of Salmon River, then to Malade and down this same to Big Snake River, and up Big Snake.[110] Trapped Goose Creek and Raft River, returned to Fort Hall and disposed of the Beaver we caught.[111] Remained there one month, and then went and joined Bridger in the Blackfoot country.

After striking the waters of the Missouri, we discovered that there were trappers in advance of us. Fifteen of us left the party for the purpose of overtaking the advance party and [to] find out who they were. Overtook them the same day, found them to be a party of trappers in charge of Joseph Gale,[112] trapping for Captain Wyatt.[113] He informed us that he had lately a fight with the Blackfeet. He had several of his men wounded, among whom was Richard Owens, but [he] was nearly well of the wounds received.

In the morning we commenced setting our traps. Knowing that our party would come on our trail, we did not consider it necessary to return and, having accomplished that for which we were sent in advance, we concluded to remain until the arrival of the main party. The men that had gone out to set traps, after having proceeded about two miles came in contact with a party of Blackfeet, were fired upon and compelled to retreat. They reached camp, the Indians in their rear. We secured ourselves and animals in the brush, then commenced the fight. We, though few in number, had the advantage of being concealed, while our enemy was exposed to view. Our main object was to save our animals.

We fought them the greater part of the day. A great number of Indians were killed. They done all in their power to make us leave our concealment, and finally set fire to the brush. The fire consumed all the outer brush and that under which we remained was not touched. I cannot

and the date should be January, 1837, not January, 1839.

104
The date of this skirmish was about February 1, 1837. See Russell, *Journal*, 52. Meek dates it January, 1836, which is one year too soon, and Carson dates it two years too late. Both Meek and Carson were speaking from memory, but Russell wrote at the time.

105
The Delaware who was killed was Manhead. See James B. Marsh, *Four Years in the Rockies or The Adventures of Isaac P. Rose* (Columbus, 1950), 137–38.

106
The trappers were camped nearly opposite the confluence of Clark's Fork with the Yellowstone, near present Park City, Montana. Russell, *Journal*, 52–53, says that Bridger took his telescope and mounted a bluff, from which he saw many Indians.

107
Meek in Victor, *River*, 196, and Russell, *Journal*, 54–55, explain two things not mentioned by Carson. Meek says that the small conical forts built by the Blackfeet would each shelter about ten warriors and it was by counting the forts that the number of the enemy was estimated. Russell also estimates the number as eleven hundred, and explains that the Indians gave up the fight because of a brilliant display of aurora borealis, which they considered an ill omen. All agree that the trappers had strongly fortified their own camp. Russell gives the date as February 24, 1837.

108
The spring of 1837 should be understood here and Lewis Fork of the Snake River, which flows through Jackson's Hole, from which point it was not far to the site of the rendezvous of 1837. Russell, *Journal*, 55–58, gives a different route for the spring hunt. Four entries in the Fort Hall Account Books, Ledger No. 2, pp. 46, 121, indicate that Carson was in the vicinity of Fort Hall between April 10 and July 5, 1837. On May 27 he traded two beaver skins and some beaver castors for supplies and, on June 6 and July 5 he made further purchases by trading in one of his traps on each occasion. From these facts, it may be concluded that he was not trapping during the spring of 1837 but was living quietly with his Indian wife, for whom he made purchases of beads. It seems probable that his daughter, Adaline, was born during this period, and that this occurrence explains his inactivity as a trapper.

109
By Northwest Company, Carson refers to the Hudson's Bay Company. The two British companies had merged in 1821, but many trappers had started with the Northwest Company and doubtless still used the term. This trip to Fort Hall and the expedition described in the next sentence must be placed in point of time by a process of elimination. The rendezvous of 1837 was on Horse Creek, but so were those of 1836 and 1835. This employment by the Hudson's Bay Company cannot have been in the fall and winter of 1836 or 1837, because Carson is known to have been with Bridger in 1836–37, and with Fontenelle and Bridger in 1837–38, as has already been established. Therefore, this hunt must have been in the late fall and early winter of 1835–36, but after the encounter of Gale's men with the Blackfeet, not before. The fact that Carson definitely describes it as a fall hunt precludes placing it in the spring of 1837, as well as the fact that during the spring of 1837, as already noted, he sold only two beaver skins.

110
The Malade River rises in southeastern Idaho and joins Bear River near Great Salt Lake. It is so called because its waters are brackish.

111
Raft River rises in extreme northwestern Utah and flows northward to the Snake. Goose Creek, easily reached from the headwaters of Raft River, is near the head of the Humboldt. This area was first trapped by Peter Skene Ogden.

112
Joseph Gale was born near Washington, D.C., in 1800. He was an experienced trapper, having gone with Ewing Young on his second trip to California and thence with him to Oregon in 1834. However, he was an unpopular leader when put in charge of this party by Wyeth. Osborne Russell is quite bitter toward him, and with good reason. Gale settled in Oregon and died there.

113
Nathaniel J. Wyeth, born January 29, 1802, was a Boston ice merchant who became interested in Oregon and first came west in 1832, taking part in the battle of Pierre's Hole. He returned two years later, built Fort Hall, and engaged in the fur business under the name of the Columbia

account for our miraculous escape from the flames. It was the hand of Providence over us that was the cause. It could have been nothing else, for the brush where we were concealed was dry and easily burned as that which had been consumed.[114]

The Indians, finding that they could not drive us from our concealment, and from the unerring aim of our rifles they were every moment losing men, then concluded to abandon the war and departed. As soon as they left, we started for our main camp, which was some six miles distant. I presume the Indians discovered the approach of the main party, and fearing that the firing would be heard and they surrounded by a considerable force, and but poor prospect of any of them getting away if they remained any longer, was the main cause of the retreat. Gale, seeing that he could not travel with his party on account of his weakness, joined us, then we moved on to Stinking Creek.[115]

The day we arrived, we lost one man, killed by the Blackfeet. That same day, I was about eight miles in advance. I saw at a distance a number of ravens hovering over a particular spot. I concluded to go and see the cause, found the carcass of a bear that had been lately killed by Indians; the trail being fresh and taking the course I wished to pursue, caused me to return. Every day, for eight or ten, we were fired upon by Blackfeet. If a trapper should get a few miles in advance, he would be fired upon, and have to return. We were surrounded by the Indians, and, finding it impossible to hunt to any advantage, we started for the North fork of the Missouri. Up said stream four days march, we overtook a large village of Flathead and Pondrai Indians.[116] A chief of the Flatheads and some of his tribe joined us and we travelled on to Big Snake River for winter quarters, and passed the winter without being molested by the Indians.

River Fishing and Trading Company, but sold out his interests to the Hudson's Bay Company in 1836 and returned to Cambridge, Massachusetts, where he resumed his ice business with the West Indies. He died on August 31, 1856. See Joseph Schafer, "Nathaniel J. Wyeth," *Dictionary of American Biography*, XX (New York, 1936), 576–77.

114
Russell, *Journal*, gives the number of Blackfeet as eighty warriors in this fight of September 10, 1835. Russell gives a more reasonable explanation of their success in this fight. He says that the trappers started a backfire. Meek in Victor, *River*, 168–69, also describes the fight and gives the names of some of the men from Bridger's party and from Gale's group, who participated. He lists Carson, Hawkins, Gale, Liggit, Rider, Robinson, Anderson, Russell, Larison, Ward, Parmaley, Wade, and Head.

115
The Stinking Creek is the Ruby River of today, and was given the more euphonious name of Philanthropy River by Lewis and Clark. It is a tributary of the Jefferson River.

116
Carson and Russell, *Journal*, 32–33, are in agreement as to the movement of Bridger's and Gale's combined parties at this time, and Russell says they left the Flathead Village on September 23, and were on Camas Creek on September 30, 1835. The Flatheads lived in the mountains of western Montana and were enemies of the Blackfeet. The Pend d'Oreilles were an allied tribe in the Idaho panhandle. Russell also speaks of

*Sketch of Carson by Brewerton, 1848.* (Courtesy of Kit Carson Museum) *See page 232.*

In the Spring [1840], Bridger and party started for rendezvous on Green River. Jack Robison and myself for the Utah country, to Robidoux's fort, and there disposed of the furs we had caught on our march.[117]

In the fall, six of us went to Grand River, and there made our hunt and passed the winter at Brown's Hole on Green River.[118] In the spring [1841], went back to the Utah country and into

meeting Francis Ermatinger with a Hudson's Bay Company party at the Indian village. This provides another reason for believing that Carson not only wintered on the Big Snake as he says, but was engaged by the British company to make a late fall hunt south of Snake River, as postulated above.

117
John Robertson, usually called "Uncle Jack," was employed on occasion by both the Hudson's Bay Company and the Rocky Mountain Fur Company, but chiefly he was a free trapper and trader on his own account. He built a cabin on Black's Fork of Green River in 1834, and resided in southeastern Wyoming until his death in 1882, when he was said to have been nearly eighty years of age. Described as "very tall, honest, jolly, slouchy and dirty, never sober except when away from liquor," he nevertheless sent money to his mother in Missouri. See Elizabeth A. Stone, *Uinta County, Its Place in History* (Laramie, 1924), 41–46, which reprints some letters to his father and mother. He left descendants by his Indian wife, Marook.

Carson could have returned in time to attend the rendezvous of 1840, but there is no evidence that he did so except for his having known Father De Smet and the difficulty of accounting for that fact in any other way.

118
The Colorado and the Gunnison were both called Grand River by the trappers. Probably the Colorado, which was nearer to Brown's Hole, is meant here.

119
The Utah country probably refers to

the New Park and made the Spring hunt.[119] Returned to Robidoux Fort and disposed of our Beaver and remained till September [1841].[120]

Beaver was getting scarce, and, finding it was necessary to try our hand at something else, Bill Williams,[121] Bill New,[122] Mitchell,[123] Frederick,[124] a Frenchman, and myself concluded to start for Bent's Fort on the Arkansas.[125] Arrived on the Arkansas about one hundred miles above the fort. Mitchell and New concluded to remain; they apprehended no danger from Indians. We continued on for the fort, arrived in a few days. Ten days after our arrival, Mitchell and New came. They were naked. The Indians run off all their animals, and stole from them everything they had.

I was kindly received at the fort by Messrs. Bent and St. Vrain, offered employment to hunt for the Fort at one dollar per day. Accepted this offer, and remained in their employ till 1842.[126] I wish I was capable to do Bent and St. Vrain justice for the kindness received at their hands. I can only say that their equals were never in the mountains. The former, after the conquest of New Mexico, received the appointment of Governor of the Territory.[127] In the revolution of 1847, [he] was treacherously killed by Pueblo Indians and Mexicans. His death was regretted by all that knew him, and for the latter, I can say that all mountaineers look to him as their best friend and treat him with the greatest of respect. He now lives in New Mexico and commands the respects of all, American and Mexican [alike].

It has now been 16 years I have been in the mountains. The greater part of that time passed far from the habitations of civilized man, and receiving no other food than that which I could procure with my rifle. Perhaps, once a year, I would have a meal consisting of bread, meat, sugar, and coffee; would consider it a luxury. Sugar and coffee could be purchased at the ren-

the area between Brown's Hole and Fort Robidoux. Had they gone farther into Utah, they would not have been able to hunt in New (North) Park, which lay in the opposite direction. It could refer to the Grand River and its tributaries, which was the country of the Bunkara Utes (also known as the Grand River Utes).

120
The year 1841 is the most probable time for the death of Waa-nibe, Carson's squaw, but whether it occurred at Brown's Hole or at Fort Robidoux is impossible to say. She had given birth to a second daughter, probably in 1840. This child died in Taos, about 1843, by falling into a kettle of boiling soap. See F. W. Cragin Papers, Notebook XII, 21. Cragin's informant was Carson's eldest daughter by his last marriage, Teresina, Mrs. De Witt Fulton Allen, in an interview on March 18, 1908, at her home in Raton, New Mexico.

121
William Sherley Williams, always known as "Old Bill," was born in Rutherford County, North Carolina, on January 3, 1787. He spent the years 1805–25 as a Baptist missionary among the Osage Indians. In 1825 he left his Osage wife and two daughters in order to accompany George Champlin Sibley's surveying expedition to Santa Fe. He remained in the mountains to engage in trapping and trading. He ranged widely from Arizona to Oregon and from Texas to the Yellowstone, sometimes with a company but usually as a free trapper. His eccentricities are well known and attracted the pens of Ruxton and Stewart. He conferred upon himself the M.T. degree, which stood for Master of Trapping. As a

guide for Frémont in the winter of 1848–49, he shares the responsibility for the disastrous end of the expedition. He was killed by Ute Indians, in March, 1848, as he and Dr. Benjamin Kern sought to retrieve some of the equipment abandoned by Frémont in the mountains. See Alpheus H. Favour, *Old Bill Williams, Mountain Man* (Chapel Hill, 1936); also Chauncey P. Williams, *Lone Elk: The Life Story of Bill Williams, Trapper and Guide of the Far West* (Denver, 1935).

122

William T. New was born in Illinois in 1802. The first knowledge we have of him as a trapper is as an employee of Bent's Fort in 1836. During the 1840's, he lived south of the Arkansas, chiefly at the Greenhorn settlement. He was living in Taos in 1850, with a wife and three daughters. He attempted to farm near Carson's place on Rayado Creek in 1850, and was killed there by Jicarilla Apaches in the spring of 1851. See Note 261, below.

123

Levin Mitchell, called Bill by a number of writers and known to the Mexicans as "Colorado" because of his red hair and florid complexion, probably came to the mountains in 1829. He was a frequent trapping companion of Carson and Meek during the 1830's. Peters, *Life and Adventures*, 162–63, says that he lived for some years among the Comanches, with the object of finding a gold mine. He was among the horse thieves at Fort Davy Crockett and went from there to California on the big horse-stealing expedition of 1840. After working for Bent in 1841–43, he became a pioneer farmer on the St. Charles River, near El Pueblo. When the area along the Arkansas was annexed to Kansas Territory in 1854, he made a trip to eastern Kansas with a view to organizing the western portion of the territory politically. He soon returned to the mountains and to his Mexican wife, but no further record of him has been found. See Janet S. Lecompte, "Levin Mitchell," *Mountain Men* (ed. by Hafen), V, 239–48.

124

A certain Frederick, called "Cut-Nose," was also among the trappers who stole horses in California in 1840, and is undoubtedly the man referred to here. Lecompte, "Levin Mitchell," *Mountain Men* (ed. by Hafen), V. The term, "a Frenchman," is not in apposition with Frederick but applies to an unnamed sixth member of the party.

H. S. Lyman, reporting the "Reminiscences of F. X. Matthieu" in *Oregon Historical Quarterly*, Vol. I (March, 1900), 78, says that Matthieu went to Bent's Fort in 1840 and that "while on this jaunt" he saw Kit Carson, who was a hunter for the fort. Matthieu's "jaunt" extended to the summer of 1842, when he went to Fort Laramie and joined a wagon train for Oregon. He outfitted at Bent's Fort and made a beaver hunt in the Laramie Mountains in the fall of 1840 and the spring of 1841, and it was undoubtedly in the fall of 1841 that he became acquainted with Carson. It is impossible that Kit could have been at Bent's Fort when Matthieu first arrived there in 1840, for he certainly knew his traveling companions, all of whom—except possibly the unnamed Frenchman—were engaged in stealing horses in California in 1840 and could not have

dezvous for two dollars per pint, and flour one dollar per pint.

In April 1842, the train of wagons of Bent and St. Vrain was going to the states. I concluded to go in with them. It had been a long time since I had been among civilized people. I arrived at the States, went and saw my friends and acquaintances,[128] then took a trip to St. Louis, remained a few days and was tired of remaining in settlements, took a steamer for the Upper Missouri, and—as luck would have it—Colonel Fremont, then a Lieutenant, was aboard of the same boat.[129]

He had been in search of Captain Dripps, an old experienced mountaineer, but failed in getting him. I spoke to Colonel Fremont, informed him that I had been some time in the mountains and thought I could guide him to any point he would wish to go. He replied that he would make inquiries regarding my capabilities of performing that which I promised. He done so. I presume he received reports favorable of me, for he told me I would be employed. I accepted the offer of one hundred dollars per month and prepared myself to accompany him. We arrived at Kansas [and] started for the Rocky Mountains. His object was to survey the South pass and take the height of the highest peaks of the Rocky Mts.[130] We travelled the course that is now travelled by the California emigrants, to Fort Laramie.

The fall before our arrival at the fort, there was a party of trappers that had joined a village of Snake Indians. They had been attacked by a party of Sioux, in which the latter was defeated and lost several men. The Sioux for revenge had collected a number of warriors, about 1000 lodges for the purpose of having satisfaction for the damage done them by the whites and Snakes. There was some Sioux at the Fort. They and the trappers and traders endeavored to per-

accompanied Carson to Bent's Fort in that year. Carson made no errors in his recollections concerning persons and although he made errors concerning dates, this is not one of them.

125
Bent's Old Fort was located six miles east of present La Junta, Colorado, but on the north, or American, bank of the Arkansas River. It was a large thick-walled adobe structure and was described by several travelers. It was built in 1834, after William Bent had wrested the Cheyenne trade from John Gantt. Prior to that time, Bent had maintained a picket post a few miles east of Gantt's Fort Cass. It is untrue that Kit Carson had a hand in building Bent's Old Fort. Such reports seem traceable to George Bent, William's half-blood son, who could have had no firsthand knowledge of the matter. Carson was never in the vicinity before 1841, except for a short time in 1833 when he was in the employment of Gantt. The fort was constructed by Mexican laborers and there is no evidence that Carson knew anything about either the making or the laying of bricks. The fort was the center of a profitable Indian trade, chiefly in buffalo hides rather than beaver, down to August, 1849, when William Bent abandoned it and built his new fort in the Big Timbers, thirty-eight miles downstream. There is no truth in the legend that Bent destroyed the Old Fort by exploding barrels of gunpowder in it, since it was used by Barlow and Sanderson as a depot on their stage line in the 1850's and 1860's.

William Bent was born in St. Louis, Missouri, on May 23, 1809. He married first the Cheyenne, Owl Woman; second, her sister, Yellow Woman; and third, Adelina Harvey, a half-blood. His partners, Charles Bent and Cèran St. Vrain were present at the fort only occasionally. However, two younger Bent brothers, George (1814–47) and Robert (1816–41) were probably at the fort at the time of Carson's arrival, although Robert was killed by Comanches shortly afterward. William Bent died at his ranch on the Purgatoire River on May 19, 1869. He was usually referred to as Colonel Bent. See McClung, *Carson–Bent–Boggs,* 98–102; and also Lavender, *Bent's Fort.*

126
Carson remained as a hunter for Bent's Fort barely eight months, if the month of his arrival and that of his departure are both counted. Peters, *Life and Adventures,* 167, says he filled the post of hunter there "for eight consecutive years." Why Peters should have falsified the record is not only a mystery but also the source of much misunderstanding. Peters' statement was followed by all the early biographers of Carson. It also allowed Oliver Wiggins and others to fabricate stories of their association with Carson and place them within this supposed period of eight years.

The eight-month period, however, was the time of Carson's second marriage, to a Cheyenne squaw known as Making-Out-Road. The marriage was not congenial and ended after a few months by her leaving him, according to the Indian divorce customs.

Carson mentions neither of his Indian wives, and Teresina Bent Scheurich denied his second marriage. However, Jesse Nelson, husband of Susan Carson, Kit's niece, was closely associated with Kit during the period 1848–56 and he affirms the second marriage as well as Carson's brief liaison with one of Jim Beckwourth's women, Antonina Luna, who later married William Tharp. The logical conclusion to be drawn is that Kit, in accordance with the moral standards of the time, concealed the knowledge of his relations with other women from the women of his family, but did not endeavor to do so among the men of the family or other male associates. For Jesse Nelson's statement, see Cragin Papers, Notebook VIII, 83. Two modern biographers, Estergreen, *Kit Carson,* and Blackwelder, *Great Westerner,* appear to find Mrs. Scheurich's repudiation of Kit's second Indian marriage convincing.

127
The reference here and in the sentence following is to Charles Bent, not to William Bent.

128
Carson not only visited relatives but he also left his four-year-old daughter, Adaline, to be cared for by his sister, Mary Ann Carson Rubey. She received some education and returned to Taos in 1852. See Blackwelder, *Great Westerner,* 99–100.

129
John C. Frémont was born on January 21, 1813, in Savannah, Georgia. He married Jessie, daughter of Senator Thomas Hart Benton, in 1841, and the Senator's interest in the Far West and his influence in Washington materially aided his son-in-law's career. Through the printing and distribution of thousands of copies of his reports, Frémont became known as the Pathfinder and Carson was the Pathfinder's guide. Frémont was the unsuccessful Republican candidate for the Presidency in 1856, and his

Area of Carson's Trapping Activities, 1831–41

suade Fremont not to proceed, that he ran a great risk, that in all probability he would meet the Sioux and that his party would be destroyed.[131]

Fremont informed them that he was directed by his government to perform a certain duty, that it mattered not what obstacles were in his advance, that he was bound to continue his march in obedience to his instruction, that he would accomplish that for which he [was] sent or die in the attempt; and if he failed, by losing his party, his government would eventually punish those that caused the failure. We continued our march [and] arrived at the South Pass. Fremont accomplished all that was desired of him and then we returned.[132] Arrived at [Fort] Laramie sometime in September. During the expedition, I performed the duties of guide and hunter. I, at Laramie, quit the employ of Fremont, he continuing his march for the States taking nearly the same route as that by which he had come.[133]

I went to Bent's Fort in January 1843, departed for Taos. In February of same year got married to Senorita Josepha Jarimilla, a daughter of Don Francisco Jaramilla.[134] I remained in Taos till April, then started for the States with Bent and St. Vrain.[135] I was hunter for the train and continued as such till our arrival at Walnut Creek.[136] There we found encamped Capt. P. St. G. Cook with four companies of Dragoons.[137] He informed us that the train of Armijo and several traders was a short distance in his rear.[138] They had [a] great number of wagons and in the party there was about one hundred men, Mexicans and Americans. They had received intelligence that a large party of Texans was at the crossing of the Arkansas, awaiting the arrival of the train for the purpose of capturing the same and kill and take prisoners of as many Mexicans as they could, in revenge of the treatment Armijo had given the Texans when in his power.[139]

Civil War career, also, was a disappointment to him. He died in poverty in New York City on July 13, 1890.

The initial meeting with Frémont was the turning point in Carson's life. He was unknown to the world beyond the mountains up to this time, and among the Mountain Men themselves he had never been a leader, although he was more experienced than most of them. Frémont was to make him famous. On the other hand, the success of Frémont's explorations is attributable, to a considerable degree, to the aptitude that Carson was to show for this kind of work. Frémont's description of Carson on this occasion is of interest. He wrote, "I was pleased with him and his manner of address at this first meeting. He was a man of medium height, broad-shouldered and deep-chested, with a clear steady blue eye and frank speech and address; quiet and unassuming." *Memoirs,* 74.

130
This was Frémont's first expedition. With the exception of Colonel Henry Dodge's expedition in 1835, no governmental exploration in the Far West had been undertaken since Major Stephen H. Long's expedition in 1820. Frémont was an officer in the Topographical Engineers. He was to choose sites for military posts along the Oregon Trail, in addition to his other duties. For a full account of Frémont's first and second expeditions see John C. Frémont, *Narrative of the Exploring Expeditions to the Rocky Mountains, in the year 1842 and to Oregon and North California in the Years 1843–1844* (New York, 1846).

They concluded to remain [and] sent word to Genl. Armijo of the predicament they were in. The Dragoons were only to guard them to the Arkansas and they wished to have [General] Armijo send troops for their protection after the departure of the American troops.

I was spoken to in regard of the carrying the letter to Armijo in Santa Fe. They offered $300.00 for the performance of the duty. I agreed to carry it. I left the train and started for Taos. Had with me Dick Owens, arrived at Bent's Fort, was informed that the Utah Indians were on my route. Owens remained at the Fort, Bent furnished me with a fine horse which I could lead and, in case I should fall in with any Indians, could mount him and make my escape. I started, discovered the Indian village without them seeing me, passed them during the night, arrived safely at Taos, gave the letters to the Alcade and he forwarded them to Santa Fe. I was to remain for an answer.[140]

Sometime before my arrival [General] Armijo had sent 100 Mexican soldiers towards the Arkansas to find out about his train and he was to proceed on after them with 600. The first party had reached the Cold Springs, were attacked by Texans, and all, with the exception of one, were killed and taken prisoner by the Texans.[141] He made his escape by having been lucky enough to catch one of the Texan's horses, and made away to report to his general; found him on the march with the 600 men. But when the Genl. heard of the defeat of his brave soldiers, his heart failed him, and he returned for Santa Fe in all haste.

I waited in Taos for four days, received the despatches from Armijo, started for the Arkansas, took with me one Mexican. When two days out, saw a large party of Indians coming towards us; they were Utahs. The Mexican advised me to mount my horse and make my escape, that the Indians had no animal that could catch him

131
The reports of hostile Sioux caused Carson to make his will. Charles Preuss the German cartographer, was inclined to scoff at this. He accuses Carson of making a great fuss about Indians in order to make himself more important. A more amusing instance of the ignorance of Preuss is found in his writing "Kid Carsten" in place of Kit Carson. That this was an error and not a joke is shown by the fact that he writes that the young of the beaver are called "Kids." Preuss also relates that Frémont and Carson quarreled about small matters; these wrangles were soon forgotten by both principals, however, and neither ever referred to them. One thing Preuss appreciated about Carson was the effort he made to bring in "fat cow," as the mountain men said, while Lucien Maxwell, the regular hunter, was content to bring in "poor bull" buffalo for eating. See Charles Preuss, *Exploring with Frémont,* translated and edited by Erwin G. Gudde and Elizabeth K. Gudde (Norman, 1958), 40, 47–49, 70.

Among the people they encountered on the way to South Pass were Jim Beckwourth, Jim Bridger, Joseph Bissonette, and Touissant Charbonneau, the son of Sacagawea, the Shoshone squaw who accompanied Lewis and Clark.

132
Among other things, they had ascended Frémont Peak [13,730 feet] in the Wind River Range. Frémont, *Narrative,* 42–47.

133
From September, 1842, to January, 1843, Carson's whereabouts are unknown. It is probable that he was

at some of the trading posts on the North Platte, or at the old Pueblo on the Arkansas, or perhaps at all of these, in turn, as he made his way to Taos by way of Bent's Fort.

134
Carson's marriage took place on February 6, 1843. George Bent and Maria de la Cruz Padilla were the canonical witnesses. The certificate, signed by Padre Antonio José Martinez, is reproduced by Father Claudius Antony, "Kit Carson, Catholic," in *New Mexico Historical Review,* Vol. X (October, 1935), 323–26. The fact that Carson had been baptized by Padre Martinez a year earlier, on January 28, 1842, is an indication that during his period as a hunter for Bent's Fort he had found time to visit Taos and begin his courtship of Josefa Jaramillo. Her father was Francisco Jaramillo, born in 1790; and her mother, Apolonia Vigil, born in 1800, was of a prominent New Mexican family. They are listed in the census of 1850 for Taos as possessing real estate valued at $217. Two sons, Luciano, nineteen, and Nicanor, eight, were still at home. Josefa is described as a native and a resident of the town of Santa Cruz de la Cañada. The same census indicates that she was born in 1830, in Río Arriba County, New Mexico, which would make her thirteen at the time of her marriage. However, McClung, *Carson-Bent-Boggs,* 71, gives her date of birth as March 19, 1828, which would make her nearly fifteen. Census records are frequently inaccurate and certainly the record is wrong in this instance.

135
Both Charles Bent and Céran St. Vrain were with their wagon train on this trip.

136
Walnut Creek flows into the Arkansas River four miles east of present Great Bend, in Barton County, Kansas. The ford at which the caravans on the Santa Fe Trail crossed the Arkansas was located here.

137
Philip St. George Cooke was born in Virginia in 1809. He graduated from West Point in 1827. From 1829, for many years, he patrolled the western frontier as a captain of Dragoons. He commanded the Mormon Battalion on its march to California, 1846–47. He was loyal to the Union during the Civil War. His *Scenes and Adventures in the Army* (Philadelphia, 1857), is a valuable source of early western history. He died in Detroit in 1895.

138
Manuel Armijo was the last Mexican governor of New Mexico. In addition to his political activities, he carried on extensive trading enterprises. He was not noted for his courage, although he was acquitted when tried in Mexico City for cowardice during the Mexican War. He died in 1853. It was Senator Armijo, the Governor's brother, who had charge of the wagon trains, which the General and Governor had approached the border in order to escort.

139
The large party of Texans was composed of 180 armed men, calling themselves the "Invincibles," under the command of Jacob Snively. They

and, as for him, he thought the Indians would not injure him and they, in all probability, would kill me. I considered the advice very good and was about to mount my horse. I changed my mind and thought how cowardly it would be in me to desert this man that so willingly offered to sacrifice his life to save mine. I told him no, that I would die with him.[142]

The Indians were rapidly approaching; one was some distance in the advance. He came to me with a smile on his countenance, the old rascal, and offered me his hand. I proffered mine but, instead of taking my hand, he had caught hold of my rifle, endeavored to take it from me. We tussled for a short time and I made him let go his hold. By this time the remainder had arrived. They kept up among themselves a loud talk. Some would ride about us examine their guns, open their pans, knock the priming of their rifles, and many manoeuvers endeavoring to frighten us or to change our positions, that they might fire and kill us before we could return the fire. We watched them closely, determined that the first that would raise his gun should be shot. They remained around us for about a half hour and seeing but little hopes of their being able to kill us without losing two of themselves, they left. I continued my journey, arrived in a few days at Bent's Fort without having met with any further difficulty. I was informed by Mr. Bent that the dragoons had caught the Texans, disarmed them, and the train continued on its march without fear, not even considering it necessary to come to the fort.

A few days before my arrival at the Fort, Fremont had passed.[143] He had gone about seventy-five miles. I wished to see him and started for his camp. My object was not to seek employment. I only thought that I would ride to his camp, have a talk, and then return. But when Fremont saw me again and requested me to join him, I

had been licensed by the Republic of Texas to invade New Mexico and prey on the trade over the Santa Fe Trail. They had been joined by a Texas colonel, Charles A. Warfield, who had recently attacked Mora, New Mexico, and had been driven off. Since Snively was on the soil of the United States, Captain Cooke disarmed the "Invincibles" and sent them back to Texas. See R. P. Crump, *The Snively Expedition* (New York, 1949); also Otis E. Young, *The West of Philip St. George Cooke* (Glendale, 1955), 109–36.

140
Carson's exploit was in vain, because General Armijo was afraid to go to the aid of the traders.

141
The advance guard of General Armijo's force consisted of about fifty men only, of whom from eighteen to thirty were reported killed by Snively's Texans. The fight took place nearer to Walnut Creek than Cold Springs, which was about ninety miles away. It was at Cold Springs that Governor Armijo was encamped with about four hundred men. Upon learning of the defeat of his advance guard, Armijo turned back, as Carson relates. The traders were aware of this and paid Carson to carry their letter of entreaty to him. It was the fact that Captain Cooke had disarmed Snively's men that enabled the traders to continue their journey, as Carson was to learn when he came back to Bent's Fort.

142
This adventure was much to Carson's credit, as well as that of the courageous Mexican. It is regrettable that Carson does not tell us the name

could not refuse, and again entered his employ as guide and hunter. I was sent back to the fort to purchase mules, I bought ten head. Fremont continued on to the Fountaine-qui-bouille[144] (Soda Springs) and went to Bent's Fort on South Fork of Platte River, where I joined him.[145]

Major Fitzpatrick, an old, experienced mountaineer, was also in his employ and about forty men. Here we separated. Fitzpatrick took charge of the main camp, with carts, etc., and went to Laramie. Fremont with fifteen men, myself in the number, struck out up Thompson's Fork and from there to Cache-la-poudre, and thence through the plains of Laramie, crossed the North Fork of the Platte below the New Park, to Sweetwater (River). We struck the stream about fifteen miles above the Devil's Gate, then we travelled about the same route as is now travelled by emigrants to the Soda Springs on Bear River.[146]

From here Fremont started to the Salt Lake for its exploration and I went to Fort Hall for provisions.[147] We were getting out. I reached the fort, was well received and furnished all that I required. I started from the fort, had one man with me, and joined Fremont at the upper end of the Salt Lake. We travelled around the East side of the lake about twenty miles, till we could get a fair view of it. We were in front of the large island of the lake and Fremont determined to go to it for the purpose of examining it. Arranged the India Rubber boat; myself and four others accompanied him. We landed safely. The island is about fifteen miles from the mainland. We remained on the island part of one day and night. We brought with us fresh water for cooking purposes. Found nothing of any great importance. There were no springs and it was perfectly barren. We ascended the mountain and, under shelving rock, cut a large cross, which is there to this day.[148]

of the brave man who shared this narrow escape with him.

143
Frémont was at El Pueblo and it was there that Carson overtook him and set off so unexpectedly on the long Second Expedition. *The Journals of Theodore Talbot,* edited by Charles H. Carey (Portland, 1931), 27, have this entry: "Fri. 21st. Fitz [patrick] and Gilpin went up to Lupton's, returning with Christopher Carson . . . He brought nine mules for Mr. Frémont, bought at Bent and St. Vrain's Fort on the Arkansas R."

144
The Fontaine-qui-bouille is today called Fountain Creek. It originates on the northwest slope of Pikes Peak and flows through Ute Pass to join Monument Creek in present Colorado Springs, and thence southward to join the Arkansas River at present Pueblo, Colorado. The Boiling Springs, from which it took its name, were seven in number, of which two were especially famous. They are located in present Manitou Springs, Colorado. They were first noted by the Chouteau–De Mun expedition of trappers in 1817, although possibly visited as early as 1811–13 by Ezekiel Williams. The Long expedition of 1820 reported on these springs, and Frémont made an analysis of their mineral content.

145
Bent's Fort on the South Platte was Fort St. Vrain, where Frémont had arrived on July 4, 1843, and to which he now returned. Sometimes called Fort George or Fort Lookout, it was built in 1837. Marcellin St. Vrain, a younger brother of Céran, was in charge of the fort at the time of Fré-

Next morning [we] started back. Had not left the island more than a league when the clouds commenced gathering for a storm. Our boat, leaking wind, kept one man continually employed at the bellows. Fremont directed us to pull for our lives, if we do not arrive on shore before the storm commenced we will surely all perish. We done our best and arrived in time to save ourselves. We had not more than landed when the storm commenced and in [an] hour the waters had risen eight or ten feet.

We now took up Bear River till we got above the lake. Then crossed it and took up Malade [River], thence to Fort Hall, where we met Fitzpatrick and party. Fremont from here took his party and proceeded in advance, Fitzpatrick keeping in rear some eight days march, and we struck for the mouth of the Columbia River.[149] Arrived safe at the Dalles on the Columbia.[150] Fremont took four men and proceeded to Vancouver's to purchase provisions.[151] I remained in charge of camp.

In the meantime Fitzpatrick joined [us]. We started for Klamath Lake.[152] A guide was employed and we arrived there safe and found a large village of Indians having the same name. We had with them a talk. We pronounced them a mean, low-lived, treacherous race, which we found to be a fact after we were in their country in 1846.[153]

Here our guide left us and we struck for California.[154] Our course was through a barren, desolate, and unexplored country till we reached the Sierra Nevada, which we found covered with snow from one end to the other. We were nearly out of provisions and cross the mountain we must, let the consequences be what they may. We went as far in the snow as we possibly could with animals, then was compelled to send them back. Then we commenced making a road through the snow. We beat it down with mallets.

mont's visit. It was the northernmost of four competitive fur-trading posts on the South Platte, the others being Fort Vasquez, Fort Jackson, and Fort Lupton, in that order. Abandoned as a permanent post in 1845 and described by Francis Parkman in 1846 as "fast falling into ruin," it was seasonally used for several years after this as a place to trade with the Arapahoes. See LeRoy R. Hafen, "Early Fur Trade Posts on the South Platte," *Mississippi Valley Historical Review,* Vol. XII (December, 1925), 335–41.

146
This was very familiar territory to Carson from his trapping years. The Devil's Gate was a gorge of the Sweetwater near the well-known Independence Rock, on the Oregon Trail.

147
Carson left Frémont for Fort Hall on August 19, and rejoined him on September 4, 1843. Frémont characterized the provisions brought by Carson as "a scanty but very acceptable supply." Richard Grant, British officer in charge of Fort Hall, was generous in his help to emigrants, who had depleted his supplies. Frémont, *Memoirs,* 201, 226.

148
Frémont called the island Disappointment, but it was later called Castle Island by the Mormons, and Captain Stansbury, in 1849, renamed it Frémont Island. Exploring Salt Lake in this small boat was more dangerous than they realized. This excursion was made on September 9, 1843. Frémont, *Narrative,* 88–90. There is a photograph of Kit Carson's cross in Dale L. Morgan, *The Great Salt Lake* (Indianapolis, 1947), opp. 94.

149
Carson accompanied Frémont and the advance party. Eleven men, including the Lajeunesse brothers, returned to St. Louis from Fort Hall, starting September 22, 1843. Frémont, *Narrative,* 94.

150
They were at Fort Boise on October 9; at the Grande Ronde on October 18; at Fort Walla Walla on October 25; and reached the Dalles on November 4, 1843. The Dalles are the Narrows of the Columbia and are still so called. Whitman was absent from his mission but they procured good potatoes at Fort Walla Walla, and Preuss records that Kit put another pot of potatoes on the fire before going to bed. Frémont, *Narrative,* 101, 105, 108, 110; Preuss, *Exploring,* 95.

151
Fort Vancouver, located near present Fort Vancouver, Washington, and across the Columbia from present Portland, Oregon, was in the charge of Dr. John McLoughlin, as it had been since its construction by the Hudson's Bay Company in 1824. It was abandoned in 1846. It was about 115 miles from the mouth of the river.

152
Frémont's decision to go to Klamath Lake was an addition to his objectives as outlined by Congress, which now had been achieved. His purpose was to investigate the mythical Buenaventura River, supposed to rise in the Great Basin and flow to San Francisco Bay. Captain Bonneville's map, published in Washington Irving, *The Adventures of Captain Bonneville, U.S.A. in the Rocky Mountains and the Far West* (New York, 1837),

The snow was six feet on the level for three leagues. We made snow shoes and passed over the snow to find how far we would have to make a road. Found it to be the distance afore stated.

After we reached the extremity of the snow, we could see in the distance the green valley of the Sacramento and the Coast Range. I knew the place well, had been there seventeen years before. Our feelings can be imagined when we saw such beautiful country.[155] Having nothing to eat but mule meat, we returned to the place from which we had sent back our animals and commenced the work of making the road. In fifteen days our task was accomplished. Sent back for the animals. They had, through hunger eaten one another's tails and the leather of the pack saddles, in fact, everything they could lay hold of. They were in a deplorable condition and we would frequently kill one to keep it from dying, then use the meat for food.

We continued our march and by perseverence in making the road, for the wind had drifted the snow and, in many places, filled up the path which we had made, we finally got across, and then commenced descending the mountain. Then we left Fitzpatrick in charge of the main party. Fremont, myself, and five or six men went ahead to Sutter's Fort for provisions.

The second day after leaving Fitzpatrick, Mr. Preus, Fremont's assistant, got lost.[156] We made search for him, travelled slowly, fired guns so that he could know where we were. We could not find him. In four days the old man returned. Had his pockets full of acorns, having had no other food since he left [us]. We were all rejoiced at his return, for the old man was much respected by the party.

We arrived safely at Sutter's Fort, three days after the return to camp of Mr. Preus. When we arrived at the fort we were naked and in as poor a condition as men possibly could be. We were well received by Mr. Sutter and furnished in a princely manner, everything we required by him.[157] We remained about a month at the fort, made all the necessary arrangements for our return, having found no difficulty in getting all we required.

About the first of April, 1844, we were ready to depart. During our stay at the fort, two of our party became deranged—I presume from the effects of starvation and through receiving an abundance. One morning one of them jumped up, was perfectly wild, inquired for his mule. It was tied close to him but he started to the mountains to look for it. After some time, when his absence was known, men were sent in search of him. Looked through all the neighborhood, made inquiries of the Indians, but could hear nothing of him. Remained a few days waiting his return, but as he did not come in, we departed. Left word with Sutter to make search and, if possible, find him. He done so and, sometime after our departure, he was found, was kept at the fort and properly cared for till he got well, and then Mr. Sutter sent him to the States.

We took up the valley of the San Joaquin on our way home, we crossed the Sierra Nevada and Coast Range, where they join, a beautiful low pass; continued under the Coast Range till we struck the Spanish trail, then to the Mohavi river, a small stream that rises in the Coast range and is lost in the Great Basin, down it to where the trail leaves the Mohavi River.[158] We arrived only on the Mohavi where we intended leaving it. In the evening of the same day a Mexican man and boy came to our camp. They informed us that they were of a party of Mexicans from New Mexico, [that] they and two men and women were encamped a distance from the main party herding horses, that they were mounted, the two men and women were in their camp, that a party of Indians charged on them for the pur-

had already disproved the existence of this river but Frémont was apparently not familiar with this development.

153
The reference is to the fighting with the Klamaths during the third expedition.

154
They reached Klamath Marsh, to the west of the lake, on December 12, 1843. Their guide was an Indian. From here they pursued a route as yet untraveled by white men, southward to Pyramid Lake in Nevada, which they reached on January 14, 1844. They continued southward till January 30, seeking the non-existent Buenaventura River, and then gave it up and decided to cross the snow-covered Sierra Nevada Mountains. Frémont, *Narrative,* 131, 137.

155
Carson saw and recognized the valley of the Sacramento and the outlines of the Coast Range on February 6, 1844. Frémont, *Narrative,* 141. The howitzer, which they had wheeled with them all this distance, had been abandoned near present Virginia City, Nevada, when they started crossing the mountains. Snow, cold, and famine beset them. They lived largely on mule meat. Frémont called February 23 their worst day, but on February 28 Charles Town, an experienced mountain man, went out of his head and Carson exclaimed, "Life yet," when he found a little grass on a hillside for the animals. On February 28, he recommended boiling a mule's head, which they did, and it was pronounced delicious by Preuss. They finally reached Sutter's Fort on March 8, 1844. Carson's de-

pose of running off their stock. They told the men and women to make their escape, that they would guard the horses. They run the animals off from the Indians, left them at a Spring in the desert about thirty miles from our camp.

We started for the place where they said they left their animals, found that they had been taken away by the Indians that had followed them. The Mexican requested Fremont to aid him to retake his animals. He [Fremont] stated to the party that if they wished to volunteer for such purpose, they might do so, that he would furnish animals for them to ride. Godey and myself volunteered with the expectation that some men of our party would join us. They did not. We two and the Mexican took the trail of [the] animals and commenced the pursuit.[159] In twenty miles the Mexican's horse gave out. We sent him back and continued on. During the night it was very dark. [We] had to dismount to feel for the trail. By sign on the trail we became aware that the Indians had passed after sunset. We were much fatigued, required rest, unsaddled, wrapped ourselves in the wet saddle blankets and laid down. Could not make any fire for fear of it being seen. Passed a miserably cold night. In the morning we arose very early, went down in a deep ravine, made a small fire to warm ourselves and, as soon as it was light, we again took the trail.

As the sun was rising [we] saw the Indians two miles ahead of us, encamped having a feast. They had killed five animals. We were compelled to leave our horses; they could not travel. We hid them among the rocks, continued on the trail, crawled in among the horses. A young one got frightened; that frightened the rest. The Indians noticed the commotion among the animals [and] sprung for their arms. We now considered it time to charge on the Indians. They were about thirty in number. We charged. I fired,

scription of this rash crossing is rather restrained. Frémont, *Narrative,* 141–51; Preuss, *Exploring,* 109–14. The route whereby they crossed the Sierras was to become known as Carson Pass. However, they had not approached it by the most direct route. See Frederick S. Dellenbaugh, *Frémont and '49* (New York, 1914), 204–29.

156 Charles Preuss was born in the principality of Waldeck, Germany, on April 30, 1803. He came to the United States in 1834, and was employed by the United States Coast Survey for five years. He became the topographer and cartographer for Frémont's first and second expeditions. He was well qualified for this work and performed it with considerable skill, despite a morose and neurotic personality. He also accompanied the ill-fated fourth expedition but declined employment on both the third and the fifth. He became ill and despondent and hanged himself from a tree near Bladensburg, Maryland, on September 1, 1854, leaving a wife and four daughters. See Preuss, *Exploring,* xix–xxix.

157 John A. Sutter (1803–80), although born in the Grand Duchy of Baden, was of Swiss parentage and was a Captain in the Swiss Army before coming to the United States in 1834. He went to California by way of Oregon, in 1838–39, and received a land grant of 49,000 acres in the Sacramento Valley from Governor Alvarado, on condition that he would establish a strong fort upon it. This he did, in the fall of 1839, on the site of present Sacramento, at the confluence of the American and Sacra-

killed one. Godey fired, missed, but reloaded and fired, killing another. There was only three shots fired and two were killed. The remainder run. I took the two rifles and ascended a hill to keep guard while Godey scalped the dead Indians. He scalped the one he had shot and was proceeding towards the one I had shot. He was not yet dead [and] was behind some rocks. As Godey approached, he raised [and] let fly an arrow. It passed through Godey's shirt collar. He again fell and Godey finished him.[160]

We gathered the animals [and] drove them to where we had concealed our own, changed horses and drove to camp, and safely arrived.[161] [We] had all the animals, with the exception of those killed by the Indians for their feast.

We then marched on to where the Mexican had left the two men and women. The men we discovered dead, their bodies horribly mutilated. The women we supposed were carried into captivity. But such was not the case, for a party travelling in our rear found their bodies very much mutilated and staked to the ground.[162]

We continued our march and met no further molestation till we arrived on the Virgin [River], where the trail leaves it. There we intended to remain one day, our animals being much fatigued. We moved our camp a mile. In looking among the mules, a Canadian of the party missed one of his mules. He started back for the camp to get it, knowing that it must have been left. He did not inform Fremont or any of the party of his absence. In a few hours, he was missed. Those of the guard said he had gone to our last camp to look for his mule. I was sent with three men to seek him. We arrived at the camp; he could not be found. [We] saw where he fell from his horse [and a] great deal of blood was seen. [We] knew that he was killed. Searched for his body but it could not be found, followed the trail of his animal to where it

mento Rivers. He called his settlement "New Helvetia," and developed his grant so that he employed hundreds of men, including Indians, Mexicans, Kanakas, and Americans. The discovery of gold on his land in 1848 caused it to be so overrun with prospectors that he was finally ruined. Congress refused to confirm his title to a second grant of 98,000 acres, which might have saved him. His last years were spent in poverty in Lititz, Pennsylvania, and he died in Washington, D. C., vainly seeking compensation from the United States government.

158
They set out on their homeward journey on March 24, 1844, with information about Walker Pass, by which they intended to leave the southern end of the San Joaquin Valley. However, their actual crossing was made, on April 14, over Oak Creek Pass, which lies between Walker Pass and Tehachapi Pass. See Frémont, *Narrative*, 152–53, 157; also H. W. Johnson, "Where did Frémont Cross the Tehachapi Mountains in 1844?" *Annual Publications of the Historical Society of Southern California*, Vol. XIII (1926), 365–73.

159
It was this quality of being willing to volunteer for extra work of any kind that distinguished Carson from the common run of his fellows.

160
Preuss, *Exploring*, 127, claims that Carson was disgruntled because Godey was entitled, under the circumstances, to both scalps. This seems to be highly doubtful. Preuss does not display a very discerning attitude toward the Mountain Men, whom he

regarded as little better than savages. Neither Frémont nor Carson gives any indication of such a feeling in describing the incident.

161
Preuss. *Exploring,* 127, writes in disgust of "these two heroes, who shot the Indians creeping up on them from behind." Frémont, on the other hand, bestows on this exploit the highest praise. He writes, "The time, place, object, and numbers, considered, this expedition of Carson and Godey may be considered among the boldest and most distinguished which the annals of western adventure, so full of daring deeds, can present." The event occurred April 25, 1844. It is fully described in Frémont, *Narrative,* 161–63.

162
The Mexican man, Andreas Fuentes, and the eleven-year-old boy, Pablo Hernandez, both accompanied the expedition. Fuentes was engaged by Frémont for his third expedition. Hernandez was cared for in the household of Senator Benton, in Washington. Although given an education, he did not turn out well. Frémont heard a report some years later to the effect that a California bandit, known as Joaquin, was actually Pablo Hernandez. If this refers to the well-known Joaquin Murrieta, as seems likely, the rumor was almost certainly erroneous. See Frémont, *Memoirs,* 409.

163
The man killed by the Paiutes was Baptiste Tabeau, described by Frémont as "one of our best men." His death was discovered on May 10, 1844. Frémont, *Narrative,* 166–67. Preuss, *Exploring,* 130, seems to have had his romantic notions of the Indians severely shaken, at last, by Tabeau's death at their hands.

164
Frémont, *Narrative,* 168, says, under date of May 12, "We considered ourselves as crossing the rim of the basin; and, entering it at this point, we found here an extensive mountain meadow, rich in bunch grass, and fresh with numerous springs of clear water, all refreshing and delightful to look upon. It was, in fact, *las Vegas de Santa Clara,* which had been so long presented to us as the terminating point of the desert. . . ." Also known as Mountain Meadows, the Vega of Santa Clara was located southwest of present Cedar City, Utah, on the headwaters of the Santa Clara River, and was the scene of the notorious Mountain Meadows Massacre, in September, 1857. See LeRoy R. and Ann W. Hafen, *Old Spanish Trail,* 72, 153, 212.

165
A few miles beyond the Vega of Santa Clara, they were overtaken by Joseph Reddeford Walker, a famous Mountain Man and Captain Bonneville's former lieutenant, with a party of eight men, who accompanied them all the way to Bent's Fort. He was more familiar with the Great Basin country but less familiar with the Rocky Mountain parks than was Carson.

166
Utah Lake, a large fresh-water lake south of the Great Salt Lake, was discovered by Padres Domínguez and Escalante in 1776. They left Utah Lake on May 27, 1844. Preuss, *Exploring,* 133, records that Carson bought an Indian boy, about twelve

crossed the river. Returned to camp, informed Fremont of his death. He, in the morning, with a party went to seek the body. Searched some time but without success. I was grieved on account of the death of the Canadian. He was a brave, noble-souled fellow. I had been in many an Indian fight with him and I am confident, if he was not taken unawares, that he surely killed one or two before he fell.[163]

We now left the Virgin, keeping to the Spanish trail till we passed the Vega of Santa Clara,[164] then [we] left the Spanish trail,[165] struck towards the Utah Lake,[166] crossed it and went to the Winty and thence to Green River, Brown's Hole, then to Little Snake River, to the mouth of St. Vrain's Fork. [We then] crossed the point of mountain and struck the Laramie River below the New Park.[167] [We] passed the New Park and on into the Old Park.[168] From there to the Arkansas River where it leaves the mountains, down it to Bent's fort.[169] [We] arrived at Bent's fort second of July, 1844, and remained until after the 4th. Then Fremont and party started for the states and I for Taos. On the 4th, Mr. Bent gave Fremont and party a splendid dinner.[170] The day was celebrated as well, if not better, than in many of the towns of the States.

I arrived in Taos and remained till March, 1845. Then Dick Owens and I concluded that, as we had rambled enough, that it would be advisable for us to go and settle on some good stream and make us a farm. We went to Little Cimarron, about 45 miles east of Taos, built ourselves little huts, put in considerable grain, and commenced getting out timber to enlarge our improvements.[171] Remained till August of same year.

The year previous, I had given my word to Fremont that, in case he should return for the purpose of making any more exploration, that I would willingly join him. He reached Bent's

or fourteen years old, from the Utes, adding that 'in a few years, he hopes to have him trained to steal horses." The Utes did a considerable business in stealing children and selling them as slaves.

167
The party was at Fort Uintah on June 3, and at Brown's Hole on June 7, 1844. Their route was up Vermillion Creek to the Little Snake River, which Frémont calls the Elkhead, to the mouth of St. Vrain's Fork, so called because Céran St. Vrain had trapped on it in 1827–28, and up this stream for a short distance. Just before reaching the St. Vrain Fork, they passed the site of the battle in which Henry Fraeb had been killed by the Sioux and Cheyennes in late August, 1841. This is at the junction of Battle Creek with the Little Snake River, just south of the Wyoming boundary in Routt County, Colorado. See Frémont, *Narrative,* 173–74; also LeRoy R. Hafen, "Henry Fraeb," *Mountain Men* (ed. by Hafen), III, 131–39. A little farther on, Carson pointed out where he and a few others had fought a Sioux party in the fall of 1839.

168
Frémont, *Narrative,* 175, under date of June 13, says, "Leaving St. Vrain's Fork, we took our way directly towards the summit of the dividing ridge . . . and reached the summit towards mid-day, at an elevation of 8,000 feet . . . and beheld a little stream . . . an affluent of the Platte, called Pullam's Fork . . . the name of a trapper, who, some years since, was killed here by the Gros Ventre Indians." John Pullum, a member of the Bean-Sinclair party from Arkan-

fort about the 1st of August, made inquiries where I was [and] heard of my being on the Cimarron. [He] sent an express to me. Then Owens and I sold out, for about half it was worth, and we started to join Fremont and we both received employment.[172]

We took up the Arkansas to where it comes out [of] the mountain, thence to Balla Salado, thence to the Arkansas, above the cañon and up to its head waters. Then crossed over to Piney River, down it to about 25 miles of its mouth, then to Grand River, crossed it, and then to [the] head of White River, down it to near where it empties into Green River.[173] Crossed Green River and went on to the Winty, up it to near where it comes out of the mountain, left it, crossed the mountain, and on to Provost Fork.[174] It was named so on account of a party of trappers having been defeated on it by a band of Indians. The trappers were under the charge of a man named Provost. His party were all killed with the exception of four.

We took down Provost [River] to the Little Utah Lake, which empties into the Great Salt Lake, followed its outlet to near the Great Salt Lake. Here Fremont made his camp, some distance south of our former encampment. There was in our front a large island, the largest of the lake.[157] We were informed by Indians that on it there was abundance of fresh water and plenty of antelope. Fremont took a few men, I being one, and went to the Island to explore it. We found good grass, water, timber, and plenty of game. We remained there some two days, killing meat and exploring [the island]. It was about fifteen miles long and in breadth about five miles. We then went back to camp. In going to the Island we rode over salt from the thickness of a wafer to twelve inches. We reached it horseback. We kept around the south side of the Lake to the last water [and] remained one day.

sas, is the trapper whose name was given to the creek. Carson's Laramie River is an error of geography; it was the North Platte, as Frémont is explicit on this point and the Laramie does not rise in North Park.

St. Vrain's Fork of the Little Snake is present Savery Creek, a curious transliteration of the original name. They followed it only a short distance, struck out for the Continental Divide, and crossed it. Pullam's Fork is now called Encampment Creek. They went down it to the present town of Encampment, Wyoming, and then turned up the North Platte and traversed New, or North, Park, crossing to Old, or Middle, Park by Muddy Pass (8,772 feet).

169 They were in New Park June 14–16; in Old Park June 17–19; and in the Bayou Salade June 21–22, 1844. Frémont says they arrived at Bent's Fort on July 1. Frémont, *Narrative,* 175–80. The crossing to the Bayou Salade, or South Park, was up Blue River and over Hoosier Pass (11,541 feet).

170 Apparently it was George Bent who entertained them with a Fourth of July dinner and celebration. Just a year earlier, July 3, 1843, Carson's wife, Josefa, and her sister, Ignacia Bent, and her children, and Cruz Padilla, George Bent's wife, had arrived at Bent's Fort from Taos in time for a similar celebration. They had been brought there by George Bent, John Hatcher, and Tom Boggs, because of a rumored anti-American uprising in Taos. Governor Armijo stifled the uprising and Josefa and Ignacia soon returned to Taos, although Mrs. George Bent remained

*Carson and Frémont, 1849.* (Courtesy of Denver Public Library) *See page 233.*

at the fort. See Lavender, *Bent's Fort,* 255–56.

171
A year earlier, Lucien Maxwell had made an attempt at farming on Rayado Creek and, about this same time, John Hatcher and Tom Boggs were trying to farm for William Bent on Ponil Creek. Carson and Owens were located between these two early ventures, near present Cimarron, New Mexico. All three were within the Beaubien and Miranda Land Grant of 1841, later known as the Maxwell Grant. Lavender, *Bent's Fort,* 245.

A Santa Fe trader encountered Carson in company with Maxwell and Tim Goodale in the fall of 1844, on the Culebra River, as they were riding from El Pueblo to Taos. They had stopped to cook supper and conversed with members of the wagon train before continuing their journey. See J. J. Webb, *Adventures in the Santa Fe Trade, 1844–1847,* edited by Ralph P. Bieber (Glendale, 1931), 63–65.

172
This was Frémont's third expedition, of which Frémont left only a reminiscent account in his *Memoirs.* Of Carson's action in joining him he wrote that "he not only came himself but brought his friend Owens to join the party. This was like Carson, prompt, self-sacrificing, and true." Frémont, *Memoirs,* 426.

173
The Piney River is the Eagle River of today. They left it near present Wolcott, Colorado, going north to cross the Colorado, probably at present State Bridge, and then went northwest to Trapper's Lake and the headwaters of White River.

The point at which they crossed the Continental Divide was somewhere above present Leadville, Colorado. It is usually assumed that it was by way of Tennessee Pass. However, a different impression is given by Thomas Salathiel Martin, a member of the expedition, who dictated his recollections in 1878. The manuscript, entitled "Narrative of John C. Frémont's Expedition to California in 1845–1846 . . . .", is in the Bancroft Library, Berkeley, California. Martin says that on or near the top of the ridge where they crossed there was a fine lake about a half-mile in width. The description fits Little Homestake Lake. Accordingly, their route followed up West Tennessee Creek, then up Homestake Creek to the lake, where they crossed the Divide just east of Homestake Peak and descended through Cold Park to another stream also known as Homestake Creek, which meets the Eagle River just below the former army post known as Camp Hale. The route is that over which the present Homestake water diversion project runs, and the crossing of the Continental Divide is about six miles west of Tennessee Pass (10,424 feet) on U.S. Highway 24. Frémont Pass (11,316 feet), about ten miles east of Tennessee Pass, was named for the explorer at a later date and was not crossed by him.

174
Provost Fork is the Provo River, which flows from the Uintah Mountains into Utah Lake. It took its name from Étienne Provost, who trapped on it in 1824, with an expedition which he led from Taos. See Morgan, *Great Salt Lake,* 68–69, 149–51.

Old Bill Williams was picked up in the Colorado mountains but re-

Fremont started Maxwell, Archambeau, Lajeunesse, and myself to cross the desert.[176] It had never before been crossed by white man. I was often hearing old trappers speak of the impossibility of crossing—that water could not be found, grass for animals, there was none.[177] Fremont was bound to cross. Nothing was impossible for him to perform if required in his explorations.

Before we started it was arranged that at a certain time of [the] next day he would ascend the mountain near his camp, have with him his telescope, so that we could be seen by him, and if we found grass or water we should make a smoke, which would be a signal to him to advance. We travelled on about 60 miles; no water or grass, not a particle of vegetation could be found, as level and bare as a barn floor, before we struck the mountains on the west side of the lake. Water and grass was there in abundance. The fire was made. Fremont saw it [and] moved on with his party. Archambeau started back and met him when about half way across the desert. He camped on the desert one night and next evening, at dark, he got across, having lost only a few animals.

Then we separated. Mr. Talbot took charge of camp.[178] His guide was Walker.[179] He was ordered to strike for Mary's River, and then follow it down to where it is lost in the Basin. Fremont took with him fifteen men to pass south of Mary's River. Both parties were to meet at the lake made by Carson River.[180]

We passed over a fine country, plenty of wood, grass, and water, only having about 40 miles to travel without water before reaching the lake, arrived at the lake and awaited the arrival of Talbot. In two or three days, he and party arrived. Here we again separated, Talbot and Walker to go through a pass to our south, cross over the Sierra Nevada to the waters of San

fused to cross the desert; Joseph Walker joined the expedition on White River and continued with it to California.

175
They followed the Jordan River to Great Salt Lake and camped within present Salt Lake City. Frémont called the large island Antelope Island. Morgan, *Great Salt Lake*, 149–51.

176
The reconnaissance party was made up of three old hands, Lucien Maxwell, a member of Frémont's first and third expeditions, Basil Lajeunesse, a favorite of Frémont's, who was with the first three expeditions and was killed on the third one, in California, and Carson. The fourth man, Auguste Archambeau, had joined the second expedition at Fort Uintah on May 27, 1844. He was an experienced trapper and a valuable addition to the party. He was born in Montreal in 1817, and ran away from home at the age of twelve to become a trapper in the Far West. In 1852 he had a trading post near Devil's Gate on the Sweetwater, and later in the decade kept a store at one of the Green River ferries, and, finally, near the site of old Fort Uintah. He returned to St. Louis in 1859 and died in 1882, of a tumor caused by a wound received while with Frémont. See F. W. Cragin Papers, Notebook V, 1, 6, 7, 8, 13; Notebook IV, 27, 28; Notebook XXVII, 57. James Reed, a nephew of Archambeau, was Dr. Cragin's principal informant, at White Rocks, Utah, August 30, 1902.

177
The belief that it was impossible to cross this desert was responsible for

Joaquin.[181] We went up Carson River to Sutter's Fort; having cross the Sierra Nevada, arrived safely at the Fort.[182] The old Captain Sutter was there and was happy to see us and furnished everything we wanted.

We remained a few days, purchased about 40 head of cattle and a few horses, then started to meet our camp. Went up the San Joaquin valley, crossed, where it came out of the mountain and then on to King's River, up it to the head waters.[183] During our march, from snow and travelling over rocks our cattle had become very tender-footed. From the head of King's River we started back for the prairie and when we arrived we had no cattle, they having all given out. Had to leave behind all except those we killed for meat. As we were getting from the mountains during the night, some Indians crawled into our camp and killed two of our mules. Next morning we started back for the fort. Through some mistake we had not found our camp, and, as we had lost nearly all our animals, it became necessary to return. The same evening we came on a party of Indians, killed five, and continued on to the fort. Arrived at the fort safely. All were afoot—lived principally on the meat of wild horses that we killed on the march. We now started for San José, only remained a few days to recruit. Got a few animals and crossed the coast range to see if we could hear anything of our party under Talbot. At San José we heard that they were on the San Joaquin. Fremont sent me and two men to meet them.[184] We met them on the San Joaquin. Guided them to San José.

After we had all got together again, we set out for Monterey to get an outfit. When we arrived within about 30 miles of Monterey, Fremont received a very impertinent order from General Castro, ordering him to immediately leave the country and, if he did not, that he would drive

Old Bill Williams' desertion at this point. However, it had been crossed by Jedediah S. Smith, from west to east, in 1826. The difficulties of the crossing were only slightly exaggerated. Smith did not choose to cross it again and he had no imitators until Frémont came along. See Dale L. Morgan, *Jedediah Smith* (Indianapolis and New York, 1953), 211–15.

178
Theodore Talbot was a Kentuckian by birth and was well educated. He had accompanied Frémont's second expedition as a sort of gentleman volunteer, possibly seeking to improve his health. He served as first lieutenant adjutant in the California Battalion and later enlisted in the artillery serving in Oregon. His military career was cut short by death, in Washington, D. C., on April 22, 1862. See Theodore Talbot, *The Journals of Theodore Talbot,* edited by Charles H. Carey (Portland, 1931).

179
Joseph Reddeford Walker was born in Roane County, Tennessee, on December 13, 1798. He went with William Becknell to Santa Fe in 1821, on the expedition that pioneered the trade over the Santa Fe Trail. He took service with Captain Bonneville in 1831 and led the famous expedition sent by him to Great Salt Lake and California in 1832. He was the discoverer of the Yosemite Valley and knew the Southwest, from the Humboldt River to the present Mexican Border, better than any other man. He died in Contra Costa County, California, October 27, 1876. See Douglas S. Watson, *West Wind: The Life of Joseph Reddeford Walker* (Los Angeles, 1934).

him out.[185] We packed up at dark, moved back about 10 miles to a little mountain, found a good place and made camp. General Castro came with several hundred men and established his headquarters near us. He would frequently fire his big guns to frighten us, thinking by such demonstrations he could make us leave.

We had in the party about 40 men armed with rifles; Castro had several hundred soldiers of Artillery, Cavalry and Infantry. Fremont received expresses from Monterey from Americans advising him to leave, that the Mexicans were strong and would surely attack us. He sent them word that he had done nothing to raise the wrath of the Mexican commander, that he was in performance of a duty, that he would let the consequences be what they may execute, and retreat he would not.

We remained in our position on the mountain for three days, had become tired of waiting for the attack of the valiant Mexican General.[186] We then started for the Sacramento River, up it to Peter Lawson's; there Fremont intended getting his outfit for the homeward trip.[187] Remained some ten days.[188]

During our stay at Lawson's, some Americans that were settled in the neighborhood came in stating that there were about 1000 Indians in the vicinity making preparations to attack the settlements; requested assistance of Fremont to drive them back. He and party and some few Americans that lived near started for the Indian encampment. Found them to be in great force, as was stated. They were attacked. The number killed I cannot say. It was a perfect butchery. Those not killed fled in all directions, and we returned to Lawson's. Had accomplished what we went for and given the Indians such a chastisement that [it] would be long before they ever again would feel like attacking the settlements.[189]

180
They were to meet at Walker Lake, in western Nevada.

181
Frémont at one point says that Kern had charge of the party guided by Walker, but at another point says it was Talbot. It was Talbot, because he made the decision to break camp and try to find Frémont. This section passed through the Owens River Valley, which Frémont named for Richard Owens, although he was not a member of this section of the expedition. Frémont, *Memoirs,* 434, 455.

182
Frémont's section crossed the Sierra Nevada range by way of Truckee Pass, soon to become known as Donner Pass, from the unfortunate experiences of the Donner party of emigrants in the winter of 1846–47. They arrived at Sutter's Fort on December 9, 1845, having had more favorable weather than in their crossing two years earlier.

183
Walker appears to have misunderstood the designation of the appointed meeting place. Frémont had specified the Tulare Lake Fork, by which he meant King's River. Walker had piloted Talbot's section over Walker Pass and they had camped on Kern River, which also discharged into Tulare Lake but on the opposite side of the lake from King's River. They had awaited Frémont at this place from December 27, 1845, to January 17, 1846. Frémont, *Memoirs,* 432–55.

184
Talbot had finally tired of waiting and moved down the San Joaquin Valley. Carson and Owens found his

party about twelve miles south of San Jose.

185
Carson is mistaken here. When Frémont went to Monterey, during the last week in January, 1846, he was courteously received by General Castro and given permission to purchase supplies. This permission was revoked by a letter from Castro to Frémont on March 12. Frémont was aware of the impending war between the United States and Mexico and by this time so was Castro, who was quite justified, under the circumstances, in requesting Frémont to leave. Carson no doubt reflects the opinion among Frémont's men at the time. The most substantial explanation of Frémont's actions during this period is to be found in Cardinal Goodwin, *John Charles Frémont: An Explanation of his Career* (Stanford, 1930).

186
Frémont had encamped and fortified his position on Gavilan (Hawk) Peak. At first he had refused to leave, but after thinking it over he had decided to set out for Oregon.

The sarcastic reference to the "valiant General" is to General José Castro (1810–60). H. H. Bancroft says, "He was by no means the cowardly, incompetent braggart that he has generally been painted." His last years were spent as a military commander of Mexican forces in Lower California.

187
Peter Lassen was born in Copenhagen, Denmark, on August 7, 1800. He emigrated to Boston about 1829 and soon settled in Missouri. In 1839 he went overland to Oregon and presently, by sea, to California. During 1842 and 1843 he worked as a blacksmith for Sutter, taking his pay in livestock. He secured a grant of land on Deer Creek, a tributary of the Sacramento River, southeast of present Red Bluff in Tehama County, California, and settled there early in 1844. For the next ten years, Lassen's Ranch was the best-known point in northern California. Lassen Peak, to the northeast, is named for him, and the Lassen Cut-Off diverged from the California Trail at Winnemucca, Nevada, and ended at the ranch. He was killed by Indians near Pyramid Lake, Nevada, in 1859. See H. H. Bancroft, *California Pioneer Register and Index, 1542–1828* (Baltimore, 1964), 216.

188
Frémont's party was at Lassen's ranch from March 30 to April 5, 1846, and again, from April 11 to April 24. Frémont, *Memoirs,* 473, 477–78.

189
Martin, "Narrative . . . ," Bancroft Library, Berkeley, says that the settlers asked Frémont for protection against a possible Indian uprising. Frémont responded by allowing all his men who wished to engage in such a campaign to be discharged, with the promise that they would be re-employed afterward. All except four, who were hired by the others to keep the camp, participated. According to Martin, they found four or five thousand Indians engaged in a war dance along the Sacramento River where it emerges from the the mountains. He says they killed over 175 of them in about three hours and the rest ran off into the moun-

We remain[ed] some time at Lawson's, received the best of treatment and finished [getting] our outfit. Started for the Columbia River by going up the Sacramento and passing near the Shasta butte.[190] Traveled on without any molestation, till we reached Klamath Lake at the upper end of it.[191]

A few days after we left, information was received in California that war was declared between the United States and Mexico. Lieutenant Gillespie, U. S. Marines, and six men were sent after us to have us come back.[192] He had traveled about 300 miles. His animals were giving out and, the rate he was traveling, he had but poor hopes of overtaking us. He then concluded to mount two men on his best animals and send them in advance. They come up to us on the lake, gave the communications to Fremont, and he, having but poor faith in the Klamath Indians, feared the situation of Gillespie and party; concluded to go and meet him. Took ten picked men, traveled about 60 miles, and met him encamped for the night.

He [Fremont] sat up till 12 or 1 o'clock reading the letters which he had received from the States.[193] Owens and myself were rolled in our saddle blankets laying near the fire, the night being cold. Shortly after Fremont had laid down I heard a noise as of an axe striking, jumped up, saw there were Indians in camp, gave the alarm. The Indians had then tomahawked two men, Lajeunesse and a Delaware, and were proceeding to the fire, where four Delaware were lying.[194] They heard the alarm. Crane, a Delaware, got up, took a gun, but not his own. The one he got was not loaded. He was not aware of it and kept trying to fire. Stood erect, received five arrows in the breast, four mortal, then fell.

The evening before I fired off my gun for the purpose of cleaning it, accidentally broke the tube, [so] had nothing but my pistol. Rushed

tains. It seems doubtful that such a preventive expedition was justified.

190
Mount Shasta (14,162 feet in altitude) in Siskiyou County, California, is an outstanding landmark. Carson's term "butte" is inadequate for such an eminence.

191
Frémont took this opportunity to connect his current survey with the one he had made in 1843–44 but he was also marking time until apprised of a declaration of war against Mexico, which would enable him to return to California in an active role.

192
Lieutenant Archibald H. Gillespie, of the Marines, U.S.N., was a native of Pennsylvania. He was wounded at San Pasqual and again at San Gabriel. He testified for Frémont at the court-martial and returned overland to California later in 1848, where he spent most of the remainder of his life. He was never prominent after 1846–49. He died in San Francisco in 1873, at the age of sixty. Bancroft, *Pioneer Register,* 159.

193
Gillespie brought messages to Frémont from President Polk, Senator Benton, and Secretary of the Navy George Bancroft, who had selected him as governmental emissary. He may also have brought verbal instructions in addition to the official letters.

194
Twelve Delaware Indians had been chosen by their tribe to accompany Frémont when he passed through their reservation in northeastern Kan-

on him, fired, cut the string that held his tomahawk. Had to retire, having no other [weapon]. Maxwell fired on him, hit him in the leg.[195] As he was turning, Step fired, struck him in the back, ball passing near the heart, and he fell.[196] The balance of his party then run. He was the bravest Indian I ever saw. If his men had been as brave as himself, we surely would all have been killed. We lost three men and one slightly wounded. If we had not gone to meet Gillespie, he and party would have been murdered. The Indians evidently were on his trail for that purpose. We apprehend[ed] no danger that night, and the men being much fatigued, no guard was posted. It was the first and last time that we failed in posting guard. Of the three men killed, Lajeunesse was particularly regretted. He had been with us in every trip that had been made. All of them were brave, good men. The only consolation we had for the loss was that if we had not arrived, Gillespie and his four men would have been killed. We lost three, so two lives had been saved.

After the Indians left, each of us took a tree, expecting that they would return. We remained so posted until daylight.[197] We then packed up, took the bodies of the dead, and started for camp of the main party. [We] had proceeded about 10 miles, could not possibly carry the bodies any farther. Went about half a mile off the trail and interred them, covering the graves with logs and brush, so that there was but little probability of their being discovered. [We] would have taken the bodies to our camp, but on account of the timber being so thick, the bodies knocked against the trees and, becoming much bruised, we concluded to bury them when we did. We met our camp this evening. They had received orders to follow our trail. Camped for [the] night. Next morning [we planned] only to go a few miles. Left 15 men in our old camp, con-

sas. Frémont, *Memoirs,* 424. He gives the names of eight of them as James Swanuck, James Saghundai, James Conner, Delaware Charley, Wetowka, Crane, Solomon Everett, and Bob Skirkett. See 58 Cong., 1 sess., *Sen. Doc. 16,* Serial 4563, p. 159. Swanock and Saghundai (Secondine) were grandson and son, respectively, of head chief William Anderson, a halfblood who had died in 1831, about a year after leading his tribe to the Kansas reservation. At this time, Swanock's father, of the same name, was the leader of a small band of Delaware trappers on the upper Arkansas River. Of Crane, Frémont says, "he was a good judge of country with a quick eye . . . usually serious and dignified, even for an Indian . . . ." Frémont, *Memoirs,* 434. The names of James Secondine and Delaware Charley appear on the muster roll of Company A of the California Battalion, but not those of the others mentioned by Frémont. In addition, the names of Richard Brown and Jim Simmonds, designated as Delawares, are on the roll of Company A. See Fred B. Rogers, "Rosters of California Volunteers in the Service of the United States, 1846–1847," *Annual Publication of the Society of California Pioneers* (1950), 17–27.

195
Frémont's account of this fight is in his *Memoirs,* 490–93. In his list of the ten men whom he took to meet Gillespie, he does not name Maxwell. Either his recollection or that of Carson must have been in error on this point. Frémont says that Godey stepped into the firelight to examine something that was wrong with his gun and that Carson cried out, "Look at that fool. Look at him, will you?"

cealed for the purpose of discovering the movements of the Indians. We had not left more than half an hour when two Indians came. They were killed and in short time their scalps were in our camp.[198]

Fremont concluded to return to California but [to] take a different route from that [by] which we had last entered the country, by going on the opposite side of the Lake. We were now encamped on a stream of the lake, nearly opposite to the place where we were encamped when we had the three men killed. In the morning, I was sent ahead with ten chosen men, with orders that if I discovered any large village of Indians to send [back] word, and in case I should be seen by them for me to act as I thought best.[199]

I had not gone more than ten miles [when] I discovered a large village of about 50 lodges and, at the same time, by the commotion in their camp I knew that they had seen us and, considering it useless to send for reinforcements, I determined to attack them, charged on them, fought for some time, killed a number, and the balance fled.

Their houses were built of flag, beautifully woven. They had been fishing [and] had in their houses some ten wagon loads of fish they had caught. All their fishing tackle, camp equipage, etc. was there. I wished to do them as much damage as I could, so I directed their houses to be set on fire. The flag being dry it was a beautiful sight. The Indians had commenced the war with us without cause and I thought they should be chastized in a summary manner. And they were severely punished.

Fremont saw at a distance the fire, [and] knowing that we were engaged, hurried to join us, but arrived too late for the sport.[200] We moved on about two miles from where the Indian village had been, and camped for the night. After encamping, Owens and twenty men were

feeling that Godey was needlessly exposing himself to danger. The third man killed was a half-blood named Denny. Frémont says further that Carson considered the Klamaths to be more daring fighters than the Blackfeet.

196
Step, who killed the brave Indian, was Joseph Stepperfeldt, a gunsmith from Quincy, Illinois. He was also a member of Frémont's fourth expedition, but little more is known of him. See William Brandon, *The Men and the Mountain* (New York, 1955), 79; also LeRoy R. Hafen and Ann W. Hafen (eds.), *The Frémont Disaster, 1848–1849* (*The Far West and the Rockies Historical Series*), (Glendale, 1960), XI, 255.

197
They remained concealed for the rest of the night. When daylight came, Carson split the skull of the dead chief with an English hatchet that hung from the dead man's wrist and Saghundai scalped him. Frémont, *Memoirs*, 490–93.

198
The Delawares blackened their faces in mourning for Crane. The stratagem was for the purpose of improving Delaware morale by giving them a chance for revenge. After they took the two scalps, Swanock said, "Very sick before, better now."

199
Frémont says he ordered Carson to avoid a fight, if possible, until the rest of the party could come up. Frémont, *Memoirs*, 494.

200
Frémont, *Memoirs*, 94, says that he

sent back to watch for Indians. In an hour he sent us word that 50 Indians had returned to camp, I suppose to hunt their lost and bury their dead.

As soon as the information was received Fremont, with six men, started to him, taking a route different from that which Owens had taken, so as to keep concealed. As we got near the camp [we] only saw one Indian. As soon as he was seen, we charged him. I was in advance, got within ten feet of him. My gun snapped, he drew his bow to fire on me. I threw myself on one side of my horse to save myself. Fremont saw the danger in which I was, run horse over the Indian, throwing him on the ground, and before he could recover he was shot.[201] I considered that Fremont saved my life for, in all probability, if he had not run over the Indian as he did, I would have been shot. We could find no more Indians and, fearing that the party seen by Owens had returned to attack our camp, we returned. Arrived, but the Indians did not make an attack.

Next morning we struck out for the Valley of the Sacramento, about four days march. Maxwell and Archambeau were traveling parallel with the party about three miles distant, hunting. They saw an Indian coming towards them. As soon as the Indian saw them, he took from his quiver some young crows that were tied thereon, concealed them in the grass, and continued approaching. As soon as he was within forty yards, he commenced firing. They did not intend to hurt him, wishing to talk, but the Indian keeping up a continuous fire and having shot rather close, they were compelled through self defense to fire on him. They done so and [at] the first shot he fell, was immediately scalped.

We kept on till we struck the Sacramento and, in passing down the river, there was ahead of us

arrived in time to participate in the battle, which undoubtedly was the case. Here Carson is claiming considerably more credit for himself than the facts warrant. According to the recollection of Thomas S. Martin, a member of Frémont's party, Carson had picked a deep place to ford the river in order to attack the Indian village and his men had got their powder wet. Frémont's arrival was extremely timely or Carson and his ten men would have been in trouble because of his impetuosity. It would seem that Carson, in his excitement, failed to take note of several essential facts. See Martin, "Narrative . . . ," Bancroft Library, Berkeley.

201 Frémont's account in his *Memoirs,* 494–95, is more precise. He shot at the Indian, and missing him, jumped his horse, Sacramento, directly upon him, so that his poisoned arrow went wild. Saghundai, following Frémont, leaped from his horse and clubbed the Indian to death. Carson, therefore, owed his life to the quick actions of both Frémont and the Delaware chief.

202 They were now out of the Klamath country but the hostility of the Klamaths towards Frémont's party had probably spread to other tribes. Frémont's account is in his *Memoirs,* 497. Kit Carson admired bravery, whether of friend or foe.

203 They arrived at Lassen's Ranch, on May 24, 1846, and left two days later. Frémont, *Memoirs,* 498.

204 They were encamped near the conflu-

a deep and narrow cañon. The Indians, supposing that we would go through it, placed themselves on each side for the purpose of attacking us as we passed. But we crossed the river and did not go into the cañon.

When we saw the Indians, Godey, myself, and another man—I have forgotten his name—took after them. We were mounted on mules. They could not be caught. One man, brave[r] than the rest, hid himself behind a large rock, and awaited our approach. We rode up near him. He came from his hiding place and commenced firing arrows very rapidly. We had to run back, being kept so busy dodging from his arrows, that it was impossible to fire. Retreated from the reach of his arrows, I dismounted and fired. My shot had the desired effect. He was scalped. [He] had a fine bow and beautiful quiver of arrows, which I presented to Lt. Gillespie. He was a brave Indian, deserved a better fate, but he had placed himself on the wrong path.[202]

Continued our march and the next day, in the evening, Step and another man had gone out to hunt. We had nothing to eat in our camp, [were] nearly starving. They saw an Indian watching the camp. I presume he was waiting so that he might steal a mule. They gradually approached him—he was unaware of their presence—and, when near enough, fired. He received his death wound and then was scalped. The hunters then returned, having found no other game. We kept on our march to Peter Lawson's, and had no difficulty on the route.[203] Then down the Sacramento to the Buttes. Here camp was made to await positive orders in regard to the war and [also] to hunt.[204]

A party was sent from here to surprise Sonoma, a military post.[205] They captured it, took one General and two Captains prisoners, several cannon, and a number of small arms. After the fort had been taken, Fremont had heard positively

ence of the Bear and Feather rivers, below present Marysville, California, until June 8, 1846. Frémont, *Memoirs,* 518.

205
The capture of Sonoma was the first overt act of Americans in California against the Mexican government. Frémont claims that it was done by a party of forty American settlers in California, but it is clear that it was done with his knowledge and support. He was camped on the American Fork by mid-June, where Ezekiel Merritt, whom he had sent to Sonoma, brought the captives later mentioned by Carson. He had also taken over Sutter's Fort and placed Edward M. Kern in command of it. Frémont, *Memoirs,* 518–21. Carson went with Frémont to Sonoma on June 24, 1846.

206
The two young Americans who were killed were named Cowey and Fowler. Reports that they had been killed in an atrocious manner are known to have been exaggerated but were responsible for the desire for retaliation among Frémont's men and Bear Flag supporters. Captain Joaquin de la Torre retreated to Sausalito, where he escaped across the bay. Three Californians, José de los Berreyesa and his twin nephews, Ramon and Francisco de Haro, were captured by Carson, Granville Swift, Jack Neil, and others at the *Embarcadero,* where they had just landed. Carson rode back and asked Frémont what should be done with them. Frémont replied, "I want no prisoners, Mr. Carson, do your duty." Carson reported this to his companions and the men were shot. Frémont, *Memoirs,* 525, says nothing of this

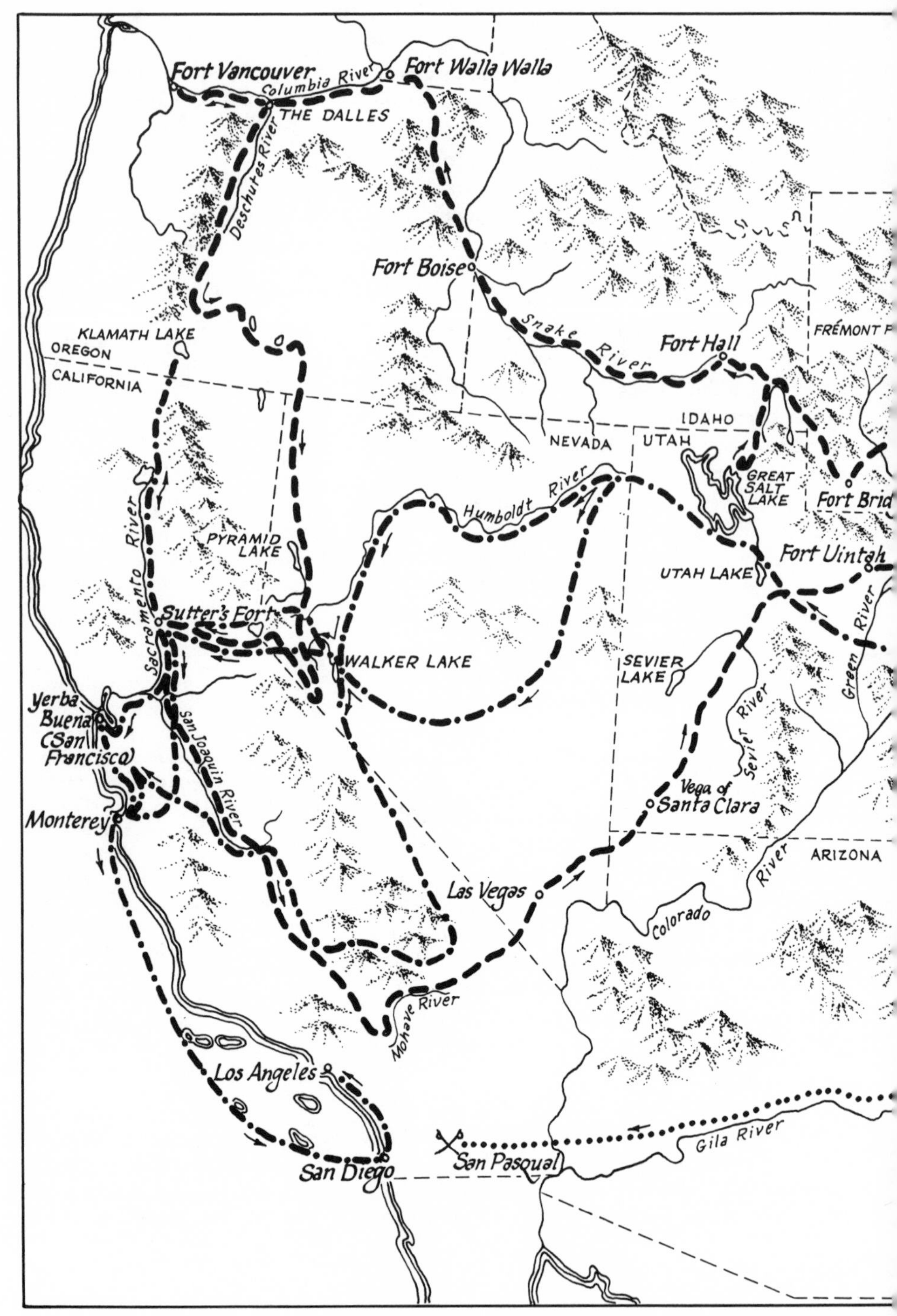
Fort Vancouver
Fort Walla Walla
Columbia River
THE DALLES
Deschutes River
Fort Boise
Snake River
Fort Hall
KLAMATH LAKE
OREGON
CALIFORNIA
IDAHO
NEVADA
UTAH
GREAT SALT LAKE
Fort Brid
FRÉMONT P
Humboldt River
PYRAMID LAKE
Sacramento River
Sutter's Fort
WALKER LAKE
Fort Uintah
UTAH LAKE
Green River
SEVIER LAKE
Sevier River
Yerba Buena (San Francisco)
San Joaquin River
Monterey
Vega of Santa Clara
ARIZONA
River
Las Vegas
Colorado
Mohave River
Los Angeles
Gila River
San Pasqual
San Diego

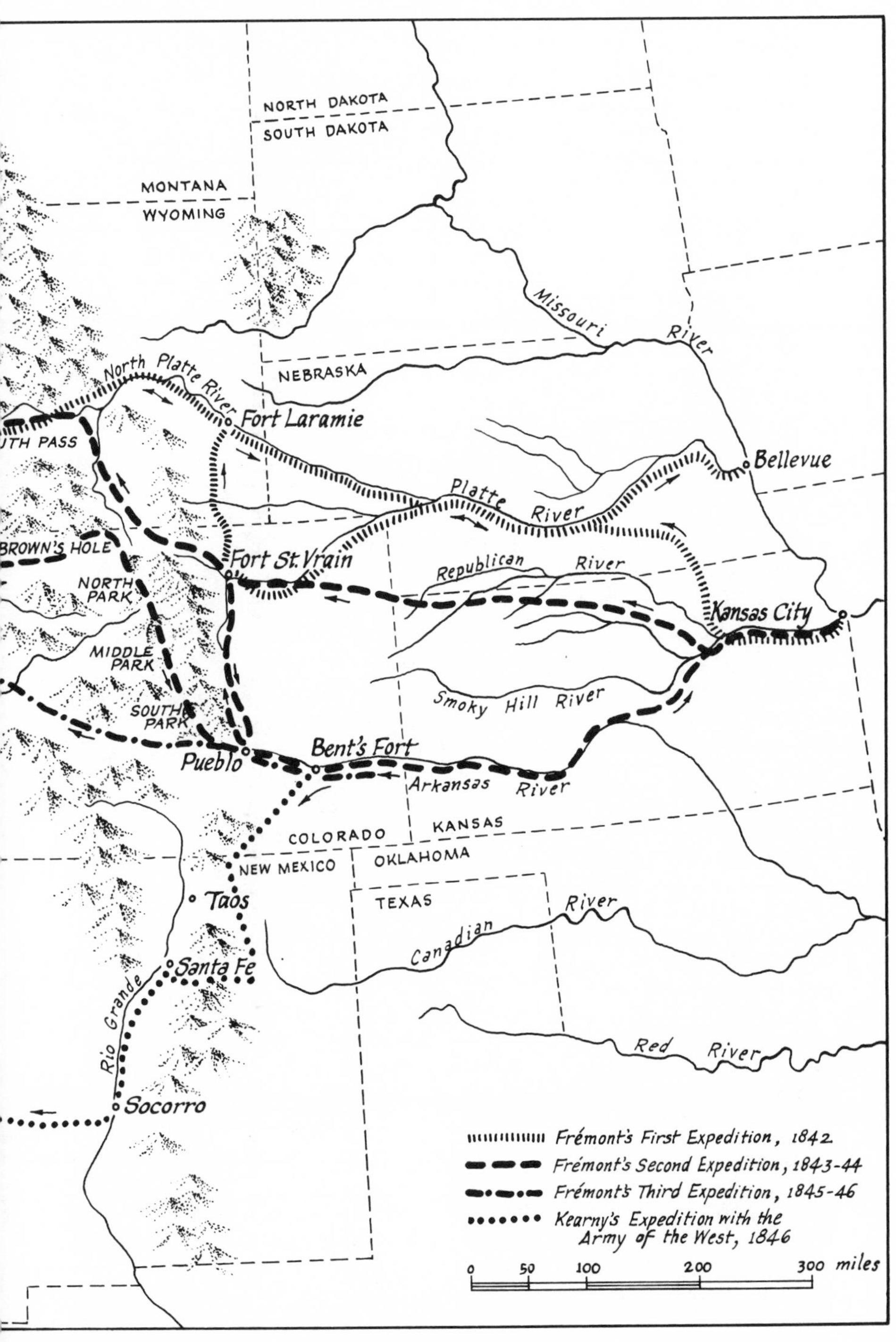


Frémont's Expeditions and Kearny's Route West

of the war being declared. [He] then marched forward to Sonoma and found it in the possession of the men he had sent in advance.

During our stay [here], General Castro ordered one of his captains and a large force from San Francisco to attack us and drive us from the country. He [the captain] came over, found two of our men that were carrying news to the settlers that Sonoma was taken and war declared, whom he brutally murdered.[206] He found that we were anxious to meet him and commenced his retreat. We followed him some six days and nights. He could not be found. He made his escape, leaving his animals, and he reached San Francisco and from there went to [the] Pueblo of Los Angeles, General Castro joining him, their object being to reorganize their forces.

Fremont left a strong force at Sonoma. All the American settlers by this time had joined him. He then departed for Sutter's fort and arrived safe. He placed the fort under military command. Left there General Vallejos, the two Captains, and an American named Leace, brother-in-law of the General, as prisoners, in charge of the gentleman to whom he gave the command.[207] [He] then departed to Monterey. It had been taken before our arrival, by the navy, under command of Commodore Sloat.[208] A few days after our arrival, Sloat left and Stockton[209] assumed the command.

Here we learned that General Castro had made his escape, had gone to Los Angeles to organize. We found that we could not catch the Mexicans by following them on land, so Fremont proposed, if furnished a frigate, to take his men to San Diego. He there would get animals and go drive the Mexican troops from Los Angeles. The frigate *Cyane* was furnished him com'd by Captain Dupont, a noble-souled fellow.[210] In four days [we] arrived at our destination. Our forces were landed, being 150 strong.

and lays the blame for the shooting on his Delaware Indians! Carson was specifically questioned about the incident by William Boggs in 1853, and gave the explanation already related, which is confirmed by an eyewitness. See William N. Boggs, "Manuscript about Bent's Fort, Kit Carson, the Far West and Life Among the Indians," edited by LeRoy R. Hafen, *Colorado Magazine*, Vol. VII (March 1930), 62–63. An account of this affair by Alexis Godey was published in the *New York Evening Post*, October 30, 1856, in defense of Frémont during his presidential campaign. Godey claims that Carson had the men shot when they resisted arrest and that letters to Captain de la Torre were found upon them. Godey was not an eyewitness, although he was near at hand. Jasper O'Farrell, a rather prominent resident of San Rafael, was an eyewitness. His statement in the *Los Angeles Star*, September 27, 1856, quoted in H. H. Bancroft, *History of California*, V (San Francisco, 1888), 171–72, confirms Carson's account of the affair. In conclusion, Frémont may be quoted against himself, as a character witness for Carson, since he said, "With me, Carson and truth are one." If Carson consulted his superior officer—and there is every reason to believe that he did so—then the responsibility for the shooting of the prisoners rests upon Frémont.

207
The prisoners were General Mariano Vallejo (1808–90), the founder of Sonoma, an able and honorable soldier and politician; his brother, Colonel Salvador Vallejo (1814–76); Colonel Victor Prudon; and Jacob P. Leese (1809–90), who had come to California from New Mexico in 1833,

Sufficiency of horses could not be procured at San Diego. Men were sent to scour the country and to press into service horses. We finally were mounted [and] started for Los Angeles. The Mexicans hearing of our approach, though they were 700 strong, fled—the Gen., Gov., and other officers for Sonora, the balance to all parts—so they did not come in contact with Americans.

We arrived within a league of the town, awaited a short time and Stockton, agreeable to the plan arranged before our departure from Monterey, arrived with a party of sailors and marines. The sailors and marines were as brave men as I ever saw and for the Com[m]odore, it is useless for me to say anything, as he is known to be the bravest of the brave. We took possession of the town, remained some time, and, on the 5 Sept. '46, I was ordered to Washington as bearer of despatches, having with me 15 men.[211]

I was ordered to go to Washington in 60 days, which I would have done if not directed by General Kearny to join him. When I got within 10 miles of the Copper Mines I discovered an Apache village. It was about 10 A.M. They were at war. I knew that by staying where we were, we would be seen, and if we endeavored to pass them, they would also see us. So I had a consultation with Maxwell and we came to the conclusion to take for the timber and approach them cautiously and, if we were seen, to be as close as possible to them at the time of the discovery. We kept on, had arrived about 100 yards of the village when they saw us. They were somewhat frightened to see us. We said we were friends, were enroute to New Mexico, wished to trade animals. They appeared friendly. We chose a good place for our camp. They visited us and we commenced trading and procured of them a remount, which was much required, our animals all having nearly given out.[212] We then

and had married Rosalia Vallejo, a sister of General Vallejo. All these men were rather favorable to the American cause, but they were detained by Frémont as prisoners for over two months. Bancroft, *Pioneer Register,* 218, 292, 365–67.

208
Commodore John D. Sloat (1781–1867) took command of the Pacific Squadron in August, 1844. He arrived at Monterey on July 2, 1846, and five days later proclaimed that California was annexed to the United States. Marines were sent ashore to raise the American flag. On July 23, 1846, Sloat turned his command over to Commodore Robert F. Stockton. C. O. Paullin, "John D. Sloat,'" *Dictionary of American Biography,* XVII (New York, 1935), 214–15.

209
Commodore Robert F. Stockton (1775–1866) was of a famous New Jersey political family. He was as romantically adventurous as Frémont, and co-operated closely with Frémont's plans. He transformed Frémont's California Battalion into the Navy Battalion of Mounted Riflemen, thus anticipating the well-known song, "Captain Jinks of the Horse Marines," by twenty-one years. He resigned from the Navy in 1850, entered politics, and became a United States Senator, 1851–53. See C. O. Paullin, "Robert F. Stockton," *Dictionary of American Biography,* XVIII, 48–49.

210
Samuel F. Dupont (1803–65), commander of the U.S.S. *Congress,* was now transferred to command the sloop *Cyane.* He became a rear admiral during the Civil War. See C. O.

Paullin, "Samuel F. Dupont," *Dictionary of American Biography,* V, 529–33.

Kit became so sea-sick during this voyage that he would never again go aboard a sailing ship.

211

Los Angeles was occupied on August 13, 1846. Stockton had assumed the title of Governor of California and now made ready to turn the office over to Frémont. Frémont, *Memoirs,* 567, says, "To insure the safety and speedy delivery of these important papers, and as a reward for brave and valuable service on many occasions, we decided to make Carson the bearer of these dispatches . . . On his way he would see his family at Taos, New Mexico, through which lay his shortest road to the frontier. It was a service of high trust and honor, but of great danger also . . . Going off at the head of his own party with *carte blanche* for expenses and the prospect of novel pleasure and honor at the end was a culminating point in Carson's life."

212

Mules are possessed of great endurance and were the preferred riding animals in the Southwest. Horses will allow themselves to be ridden to death, but burros will not. In respect to this trait, mules resemble their paternal, or asinine, ancestry. Carson's statement in Frémont's *Memoirs,* 585, that he had worn out and killed thirty-four mules up to the time of his meeting with Kearny, must be understood to mean that he had shot some of the animals, either in exasperation or in the belief that they would die anyway, when they had refused to go any farther. Some

started and in four days arrived at the first settlements. At our departure from California we had only 25 lbs. of dried meat, having a quantity of pinola [a mixture of parched corn meal and the sweet flour of mesquite beans]. At the River village we got some corn. We would dry the corn by the fire, parch the corn, then eat it. Not having other food during the trip, we suffered considerably for food.

On the 6th of October, '46, I met General Kearny on his march to California.[213] He ordered me to join him as his guide. I done so, and Fitzpatrick continued on with the despatches.

On the 18 ]15[ of October we left the Rio Del Norte, Decr. 3 [2] arrived at Warner's Ranch, and marched on for San Diego.[214] On the 6th we heard of a party of Californians encamped on our route, probably one hundred in number. When we arrived within ten or fifteen miles of their camp, General Kearny sent Lieut. Hammond, with three or four Dragoons, ahead to examine their position.[215] He went, was accidentally discovered, saw the encampment as reported. They were in an Indian village. He then returned to us and gave the information found. The General then determined to attack them. We packed up about one o'clock in the morning and moved on. When within a mile of their camp, we discovered their spies that were out watching the road and our movements. The trot and then the gallop was ordered to pursue the spies. They retreated to their camp.

I was ordered to join Capt. Johnston.[216] He had fifteen men under his command. We were to proceed in advance. Our object was to get the animals belonging to the Californians.

Captain Moore, having a part of two companies of Dragoons and a party of twenty five volunteers that had come from San Diego, was ordered to attack the main body.[217] They were attacked, only fought about ten or fifteen minutes, then they retreated.

When we were within 100 yards of their camp, my horse fell, threw me, and my rifle was broken into two pieces. I came very near being trodden to death. I being in advance, the whole command had to pass over me. I finally saved myself by crawling from under them. I then ran on about 100 yards to where the fight had commenced. A Dragoon had been killed. I took his gun and catridge box and joined in the melee. Johnston and two or three of the dragoons were then killed. The Californians retreated, pursued by Moore, for about three quarters of a mile. Moore had about 40 men mounted on horses, the balance on mules.

Two or three days before, we [had] heard of a party of Californians that were enroute to Sonora. Lieutenant Davidson and twenty-five dragoons and I were sent to surprise them.[218] Done so, and captured 70 or 80 head of animals, from which Moore got some 40 horses that were gentle and on which he mounted his men. The command, in the pursuit, had got very much scattered. The enemy saw the advantage, wheeled and cut off the forty that were in advance, and out of the forty, killed and wounded thirty-six. Captain Moore among the slain, also Lt. Hammond. Gen. Kearny was severely wounded and nearly every officer of [the] command was wounded.[219]

Lieut. Davidson, in charge of two Howitzers, came up; before he could do anything every one of his party were killed or wounded, and one piece taken by the enemy. They captured it by lassoing the horse, fastening the lasso to the saddle, and then running off. They got off about 300 yds. and endeavored to fire it at us, but could not. It was impossible for Lieut. Davidson to do anything, having lost all his men, and one piece [of artillery], and was himself lanced several

were certainly killed for food. However, not all of the mules were killed, since Carson recovered two of them on October 22, after an interval of two weeks, as he made the return trip with Kearny. The mules were in good condition. See Henry Smith Turner, *The Original Journals of Henry Smith Turner,* edited by Dwight L. Clarke (Norman, 1966), 88.

213
General Stephen Watts Kearny (1794–1848) was on his way to California with full authorization from President Polk to supersede the American authorities then in power. Upon learning from Carson that a civil government had been established he reduced his already small force by two-thirds, retaining only about a hundred dragoons. Kearny wanted Carson's services because he had been over the route, as Fitzpatrick had not. Carson says that he "prepared everything to escape in the night" rather than obey Kearny, but that Lucien Maxwell persuaded him to obey rather than desert. Frémont, *Memoirs,* 585–86. He made a full statement at the request of Senator Benton, but said he would have preferred to give his evidence "face to face with General Kearny." The meeting of Carson with Kearny on the trail took place near Socorro, New Mexico. A recent biography of Kearny is Dwight L. Clarke, *Stephen Watts Kearny: Soldier of the West* (Norman, 1961). The route over which Carson guided Kearny is detailed in George Ruhlen, "Kearny's Route from Río Grande to the Gila River," *New Mexico Historical Review,* Vol. XXXII (July, 1957), 213–30.

times through the clothing and one passing through [the] cantel of his saddle, which if the Californian had not missed his aim he, also, wound be numbered among the slain.

We rallied in a point of rocks near where the advance had been defeated, remained there that night, the reason [being we] dare not move on, and having a number of dead to bury. The dead were buried at the hours of 12 and 1 o'clock that night. Next day we moved on.

I had command of about 15 men and was ordered in advance. Marched about seven miles. During the night, the Californians had received reinforcements. They were now about 150 strong. During the day they would show themselves on every hill ahead of us. Late in the evening we [were] still on the march, being within about 400 yards from the water where we intended to camp. They then charged on us, coming in two bodies. We were compelled to retreat about 200 yards, to a hill of rocks that was to our left. After we had gained our position on the hill, the Californians took another hill about 100 yds. still to our left, and then commenced firing. Captains Emery[220] and Turner[221] took the command of what dragoons we had, charged the enemy on the hill, routed them, giving us full possession of their position; there [we] remained for the night.

The day on which we had the first fight, Kearny had sent three men as express to San Diego to Com[m]odore Stockton. This morning they had returned. Within five hundred yards of our camp, [they] were taken prisoners by the enemy in our sight. The day previous, the horse of a Mexican Lieutenant was shot and he [was] taken prisoner. The parley was sounded and [we] then exchanged the Lieutenant for one of our men that was prisoner.[222]

The place in which we were stationed had barely water enough for the men to drink. We

214 The party reached Warner's Ranch on December 2, 1846. Its proprietor was a Connecticut Yankee, Jonathan Trumbull Warner (1807–95), who came to Santa Fe in 1831 and traveled on to California with David Jackson. He resided on the ranch from 1844, when his grant was confirmed, until 1857, when he lost it. See J. J. Hill, *The History of Warner's Ranch and Its Environs* (Los Angeles, 1927).

215 Lieutenant Thomas C. Hammond, Company K, 1st U.S. Dragoons, died of his wounds at San Pasqual. Bancroft, *Pioneer Register,* 177.

216 Captain Abraham R. Johnston, Company C, U.S. Dragoons, was killed at San Pasqual. Bancroft, *Pioneer Register,* 252.

217 Captain Benjamin A. Moore, Company C., U.S. Dragoons, was also killed at San Pasqual. Bancroft, *Pioneer Register,* 252.

218 Lieutenant John W. Davidson served on the Pacific Coast till 1859, was brevetted brigadier general, and died in Minnesota in 1881. Bancroft, *Pioneer Register,* 115.

219 This statement is correct. Most of the damage done was by lances, in the use of which the riders of Southern California were adept. Only Captain Moore and the dragoon whose gun Carson took for himself are known to have been killed by gunshot.

had nothing to eat but mule meat. The animals were turned loose. As soon as any would get from the reach of our guns, they would be driven off by the enemy. The Mexicans had command of the water, probably about 500 yds. in our advance. Kearny concluded to march on, let the consequences be what they would. About 12 o'clock we were ready to march, the wounded in ambulances [litters]. The enemy, seeing our movements, saddled up, formed in our rear 500 yards, the men being placed about 10 feet apart so that our artillery could do them but little damage.

Kearny had a council with his officers. They all knew that as soon as we would leave the hill we would again have to fight, and, in our present condition, it was not advisable. They came to the conclusion to send for reinforcements to San Diego. Lieut. Beale, of the navy, and myself volunteered to undertake to carry the intelligence to Stockton.[223]

As soon as dark, we started on our mission. In crawling over the rocks and brush, our shoes making noise, we took them off; fastened them under our belts. We had to crawl about two miles. We could see three rows of sentinels, all a-horseback. We would often have to pass within 20 yards of one. We finally got through, but had the misfortune to have lost our shoes—had to travel over a country covered with prickly pear and rocks. Got to San Diego the next night.[224] Stockton immediately ordered 160 or 170 men to march to Kearny's relief. They were under the command of a Lieutenant, had one cannon, which was drawn by the men by attaching to it ropes. I remained at San Diego, Lieut. Beale was sent aboard of [the] frigate *Congress*, had become deranged from fatigue of the service performed. [He] did not entirely recover for two years.

The next night the reinforcements reached

220
Lieutenant William H. Emory, of the U.S. Topographical Engineers, testified for the prosecution at the Frémont court-martial. His *Notes of a Military Reconaissance* (1848) is well known to students of western history. He rose to the rank of major general during the Civil War. Bancroft, *Pioneer Register,* 130–31.

221
Captain Henry S. Turner, 1st U.S. Dragoons, also testified for Kearny at the trial of Frémont. He resigned from the army soon afterward, and engaged in banking in San Francisco for a time. Bancroft, *Pioneer Register,* 360. *Turner's Journals* covers his service in New Mexico and California during this period. Carson made an error of two days in calculating the distance between the Pima village and the mouth of the Gila River. Since he had estimated it would require two more days than it actually took, everyone was happily surprised. Turner, *Journals,* 116.

222
The leader of the express was Carson's old friend and companion, Alexis Godey. Before his capture, Godey had cached Stockton's reply in a hollow tree, where it was found some years later. It is now in the Gaffey Manuscripts, the Huntington Library, San Marino, California. Stockton's letter made excuses for not sending immediate aid, but a force of 180 men was sent to his relief before the second express of Carson and Beale reached San Diego. Thomas H. Burgess, a Kentuckian who had come to California in 1845, was the man exchanged for the Mexican lieutenant. General Pico refused to exchange Godey, and Burgess

Kearny. They lay by during day, traveled by night. The enemy, however, discovered their approach, then fled. Kearny and party then joined and moved on to San Diego, having no further molestation. Remained in San Diego about a month or so, till the wounded recovered. Then a force of 600 men were organized and started for Los Angeles under Stockton and Kearny. There were at Los Angeles about 700 Mexicans. On the 8th January '47, we arrived within 15 miles of Los Angeles. The Mexicans had a good position, being in command of a hill where we had to pass the river. We had two pieces of cannon. Stockton directed them. The Mexicans only stood a few rounds, retreated, and crossed the river. [We] took possession of the hill and encamped for the night.[225]

On the 9th we approached within three miles of the Pueblo, having to fight during the day. Nothing, however, was necessary to be employed [except artillery]. They could not make their appearance near us but Stockton, from his unerring aim of his guns, would make them leave.[226]

On the 10th we took possession of the Pueblo. The place was evacuated by the Mexicans. They went to attack Fremont. He was thirty [miles] distant from the Pueblo, on the march thither with about 400 men that he had raised in the vicinity of Monterey. They met Fremont, would not fight him, surrendered to him in preference to any other of the commanders.

On the 12th, I think, Fremont joined us at Los Angeles.[227] We remained there during the winter without any further molestation. As soon as Fremont joined, I left Kearny, and joined him. In March, I started as bearer of despatches for the War Dept.[228] Lieutenant Beale went with me with despatches for the Navy Dept. Beale, during the first 20 days, I had to lift him on and off his horse. I did not think he could live, but I took as good care and paid to him as much at-

could not say whether help was on the way or not. This made Carson's and Beale's effort seem necessary although, had the facts been known, it was not. See Frémont, *Memoirs,* 586–88.

223 Lieutenant Edward Fitzgerald Beale (1822–98) was the grandson of Commodore Thomas Truxtun, and his father, George Beale, was also a naval officer. Beale afterward made six more overland transcontinental crossings, an unusual record for a naval officer. He was in charge of the famous experimental use of camels in the southwest. Later he engaged in extensive ranching operations in California. Beale's Delaware Indian servant was also volunteered by his master for this service. See Stephen Bonsal, *Edward Fitzgerald Beale* (New York, 1912).

224 The fact that the trip was unnecessary does not obscure the extremely difficult and truly heroic nature of this exploit. The Indian boy was the first to come in; Beale was second, but he had to be carried to Stockton by the sentries; Carson was last, but in somewhat better shape. The commemorative tablet in the Smithsonian Institution, Washington, D. C., does not depict the Indian nor mention him, which is an inexcusable omission. See Frémont, *Memoirs,* 588–89; also Sabin, *Kit Carson Days* (1914), 288–94.

225 This action was the battle of San Gabriel, which occurred on January 8, 1847. Some four hundred of the American force were sailors and marines. Stockton had six cannon altogether.

tention as could [be] given to anyone in the same circumstances and, before our arrival [be had] got so far recovered that he could assist himself. For my care, I was trebly repaid by the kindness and attention given me by his mother, while I was in Washington.

On the River Gila, we were attacked by the Indians. During [the] night they sent a good many arrows into our camp, but without effect. As soon as they commenced, I directed the men to hold before them pack saddles and not to speak a word, so that the Indians could not direct their aim by hearing us, for them not to return the fire but let the Indians approach, and then use our rifles as clubs. The Indians did not approach, but, finding they done no execution, they left before morning and we continued our journey. Had no further difficulty and arrived at Washington in June.

At St. Louis I had the honor of an introduction to Col. Benton and was invited by him that during my stay in Washington to remain at his home. I accepted of his invitation and, during the time I was there, received the very kindest of treatment.[229]

I remained in Washington some time, received the appointment of Lieut. of Rifles, U. S. Army, from President Polk and was ordered back to California as bearer of despatches.[230] Lt. Beale [went] with me, but, on account of his illness, he was compelled to return from St. Louis. When I arrived at Fort Leavenworth I was furnished an escort of fifty men, volunteers, the Comanche Indians being at war. I came on to Pawnee Rock without any difficulty. Was encamped about 300 yards from a company of Volunteers enroute for New Mexico having with them a very large train of wagons.

At daylight the men of said company were leading out their horses to picket them in new grass. They were attacked by a party of Comanches and had 26 horses and all their cattle driven



226
This was the battle of Los Angeles, which ended the fighting in California.

227
Frémont's arrival was on January 14, 1847.

228
The date of Carson's departure was February 25, 1847.

229
Jessie Benton Frémont lived at her father's Washington house and came to know Kit well and to be very fond of him. She tells of reading the poetry of Burns and of Byron to him, and of his comments on certain poems. She also tells of his embarrassment at meeting Washington ladies, who might disapprove of his having been a squaw man. He told her that his first wife always had warm water ready for his feet when he came in from hunting or trapping. See Frémont, *Memoirs,* 74; also Jessie Benton Frémont, *The Will and the Way Stories* (Boston, 1891), 40–41.

A story of Carson's life, evidently based on an interview given by him, appeared in the *Washington Union* during the summer of 1847. It was reprinted in the *Supplement* to the *Connecticut Courant,* July 3, 1847. It is reproduced in Appendix B, below.

230
Carson saw President Polk on two occasions, June 7, and July 14, 1847. He told the President about the quarrel between General Kearny, on the one side, and Commodore Stockton and Frémont, on the other. The President confided to his diary that he thought Kearny in the right but he

off. The cattle taking a turn near our camp, I was enabled to retake them from the Indians. I lost two horses, but through fault of my men having the rope in their hand and wishing to fire at the Indians—they let [the] horses go.

The [volunteer] company lost 26 [horses] and would have lost all of their cattle if I and my party had [not] been there to assist them. Also had three men wounded. I lost two horses as before stated. The volunteers were under the command of Lieut. Mulony.[231]

We then continued our march and arrived at Santa Fe without any difficulty. There I left my escort and hired sixteen men and continued my journey to California. At Muddy Creek, a tributary of the Virgin River, there were about 300 Indians collected. They wanted to come into my camp. I would not permit them. I told them that the fall before they had killed seven Americans, that they were of treacherous character and could not be trusted, and that I would not allow myself to be deceived by them—that their object was to come to me friendly and then kill my party. I told them to retire, if not, I would fire on them. I was compelled to fire. One Indian was killed and the balance went off. I had no more trouble on the road, only having got out of provisions and had to eat two mules.

Arrived at Los Angeles in October, then went on to Monterey and delivered the despatches to Colonel Mason, 1st Drag[oon]s, officer in command.[232] Remained a few days and was ordered back to Los Angeles. Shortly after my arrival I was assigned to duty with the Dragoons under command of Capt. Smith.[233] The greater part of the winter I passed in the Tejon Pass. Had twenty five men under my command guarding the Pass, to prohibit Indians from taking through stolen animals. It being the main pass, they would have [to] go through in case they committed any depredations.

did not tell Kit his views, because Kit was obviously on the other side. See James K. Polk, *The Diary of James K. Polk,* edited by Milo M. Quaife, III (Chicago, 1910), 52, 54, 61.

231 This was S. D. Mullowny, 1st Lieutenant, 3rd Missouri Mounted Volunteers. See Heitmann, *Historical Register,* II, 63.

232 The scene had changed in California while Carson had been away. Commodore Stockton and General Kearny had both departed for Washington, and Frémont had gone there, also, to face a court-martial. Kearny had appointed Colonel Richard B. Mason, of the 1st U.S. Dragoons, to act as military governor of California. A young lieutenant destined to become famous, William Tecumseh Sherman, has left a description of this arrival of the first overland mail in his *Memoirs of General William T. Sherman,* I (New York, 1886), 46–47. In common with nearly everyone else, Sherman was surprised at the unprepossessing appearance of Carson, whose fame by this time was considerable. He wrote, "I cannot express my surprise at beholding a small stoop-shouldered man with reddish hair, freckled face and soft blue eyes, and nothing to indicate extraordinary courage or daring. He spoke but little and answered questions in monosyllables."

233 Andrew Jackson Smith (1815-97), captain in the 1st U.S. Dragoons, came to California with the Mormon Battalion. He saw much service on

In the Spring I was again ordered to Washington as bearer of despatches.[234] I reached Grand River without any serious difficulty. Then, the river being high, I lost in rafting it, one raft, which had on it six rifles and a number [of] riding and pack saddles. Lieut. Brewerton was with me.[235] It was near sundown when the raft was lost. Some of [the] men were on the opposite bank, the Lieut[enant] among the number. They were nearly naked, had to remain in that situation during the night, and [in] the morning I sent a man over [to] them with an axe so that they could make another raft. They, after some labor, made one, and crossed.[236] We then continued our march, some of the men having to ride bareback until we arrived at Taos.

About fifty miles of Taos, we met several hundred Utah and Apache Indians.[237] They showed demonstrations of hostility. We retired into the brush, would only allow a few of them to approach us, informed them that if they were friends that they should leave, that we were naked and in a destitute condition, and could give them nothing. They evidently left us, when they saw we had nothing. That night, I moved on about ten miles and met a party of volunteers on their pursuit of the Apaches. Next day reached Taos, then to Santa Fe, found Colonel Newby, of Illinois Vol[un]t[eers], in command.[238] He rendered me all the assistance I required, informing me that the Comanches were still at war and were in parties of from two and three hundred, watching the roads.

I discharged all my men but ten, retaining the best, and then returned to Taos and departed for the States.[239] Keeping north of the Comanche range, I reached Bijoux, a tributary of the Platte, [traveled] down it to within twenty five miles of the south fork of the Platte, left Bijoux and struck for the Platte, kept down it to Fort Kearney, then left it and struck for the Republican

the frontier before the Civil War, in which he became a major general. See Thomas M. Spaulding, "Andrew Jackson Smith," *Dictionary of American Biography,* XVII (New York, 1936), 236–37.

234
The trip was made over the Old Spanish Trail and Carson told Brewerton of certain adventures with Frémont as they came to his mind, whenever they passed the places where the events had occurred. They met Joe Walker in Utah again. They took the east branch of the trail from Sevier River to Salina Creek in Utah, and in Colorado they took the north branch of the trail by way of the Gunnison River and Cochetopa Pass.

235
Carson set out from Los Angeles on May 4, 1848, with twenty-seven men, including Lieutenant George D. Brewerton, whose lively and detailed account of the trip as far as Taos was published under the title "A Ride With Kit Carson" in *Harper's Magazine,* Vol. VIII (August, 1853), 307–45. Brewerton (1827–1901), was born in Rhode Island, the son of General Henry Brewerton. He resigned his commission on December 31, 1852, and embarked on a journalistic career and studied law. He served in the Civil War, during which he wrote several manuals of military training. He was an active Baptist minister in 1866–67, and in his later years did landscape painting. His narrative has been edited, in book form, by Stallo Vinton, and published under the title *Overland with Kit Carson: a Narrative of The Old Spanish Trail in 1848* (New York, 1930).

236
Brewerton tells of their difficult crossing of Grand River and says that they had a similar but less difficult experience crossing Green River two days later. They would necessarily have crossed Green River first, however, so he may have confused the difficulties involved, as well as the identity of the rivers. Carson mentions only the crossing of the Grand, which was more likely to have had a turbulent flow of water. Brewerton credits Auguste Archambeau, a strong swimmer, with having saved his life when the raft capsized.

237
Brewerton says the Indians numbered 150. Carson judged correctly that this was a hostile band and acted accordingly. They were met in the San Luis Valley. Carson was already a celebrated character, but Brewerton's article further enhanced his reputation.

238
Colonel Edward W. B. Newby, of the 5th Illinois Volunteers, commanded at Fort Marcy at this time. Heitman, *Historical Register,* II, 63.

According to the *Santa Fe Republican,* June 27, 1848, Carson arrived in Santa Fe on June 19, 1848, after a trip made in forty-one days from Los Angeles. From the date of departure, the forty-first day would fall on June 14. It seems probable that June 14 was the time of arrival at Taos, where Carson remained a few days before going to Santa Fe.

239
Jesse Nelson (1827–1923), who married Susan Carson, daughter of Kit's brother Bob, made this trip from Taos to Fort Leavenworth. He mentions other residents of Taos who did so, including Louis Simmons, who later married Kit's half-blood daughter, Adaline. Nelson mentions only Auguste Archambeau of Kit's companions from California, but says Kit kept eight of them. He mentions seven, including himself and Simmons, who joined the party at Taos or at Santa Fe. See F. W. Cragin Papers, Notebook VIII, 51, 75, 77. Cragin interviewed Nelson on July 9, 1908, at Smith's Canyon Ranch in Colorado.

240
The unusual route taken was to avoid the hostile Comanches, of whom Colonel Newby had warned Carson. Jesse Nelson says that Fort Kearny was a sod fort at this time. F. W. Cragin Papers, Notebook VIII, 51, 75, 77. Kearney is the spelling used for the present Nebraska town at the same location.

241
The *St. Louis Reveille,* July 31, 1848, noted Carson's arrival in St. Louis, apparently on that date, and mentions that rumors of his death had preceded his arrival, an indication of the danger from Comanches along the usual Arkansas River route. It also gives June 14 as the date of his arrival in Santa Fe, which confirms the conjecture that he had actually arrived in Taos on that date.

Carson says nothing of his stop in St. Louis on the way east and nothing of his stay in Washington. He is known to have carried a copy of the *California Star* containing an account of the discovery of gold on Sutter's property and probably carried letters announcing it, as well. Other messages and papers with the same news are known to have arrived in-

Fork and from thence to Fort Leavenworth, having had no trouble on the march.[240] Thence to Washington and delivered my dispatches.[241] Returned to St. Louis. Remained a few days and started back for New Mexico. Arrived there in October 1848.

When I reached Santa Fe, when on my way to Washington with despatches, I was informed by Colonel Newby that my appointment of Lieutenant was not confirmed by the Senate and I was advised by many of my friends to deliver to the commanding officer the despatches and not take them through. I considered the matter over, and, as I had been entrusted with the despatches, chosen as the most competent person to take them through safely, I determined to fulfill the duty.[242] That mattered not to me if, in the discharge of a duty of service beneficial to the public, whether I was of the rank of Lieutenant or holding the credit of an experienced mountaineer. Having gained much honor and credit in performance of all duties entrusted to my charge, I would on no account wish to forfeit the good opinion of a majority of my countrymen because the Senate of the United States did not deem it proper to confirm on me an appointment of an office that I never sought, and one which, if confirmed, I would have resigned at the termination of the war.

I was with Fremont with 1842 to 1847. The hardships through which we passed I find it impossible to describe, and the credit which he deserves I am incapable to do him justice in writing. But his services to his country have been left to the judgment of impartial freemen, and all agree in saying that his services were great and have redounded to his honor and that of his country.

I have heard that he is enormously rich.[243] I wish to God that he may be worth ten times as much more. All that he has or may ever receive,

dependently, and it is difficult to assign priority.

Carson's old friend and fellow trapper, Joe Meek, was in Washington at this time to inform the President of the Whitman Massacre, in which his half-blood daughter, Helen Mar, had been one of the victims, and to request the Federal Government to aid Oregon Territory in dealing with the Cayuse Indians. President Polk, whose wife was Meek's cousin, furnished Joe with several hundred dollars, some of which he loaned to Kit, who renewed his friendship with Meek and also with the Bentons and the Frémonts. Godey and Owens, who had attended Frémont's court-martial, had probably left the capital before Carson arrived, but it is strange that he makes no mention of Meek, who refers to Carson frequently in his own memoirs. See Victor, *River,* 458.

242
President Polk had appointed Carson to a lieutenancy on the occcasion of their second conversation at the White House, June 14, 1847. The action of the U.S. Senate in refusing to confirm the appointment is characterized by Milo M. Quaife as an "act of vindictive meanness." It was also an instance of collective stupidity. The fact that Carson delivered the dispatches in spite of having learned in Santa Fe that he had been refused the appointment is proof that he deserved this small reward, whether the Senate thought so or not.

243
Frémont had purchased the Mariposa Grant, of seventy square miles, in California and was living upon it. Valuable gold mines were found on it, and at the time Carson dictated

he deserves. I can never forget his treatment of me while in his employ and how cheerfully he suffered with his men when undergoing the severest of hardships. His perseverance and willingness to participate in all that was undertaken, no matter whether the duty was rough or easy, is the main cause of his success. And I say, without fear of contradiction, that none but him could have surmounted and succeeded through as many difficult services, as his was.

I remained at Taos during the winter.[244] I made two trips during the time with Colonel Beall, 1st Drag[oon]s in command of troops in pursuit of Indians.[245]

The Colonel had ordered a command, previous to his departure, to pursue the Indians, to cross the mountains. They had advanced some distance and found it impracticable to cross. The officer in the command was advised by his guides to return, that it was utterly impossible to proceed. He returned, reported to Colonel Beall the impracticability of the route—the cause of his return. The Col[onel] replied that there was no such word as "impracticable" in the soldier's vocabulary and that nothing ought to be impossible for the 1st Dragoons to accomplish. He immediately assumed the command, I was employed as his guide, and we departed; and after surmounting many difficulties and passing through severe hardships, we finally accomplished the object of the expedition and returned to Taos.

On our return, after passing through the Sangre de Cristo Pass, an Apache village was discovered. Two chiefs were captured. The Colonel held a talk with them. They made promises of peace and friendship and were liberated.[246] We then continued on and arrived at Taos. Remained till February [when] Col. Beall heard [that] a large number of Indians were encamped on the Arkansas, agreeable to treaty

his memoirs Frémont was reputed to have been worth ten million dollars. He subsequently lost it all in railroad promotion schemes. The feeling of esteem between Frémont and Carson was mutual and neither ever said a harsh word about the other.

244
The winter of 1848–49 is indicated here. However, it was probably in the late fall of 1848, after his return from Washington in October, that Kit was employed by William Bent to go with Robert Fisher and several others to the former Bent trading post known as Adobe Walls in present Hutchinson County, Texas. They were to endeavor to reopen trade with the Comanches, but were forced to abandon the project by the hostility of the Kiowas. See Lavender, *Bent's Fort,* 309.

When Frémont came in to Taos in late January, 1849, from the hopeless dissolution of his fourth expedition in the La Garita Mountains of southern Colorado, he found Owens, Maxwell, and Carson at Beaubien's store. He stayed a few days at Carson's house, while Godey performed the rescue work that he himself should have been engaged upon, and then went on to California by a more southerly route. At this time Carson considered going to California to settle, but could not decide to break off his connections with Maxwell. See Hafen and Hafen (eds.), *The Frémont Disaster,* XI, 206.

245
Benjamin Lloyd Beall attended West Point but left in 1818 and did not graduate. He served in the Mexican War and, afterward, in California and Oregon. He supervised the building of many frontier forts, from Tex-

made by United States and Mexico; the former was supposed to deliver to the latter all the Mexican captives held by Indians of the former nation.[247] It was the intention of the Colonel to visit those Indians, to endeavor to have them deliver up all Mexicans held captive peaceably if he could, forcibly if he must. His command consisted of two companies of Dragoons and I was his guide.

We arrived at the Arkansas, found encamped there four nations of Indians, some two thousand souls. He stated to the Indian agent the object of his having come there and was informed that it would be useless to demand of them the captives at present, that they surely would refuse and force would be necessary, and the Indians being in such force, that he would fail in his object if he undertook to fight with such numbers against him.

It took a great deal of persuasion to cause the Colonel to desist from making the attempt, but as the Agent, traders, and officers of his command were opposed to his attempting to make them give up the captives with such [an] inferior force at his command, he finally concluded not to demand the prisoners but leave it for some other day—that the object, in all probability, would be gained by having a treaty with them and the delivery of the captives one of the articles.

We then marched up the Arkansas to the mouth of the Huerfano, then through the Sangre de Cristo Pass, thence to Taos.[248]

In April, Mr. Maxwell and I concluded to make a settlement on the Rayado.[249] We had been leading a roving life long enough and now was the time, if ever, to make a home for ourselves and children. We were getting old and could not expect to remain any length of time able to gain a livelihood as we had been [for] such a number of years. Arrived at Rayado, com-

as to California. He became lieutenant colonel of the 1st Dragoons in 1855. During the Civil War he had two sons in the Union Army and one in the Confederate Army. Heitman, *Historical Register*, I, 202.

246
This campaign was probably conducted in December, 1848. The route through the Sangre de Cristo Pass approached the mountains from the north, up the Huerfano River and Oak Creek, but near the summit it joined present La Veta Pass and the western descent of the two was identical, down Sangre de Cristo Creek. The village was that of some Jicarilla Apaches who, during this period, were allied with the Mohuache Utes, and both were hostile in the early 1850's. The chiefs were set free by Carson's advice.

247
In late October, 1848, as he traveled west on his fourth expedition, Frémont had found an estimated thirty-five hundred Indians (six hundred lodges) camped in the Big Timbers along the Arkansas, some thirty-five miles below Bent's Fort. They were Cheyennes and Arapahoes who dwelt chiefly to the north of the river and Kiowas and Comanches from the former Mexican territory south of the river. Either they had continued to camp there until February, 1849, or they had assembled there again when Beall decided to try to treat with them. These are the four nations that Carson mentions, but there were probably some Jicarilla Apaches among them, also. See Lavender, *Bent's Fort*, 308.

248
The Huerfano River enters the Ar-

menced building and making improvements, and were in a way of becoming prosperous.

In October, the train of Mr. White was attacked by the Jicarilla Apache Indians.[250] He was killed and his wife and child taken prisoner. A command was organized in Taos, Leroux[251] and Fisher[252] as guides. When they reached Rayado, I was employed as one of the guides. We marched to where the depredation had been committed, then took their trail. I was the first man that found the camp where the murder had been committed. Found trunks that were broken open, harness cut, etc., everything destroyed that the Indians could not carry with them. We followed them some ten or twelve days. It was the most difficult trail that I ever followed. As they would leave the camps, they, in numbers from one to two, went in different directions, to meet at some appointed place. In nearly every camp we would find some of Mrs. White's clothing, which was the cause of renewed energy on our part to continue the pursuit.

We finally came in view of the Indian Camp. I was in advance, started for their camp, calling to the men to follow. The comdg. officer ordered a halt, none then would follow me.[253] I was informed that Leroux, the principal guide, told the officer in command to halt, that the Indians wished to have a parley.[254] The Indians, seeing that the troops did not intend to charge on them, they commenced packing up in all haste. When the halt was ordered the comdg. officer was shot; the ball passing through his coat, gauntlets that were in his pockets, shirts, and to the skin, doing no serious damage, only making him a little sick at the stomach. The gauntlets saved his life, leaving to the service of his country one more gallant officer. As soon as he recovered from the shock given him by the ball, he ordered the men to charge, but the order was too late for the desired effect. There was only one Indian in the camp;

kansas River from the southwest near Boone, Colorado, about twenty miles east of Pueblo.

249
The Rayado was the name of a small stream and its mountain valley, about fifty miles east of Taos. It takes its name from a Comanche Indian chief of the early nineteenth century. Maxwell had begun operations there somewhat earlier. The Rayado Valley lay south of Carson's previous attempt at farming on the Little Cimarron.

250
James M. White had formerly engaged in trade over the Santa Fe Trail for some years. On this occasion he was traveling with a caravan headed by Francis X. Aubry, who, a year earlier, had made a celebrated ride from Santa Fe to Independence, Missouri, a distance of 780 miles, in the record time of five days and sixteen hours. It being late October and the caravan having passed the Point of Rocks, beyond which there was usually no danger from Indians, White moved ahead of the slow wagon train with his wife and small daughter in a dearborn, with an escort of four men on horseback. The men were all killed, and two weeks later, when the news reached Taos, the military rescue party was organized.

251
Antoine Leroux, also called Joaquin and Watkins Leroux, was born in St. Louis about 1801. He is thought to have come to Taos in 1824, where he lived the life of a trapper. He married Juana Catarina Valdez de Vigil in 1833, and became the recipient of a land grant. He knew the Navaho country west of Taos better than any

he, swimming into the river hard by, was shot. In about 200 yards, pursuing the Indians, the body of Mrs. White was found, perfectly warm, had not been killed more than five minutes—shot through the heart with an arrow. She evidently knew that some one was coming to her rescue. She did not see us, but it was apparent that she was endeavoring to make her escape when she received the fatal shot.

I am certain that if the Indians had been charged immediately on our arrival, she would have been saved.[255] The Indians did not know of our approach and perhaps, not paying any particular watch of her, she could [have] run towards us, the Indians fearing to pursue. She could not possibly have lived long, for the treatment she had received from the Indians was so brutal and horrible that she could possibly last but a short period. Her life, I think, should never be regretted by her friends. She is surely far more happy in heaven, with her God, than among friends of this earth.

I do not wish to be understood as attaching any blame to the officer in command or the principal guide. They acted as they thought best for the purpose of saving the life of Mrs. White. We merely differed in opinion at the time. But I have no doubt that they now can see that if my advice had been taken, the life might have been saved, for at least a short period, of the much lamented Mrs. White.

We, however, captured all their baggage and camp equipage—many running off without any of their clothing—and some animals. We pursued the Indians for about six miles on a level prairie. One Indian was killed and two or three Indians taken prisoner. I have much regretted the failure of the attempt to save the life of so greatly esteemed and respected a lady. In camp was found a book, the first of the kind I had ever seen, in which I was made a great hero, slaying

other mountain man. He and Carson were the most trusted and reliable guides for army expeditions in the southwest. Leroux died at his ranch two miles west of Taos in 1861, and was buried in Taos. See Forbes Parkill, *The Blazed Trail of Antoine Leroux* (Los Angeles, 1965).

252
Robert Fisher was born in Virginia in 1807, and he, also, came to Taos in 1824. For many years he was one of the most trusted men employed at Bent's Old Fort on the Arkansas River. During the summer of 1849 he and Carson were employed by William Bent to endeavor to reopen the trading post of Adobe Walls in the Texas Panhandle, but were forced by the Comanches to abandon it. Fisher was married to Rumalda Lopez and had several children, but in 1850 he left his family to go to the California gold fields, where he died. See Harvey L. Carter, "Robert Fisher," *Mountain Men* (ed. by Hafen), IV, 97–102.

Dick Wootton and Tom Tobin were also among the guides employed. For Wootton's account of this affair see Howard L. Conard, *Uncle Dick Wootton* (Chicago, 1890), 205–14.

253
Major William N. Grier, West Point, 1835, of the First U.S. Dragoons, was in command. He was stationed at Taos at this time, and saw several years service in the Southwest. Like Carson, he was brevetted brigadier general during the Civil War. Heitman, *Historical Register,* I, 478.

254
Dick Wootton, who exhibits some envy of Leroux's reputation, never-

Indians by the hundred, and I have often thought that as Mrs. White would read the same, and knowing that I lived near, she would pray for my appearance and that she would be saved.[256] I did come, but had not the power to convince those that were in command over me to pursue my plan for her rescue. They would not listen to me and they failed. I will say no more regarding the matter, attach no blame to any particular person, for I presume the consciences of those that were the cause of the failure have severely punished them ere this.

We returned and arrived at Taos in November. On the return we had the severest snow storm that I ever experienced. Had one man frozen to death. We were trying to make Barclay's fort on the Mora but, on account of the wind, we could not keep our course, but happily arrived at some timber near Las Vegas.[257] I learned that in the same storm many of the Indians that we had been pursuing perished. After the storm we went in to Las Vegas. Captain Judd was in command of the post and from there the command marched for Taos and I proceeded to Rayado, where I remained till Spring.[258]

During the winter there was a detachment of ten dragoons commanded by Leigh Holbrook stationed at the Rayado.[259] Sometime during the month of March, a party of Indians came and attacked the rancho that was about two miles distant where we had our animals that were gentle kept to graze. There were two men in charge; both were severely wounded. One, however, made his way to the Rayado and gave the report. The Dragoons, three Americans, and myself immediately saddled up and proceeded to the Rancho. It was night when we arrived. Remained until morning, then took the trail of the animals that was driven off, followed it at a gallop for 25 miles and discovered, at a distance, the

theless, does not attribute the halt to his advice. He attributes it to the fact that Grier was hit and momentarily confused. Conrad, *Uncle Dick,* 205–14.

255
All of the mountain men agreed on this point, from their knowledge of Indians and their ways.

256
It seems probable that the book was Charles Averill, *Kit Carson, Prince of the Gold Hunters* (1849), perhaps the earliest of a long line of thrilling dime novels which exploited the imaginary as well as the real adventures of Carson. Carson, of course, was never a gold hunter. There is no proof that the book belonged to Mrs. White, whose child was never recovered. Kit's reflections indicate a laudable, but rather touching, feeling that he had to live up to his heroic fictional reputation.

257
The resident proprietor of Barclay's Fort, at the junction of the Mora and Sapello Rivers, made these two entries in his diary: "Nov. 23 All day look for Major Greer of course in vain. Fisher and some others got here this evening. Nov. 25 Major Greer Kit Carson and Watkin La Roux from Las Vegas. After noon major and Kit back to Las Vegas." Alexander Barclay Papers, The Bancroft Library, Berkeley, California.

Barclay's Fort was built in 1848, by Alexander Barclay and his partner, Joseph Doyle. Barclay, an Englishman, had formerly been a clerk at Bent's Fort and was one of the founders of El Pueblo, in 1842, and of Hardscrabble, in 1844. He died in late 1856.

Indians. During the pursuit, some of our animals gave out and were left on the trail.

We approached the Indians cautiously and, when close, charged them; killed five, the other four made their escape. We recovered the stolen animals, with the exception of four, and then returned. Two of the men with me at the time [have] since [been] killed by the same tribe of Indians; Sergt. Holbrook, a gallant and brave soldier, was killed in the battle of Ceneguilla[260] in 1854, and William New, a brave and experienced trapper, was killed at the Rayado a few months after our pursuit of [the] Indians that had stolen the animals from the Rayado.[261]

On the 5th May 1850, Tim Goodel and I started to Fort Laramie with forty or fifty head of mules and horses to trade with the emigrants.[262] Arrived about the first of June, remained about a month, disposed of our animals to good advantage.[263] Then we separated, Goodel going to California, I for home. Arrived at the Greenhorn, a tributary of the Arkansas, had with me one Mexican boy.[264] I learned there that the Apaches were on the road which I had to travel, watching it for the purpose of murdering those that might pass. I remained about six days to recruit my animals; I could get no one to accompany me but one man, Charles Kinney, and then started.[265]

The first night I travelled about forty miles through the mountain[s], reached the River Trinchero.[266] Had the animals concealed in the brush, some distance from the road, and I ascended the highest cottonwood tree for the purpose of watching for the Indians. I remained in that position during the entire day. Sometimes I would fall asleep, and nearly fall, but would recover in time and continue my watch. Near evening I saw a large body of Indians about one half mile distant. They had not as yet discovered our trail. I descended the tree. We saddled up, and

258
Captain Henry B. Judd, West Point, 1839, of the Third U. S. Artillery, served in New Mexico, 1848–50. Heitman, *Historical Register*, I, 548.

259
Sergeant Holbrook's account of this fight is found in Sabin, *Kit Carson Days* (1914), 351–52.

260
Carson gives a subsequent account of the battle of Cieneguilla. See Note 291, below.

261
New's death was in May, 1850—not 1849, as some writers have it. He is listed in the U.S. Census for Taos County in 1850, and was at Barclay's Fort on January 11, 1850. Alexander Barclay Papers. See Harvey L. Carter, "Bill New," *Mountain Men* (ed. by Hafen), V, 249–54.

262
Tim Goodale was a trapper and trader who lived at Greenhorn in the 1840's. He went to California in 1850 and again in 1853, with the Carson-Maxwell-Hatcher sheep drive. In 1858 he guided for Colonel Randolph B. Marcy, and later for Major E. L. Berthoud. He lived northwest of Denver on Boulder Creek in 1860, and at La Porte, Colorado, on the Cache La Poudre until 1864, when he removed to the Bitterroot Valley in Montana, where he died. He is said to have been from Illinois, well educated, and to have had a succession of Indian wives. F. W. Cragin Papers, Notebook IV, 13, 53, 54, 55; XXVII, 30, 58, 65, 76.

263
Peters, *Life and Adventures*, 356–57,

proceeded on our journey, keeping in the brush some distance of[f] the road till dark. Then I took the road and travelled to Red River, got there at daylight in the morning, and that evening went to Taos.[267] Remained a few days and departed for the Rayado.

During my absence the Indians had run off every head of stock on the Rayado.[268] Troops were stationed there at the time, but the Indians came in such force that they feared to attack them. Shortly afterwards, there was a command sent in pursuit, commanded by Major Grier. They killed some of the Indians and recovered all the stock except that which had been killed by the Indians.

I remained at the Rayado till fall, nothing having transpired of any moment except my following of an American that had organized a party for the purpose of murdering, on the plains, Mr. Saml. Weatherhead and Mr. Elias Brevort, that were supposed to have a large amount of money.[269] Fox was the name of their leader. The object of the party was discovered by Fox, when in Taos, trying to get a man to join him. He stated to him that which was to be done. He refused to go, and, when he thought Fox had gone sufficient distance not to be apprehended, he stated what Fox had informed him.

Lieut. Taylor, 1st Dragoons, was in Taos at the time [and] came to me saying that he wished Fox apprehended for debt and requested me to pursue him for that purpose.[270] I refused. Then he stated the true cause of his wishing him apprehended, which informed that he [Fox] and a party of men were travelling in company with Weatherhead and Brevort, and that it was their intention to murder them as soon as they reached the Cimarron, then go to Texas. I immediately agreed to go, when I knew their object. Ten dragoons was given me. We marched on till one o'clock that night. Met Capt. Ewell in command

tells an amusing story of an emigrant who had heard that Kit Carson was at Fort Laramie and wanted to see the celebrity. He was so disappointed in the disparity between the actual Carson and what he had imagined his hero's appearance to be that he turned away in disgust, remarking, "You aint the *kind* of Kit Carson I'm looking for."

264
In the 1840's there was a small settlement of trappers and their squaws and children about twenty-five miles south of Pueblo, Colorado, where the Taos Trail crossed Greenhorn Creek. The creek took its name from the Comanche chief, Cuerno Verde, who was killed in battle there with Governor Anza of New Mexico in 1779. The creek flows into the St. Charles or San Carlos River a few miles before that stream joins the Arkansas River.

265
Charles Kinney may be the Carlos Quinto of New Mexican records, in which case he was baptized at Taos in 1828, at the age of twenty-five, and later lived in Mora, New Mexico, with his Mexican wife and two children. Kinney was employed at Fort Jackson, on the South Platte, by Sarpy and Fraeb in 1838, and at Fort Lupton in 1841-42. He was living at Greenhorn from 1847 to 1850, but appears to have guided emigrants to Salt Lake City during this period, being described as "an old Mountaineer and a reliable brave gentleman," which agrees with Carson's opinion of him. See Janet S. Lecompte, "Charles Kinney," *Mountain Men,* ed. by Hafen, IV, 169–71.

of recruits enroute for New Mexico.[271] Stated to him the object of [my] journey. He then joined me with twenty five men.

Came to the camp of Mr. Weatherhead and Brevort, entered it cautiously, arrested Fox, remained there that night. Capt. Ewell then took charge of Fox and returned to his camp. Weatherhead and Mr. Brevort then selected fifteen men of his party in whom he had confidence, and directed the remainder to leave. There were about fifty men of their party. I have not the least [doubt] but that they would have been murdered if these men had not been driven from their party.

They told me that anything I would ask of them would be freely given. I demanded nothing for my trouble, considering having done a good act, thereby saving the lives of two valuable citizens, was reward sufficient. However, in the Spring following they made me accept, as a present, a pair of splendid silver mounted pistols.[272]

I returned to Rayado with Fox; turned him over to the proper authorities. He was then taken to Taos and confined, but nothing positive could be proven against him, and he was liberated.

I remained in Rayado till March and then started for St. Louis, took with me twelve wagons of Mr. Maxwell for the purpose of bringing out goods for him. Arrived at Kansas May 1.[273] [I] proceeded to St. Louis, purchased the goods, then returned to Kansas, loaded the wagons, and started for home. I concluded to take the Bent's Fort trail on account of water and grass being in greater abundance thereon.

About fifteen miles before we came to the crossing of the Arkansas, I fell in with a village of Cheyenne Indians.[274] They were at the time hostile to the United States, on account of one of the officers of Colonel Sumner's command (that was about ten days march in my advance) hav-

266
Kit traveled over Sangre de Cristo Pass and down the Trinchera River, which flows to the Río Grande.

267
Red River refers to the small New Mexican settlement of that name, located on the Río Colorado or Red River, a tributary of the Río Grande. It was about twenty eight miles by the trail from Red River to Taos. The name was changed to Questa in 1884 when a post office was established there.

268
It was during this time that Bill New had been killed.

269
Elias Brevoort, "The Santa Fe Trail," a manuscript in The Bancroft Library, Berkeley, California, has a detailed account of this affair, written in 1884. Brevoort, who was born in Detroit in 1822, had been an Indian trader for seven years. In 1850 he made his first trip to Santa Fe and, having disposed of his goods, was returning to Kansas City. He mentions Samuel Weatherhead, of Baltimore, and a lawyer named Tully, of San Francisco, as traveling companions—not as partners. All these men had considerable sums of gold, amounting, in all, to more than $40,000. Brevoort says that the informer was an actual accomplice of Fox, who had been left behind because he was ill and who, thinking he was dying, turned informer.

270
Lieutenant Oliver H. P. Taylor, West Point, 1846, of the First U.S. Dragoons, was killed on the Spokane

ing flogged an Indian Chief of their tribe.[275] The cause to me [was] unknown, but I presume courage was oozing from the finger ends of the officer and, as the Indians were in his power, he wished to be relieved of such [a] commodity.

As an Indian very seldom lets pass an injury done him unavenged, and it matters not who may be the victim so that it is of the same nation, I unfortunately, happened to be the first [American] that passed them since the insult was given them. On me they intended to have retaliation.

I had travelled about twenty miles from their village. They pursued me. I was encamped. They came to me by one[s], two[s], and threes till twenty arrived. I thought them friendly, not having known that which had been done them. Wished to treat them with kindness and invited them to sit down and smoke and talk. They done so. They then commenced talking among themselves, and I understood them to say that while I would be smoking and not on my guard they could easily kill me with a knife, and as for the Mexicans with me, they could kill them as easily as buffalo.

I was alarmed. [I] had but fifteen men, two Americans and thirteen Mexicans; of the latter I had [a] poor opinion of their bravery in case I was attacked. I informed the Indians that [I knew not] the cause of their wishing my scalp, that I had done them no injury and wanted to treat them kindly, that they had come to me as friends and I now discovered that they wished to do me injury, and that they must leave. Any refusing would be shot, and, if they attempted to return, that I would fire on them.[276] They departed and joined those that were in sight on the hills. I then ordered my men to hitch up and commence our march. We moved on, the drivers carrying in one hand their rifles and in the other their whips. I travelled on till dark, encamped, and started an express to the Rayado.

Expedition, May 17, 1858. Heitman, *Historical Register*, I, 948.

271
Captain Richard S. Ewell, West Point, 1836, was a Captain of the 2nd Dragoons in the Mexican War. He became a Lieutenant General in the Confederate Army. Heitman, *Historical Register*, I, 410.

272
Brevoort, "The Santa Fe Trail," manuscript in The Bancroft Library, Berkeley, says that the murder and robbery were to have been carried out the next night following the apprehension of Fox, who was never prosecuted because the informer had recovered from his illness and had left New Mexico. Brevoort dwells on Carson's modesty in declining a reward. The pistols were specially made at the Colt factory and were suitably inscribed. Concerning Fox, Brevoort says he was "of the dismissed dragoons," which affords an explanation of the interest of the military in the matter.

273
Kansas refers to the present site of Kansas City, Missouri, then just a small village, but beginning to rival Independence and Westport commercially.

274
The crossing of the Arkansas was at Chouteau's Island in western Kansas.

275
Jesse Nelson, who accompanied Kit on this trip, gives an account of this incident in F. W. Cragin Papers, Notebook VIII, 61, 65. He says that the officer had the Indian flogged for having stolen his wife's ring. This

Next morning I moved on till 12 o'clock, stopped to noon, and five Indians were approaching my camp. I ordered them to halt when within 100 yards, but I eventually let them come in so that I could speak more freely to them. As soon as they came in, I informed them that I had the night before sent an express to Rayado, that he had gone for the troops that were stationed there and that among them I had many friends, that they would surely come to my relief, and if I were killed they would know by whom, and that my death would be avenged.

They departed, examined the road, and [finding] that all I said was true, and he [the express] had advanced so far that they could not overtake him, they concluded to leave me, fearing the arrival of the troops. I am confident I and my party would have been killed by the Cheyennes, for they were a large number around me, if I had not sent forward for assistance, and the only reason they had of attacking me was, as I afterwards learned, the difficulty among them caused by the conduct of an officer of Col. Sumner's command.

My express reached Col. Sumner the third day, gave to the Colonel the letter which he had, but [as he] would send me no aid, the express continued on and arrived at Rayado the next day.[277] My letter was given to Major Grier, the commanding officer. He immediately detailed Lt. Johnston and a party of men to march to my aid.[278] When Lt. Johnston met Sumner he asked him where he was going, was informed to my aid; the conscience of the gallant old Colonel then, I presume, troubled him. He had refused me aid two days previous and, in all probability, I and [my] party was murdered. He concluded to send Major Carleton and thirty men with him.[279] [Sumner knew] that Johnston, a noble and brave officer, could meet the Indians, have a fight, and all knew that, if such was the case, the affair would be properly managed and that

was the beginning of Cheyenne hostility to the whites—up to this time they had been friendly.

276
Nelson says that a big Indian brandished a hatchet over Kit's head, that Nelson had his gun leveled at this Indian, and that another Indian had a bow, with the arrow pulled back to the head, aimed at Nelson. See Nelson's account, F. W. Cragin Papers, Notebook VIII, 61, 65. The situation was really saved by Ah-man-nah-ko, son of the Cheyenne chief, Old Bark, who recognized Carson and averted the crisis temporarily. However, he warned Kit that the Cheyennes would try to ambush him later on, which caused Kit to send the rider to Rayado for help. The second encounter verified the warning. There is a drawing of Ah-man-nah-ko and his wife in Lieutenant J. W. Abert's *Report,* 30 Cong. 1 Sess., *House Exec. Doc. 41,* Serial 517.

277
Colonel Edwin V. Sumner (1797–1863) was a native of Boston, Massachusetts. His career as an army officer began in 1819, and he was a Captain in the 1st Dragoons from the time of its organization in 1833. He served in the Mexican War and served as major general of Volunteers in the Civil War. To his soldiers on the frontier, he was known as the "old bull of the woods." Heitman, *Historical Register,* I, 936.

278
Lieutenant Robert Johnson, of the 1st Dragoons, was a member of the West Point class of 1846. A native of Virginia, he joined the Confederate Army in 1861. He died in 1902. Heitman, *Historical Register,* I, 578.

he would receive great praise. The Colonel wishing to have a hand in the matter, he concluded to send Carleton. But to the Colonel I do not consider myself under any obligations; for by his conduct two days previously he showed plainly that by rendering aid to a few American citizens in the power of Indians, enraged by the conduct of some of his command, was not his wish.

But I am thankful to Carleton and Johnston [for] the kindness they showed me on their arrival and by their anxiety and willingness to punish the Indians that wished to interrupt me. Major Grier, a gentleman and a gallant soldier, is entitled to my warmest gratitude for the promptness [with] which he rendered assistance and cordially showed his capability of performing the high duty to which he was appointed. It plainly showed his noble heart and that reliance can be placed on him in the hour of danger.

The services of the troops were not required, for the Indians knew they would come, so on their arrival, they were not in striking distance. The troops came up to me about twenty-five miles of Bent's Fort. They returned, I in company with them, to Rayado. I then delivered to Mr. Maxwell the wagons and goods and remained till March.[280]

Mr. Maxwell and I rigged up a party of eighteen men to go trapping, I taking charge of them. We went to the Balla Salado, then down the South Fork to the Plains, through the Plains of Laramie to the New Park, trapped it to the Old Park, then again to the Balla Salado, then on the Arkansas where it goes out of the mountain, then followed on under the mountain, thence home to the Rayado, through to the Raton Mountain, having made a very good hunt.[281]

I remained at Rayado during the fall and winter. In February '53, I went to the Rio Abajo and purchased sheep.[282] Returned with them to

279
Major James Henry Carleton, of the 1st Dragoons, began his military service in 1839. He served in the Mexican War, fighting at Buena Vista. He was brigadier general of Volunteers in New Mexico Territory from 1862–65, during which time Carson served under him. He died in 1873. Heitman, *Historical Register,* I, 282.

280
Jesse Nelson further says that Kit's daughter, Adaline, returned from Missouri to Rayado with him on this trip. Carson purchased the old hospital at Rayado from the government in 1851, when the troops were moved from there to the newly established Fort Union. Both the Carsons and the Nelsons lived in it. At this time Maxwell was supplying the army with hay and other provender at high prices and Carson shared, to some extent, in his prosperity. F. W. Cragin Papers, Notebook VIII, 49, 75, 83. When Kit was away from Rayado, Josefa usually returned to Taos to visit her relatives there.

281
This trapping expedition was in the nature of a last farewell to the old way of life, like that which Sir William Drummond Stewart and William Sublette had made in 1843. It was the only trapping party that Kit Carson ever headed. There is no clue to the identity of the other members, but it may have included some of those who went to California on the sheep drive in the following year. Since it was "a good hunt," it may have provided Carson with money to buy sheep, which otherwise he would not have had.

the Rayado. Then I started for California.[283] There was with me Henry Mercure, John Bernavette, and their employees.[284] We had about 6,500 head of sheep. Went to Fort Laramie, then kept the wagon road that is travelled by emigrants to California, arrived about the first of August, having met with no serious loss. Sold our sheep to Mr. Norris at $5.50 a head, doing very well.[285]

I heard so much talk of the great change that had taken place at San Francisco, I concluded to go down, and when I arrived I would not have known the place if I had not been there so often before.[286]

Maxwell came on shortly after me to California. Disposed of his sheep in Sacramento. But on Carson River he sent to me an express, which I received at Sacramento, requesting me to await his arrival and then we would travel together home by way of the Gila. He arrived. I went down to Los Angeles by land. He took the steamer. I would not travel on the sea, having made the voyage on that in 1846, and I was so disgusted with it that I swore that it would be the last time I would leave sight of land, when I could get a mule to perform the journey. Arrived safely at Los Angeles, Maxwell having arrived some fifteen days before me. Made the necessary preparations, and then started for New Mexico.

[We] came to the Pima village and, on account of the scarcity of grass, we continued up the Gila to the mouth of the San Pedro, up it three days and from there we took a straight course for the copper mines, and then [onto] the Del Norte, thence home through the settlements of the Rio Abajo. Arrived at Taos Decr. 25th, 1853.[287]

On my way home, I saw the Mormon Delegate to Congress and by him I was informed that I had received the appointment of Indian

282
In New Mexico the principal settlements were in the valley of the Río Grande. Those lying south of Santa Fe were referred to as the Río Abajo, while those lying north of the capital were known as Río Arriba. Ralph E. Twitchell, *Leading Facts of New Mexico History,* II (Cedar Rapids, 1912), 146.

283
This was not the first sheep drive to California. Dick Wootton, with twenty-two employees, had driven nine thousand sheep to Sacramento from Taos a year earlier, in 1852. He went by a shorter route and made the trip in 107 days. See Conard, *Uncle Dick,* 249–62.

The big drive of 1853 was in three sections, of which the first was that of John L. Hatcher, the second, that of Carson, the third, that of Maxwell. Hatcher set out on January 29 and arrived June 29, 1853. Carson and Maxwell set out more than a month later. Carson arrived September 5, 1853, and Maxwell several days later. *San Francisco Herald,* September 5, 1853. Carson apparently deviated somewhat from the established trail in order to have better forage. *Daily Alta California,* August 9, 1853, reports that an emigrant train passed Carson in Carson Valley on a new road he had laid out from the Sweetwater. A new ferry over Green River, six miles above the regular crossing, took Carson's animals across free of charge and named the road to the ferry "Kit Carson's Cutoff," hoping for patronage from others because of Carson's fame. F. W. Cragin Papers, Notebook XXVII, 57. Cragin interviewed William Shortredge, one of the ferry proprietors, in Fort Collins, Colorado, November 24, 1903.

Agent.[288] After my arrival at Taos, I accepted the appointment, giving the necessary bond.

In February, 1854, the Jicarilla Apache Indians showed [a] disposition of hostility. Lieut. Bell, 2d Drag[oon]s, had a fight with them on the waters of Red River, in which there was one or two soldiers killed and some wounded but, in the affray, he killed a number of Indians, and they retreated.[289] He had charged them once or twice and they could not stand, although superior in number.

In March I proceeded to Santa Fe on business pertaining to my office. Before my departure a large party of Jicarilla Apaches had come within twenty miles of Taos. I had seen a number of the Chiefs and they all pretended friendship, but, during my absence, they became hostile. Lieut. J. W. Davison, 1st Dragoons, and sixty Dragoons of F and I Companies were ordered against them. He overtook them in the Embudo Mountains, about 20 miles southwest of Taos.[290] The Indians evidently, from the preparations they had made and having chosen such an advantageous position, intended to fight the troops sent against [them], if they did not come in force.

Lt. Davidson had sixty men and there were seventy five or eighty lodges of Indians. He marched to them. They immediately saw his small force and surely came to the conclusion to fight, for when a few men were sent in advance they did not speak to them in a friendly manner and [were] showing demonstrations of hostility. Lieut. Davidson was compelled to attack them. I know Davidson, having been in engagements when he done a prominent part, and I know him to be as brave as an officer can be; and from the men that were in [the] engagement of that day I have been informed by all that, during the fight, he never took ambush and that when in retreat he directed his men to take shelter as best

Carson's daughter, Adaline, had recently been married to Louis Simmons, a former trapper, and they went to California with Kit at this time, and did not return. F. W. Cragin Papers, Notebook I, 24. Jake Beard, who also made the trip, was Dr. Cragin's informant, at El Paso, Texas, October 1, 1904. Jesse Nelson said that Adaline was a wild girl and did not behave properly, and that Simmons left her. F. W. Cragin Papers, Notebook VIII, 75. Adaline is said to have married George Stilts afterward, and to have died near Mono Lake, California, in 1860. McClung, *Carson-Bent-Boggs,* 70.

284
Henry Mercure and John Bernavette were Carson's financial partners in this enterprise. The U.S. Census for Santa Fe, 1850, lists Mercure as a merchant of that city, age 28, in partnership with his brother, Joseph, age 32. They were born in Canada. Henry Mercure had served with Carson as a member of Company A of the California Battalion. See Fred B. Rogers, "Rosters of California Volunteers . . . ," *Annual Publication of The Society of California Pioneers* (1950), 22.

John Bernavette appears in the U.S. Census for Taos, 1850, as Juan Bernadet. He was a merchant of Taos, 30 years of age, with a wife and child, and with real estate valued at $2,500. His birthplace is given as Spain.

285
Samuel Norris, reputed to have been German or Danish in origin, came to California by sea in 1845 and became a trader at New Helvetia and at San Francisco. For a time there was a firm known as Shelby and Norris. After

they could but that he, fearing no danger, remained exposed to the fire of the Indians.

The Indians had position on the side and top of the mountain; the troops were on the bank of a small stream below. With horse the Indians could not be reached. They therefore had to dismount, only leaving a few men to guard the horses. The troops ascended the mountain, drove the Indians from their position, but lost five men killed. The Indians were in great force, had the troops surrounded, and made an attempt to secure their horses, but, by the timely arrival of Davidson, they failed. The Indians were firing on the troops from every direction. They could not be seen [as they] were concealed behind trees in the brush.

The troops charged them several times, but those whom they charged would retreat and join those in the rear. Finding that it was impossible to do any execution on account of the situation in which he was placed, and having lost several men in killed and wounded, he was compelled to retreat, though reluctantly on his part, but the officer with him, seeing the deplorable condition of his men, caused him to give up the idea of maintaining his position. The retreat was sounded, the Indians, in great numbers, in pursuit. The troops had to wheel about several times to charge the Indians. They finally succeeded in reaching the main road to Taos, but lost in killed twenty two soldiers and nearly every one of the command wounded. The number of Indians killed during that day has never as yet been ascertained, but there is no doubt but a great number of them were slain.[291]

I returned to Taos the next day after the fight, having passed near the place where it had been, but did not meet any Indian. They had all fled and took a direction west across the Del Norte.

On the 4th day of April, 1854, Lieut. Colonel Cooke, 2nd Dragoon, organized a command for

1857, Norris wandered about the world a great deal, but often came back to San Francisco. Bancroft, *Pioneer Register,* 263. The sheep bought by Norris had cost less than fifty cents per head.

286
In his six years since Carson had seen San Francisco, it had grown from a few hundred to about forty thousand people, as a result of the gold rush. Kit also visited friends and relatives living in the Russian River Valley at this time.

287
Their return was reported in the *Santa Fe Weekly Gazette,* December 31, 1853.

288
The delegate to Congress from Utah Territory was John M. Bernhisel. He served in this capacity from 1851 to 1859. H. H. Bancroft, *History of Utah* (San Francisco, 1891), 484.

289
Although both Quaife and Grant render this officer's name as Beall, it is clearly "Bell" in the manuscript and not to be confused with Lieutenant Colonel Benjamin Lloyd Beall, already identified in Note 245, above. The reference here is to Lieutenant David Bell, of Ohio, West Point, 1847, who died December 2, 1860. Heitman, *Historical Register,* I, 207. Carson is nearly always correct, not only in regard to the names of officers, but also in regard to their rank.

290
A stand had been made at Embudo by the supporters of the Taos Rebellion in 1847.

Carson had known Lieutenant

the purpose of pursuing the Indians and giving them such chastisement as they deserved.[292] He employed a company of forty Pueblo Indians and Mexicans under command of Mr. James H. Quinn,[293] as Captain, and John Mostin, as his Lieutenant.[294] They were men in every way qualified to perform the service for which they were employed, and that was to proceed some distance in advance of the main body and act as spies and keep the trail of the Indians. I accompanied the march as principal guide.

The march was taken up on the 4th and reached Arroyo Hondo, some ten miles north of Taos, then took down said stream to where it empties into the Rio Grande, having passed through a deep and difficult cañon for the passage of troops. The Del Norte River was high but it had to be crossed. The bed of the river is full of large rocks and, in crossing, the horses would sometimes be only to their knees in the water and then have to step off of a rock. They would be over their backs and would necessarily have some trouble in ascending the next rock.

I took the lead and finally crossed. The troops then commenced their passage and crossed, meeting with no very serious accident more than two or three dragoons were nearly drowned [in helping] to cross the Infantry. The Dragoon horses had to be recrossed for the purpose of getting them [the infantry] over. It was finally done, I crossing and recrossing the river about twenty times. The command had all crossed.

We had now to ascend from the river. The cañon is at the lowest calculation 600 feet high, but, by leading the animals cautiously through the different windings of the trail, we ascended. [We] continued our march over a plain in which there were many cañons and deep ravines destitute of water and grass, till we arrived at Sirvilletta, a small Mexican town, where we encamped, and forage was purchased for the ani-

Davidson since the battle of San Pasqual.

291 This is the battle of Cieneguilla, which occurred on March 30, 1854. Although his losses were heavy, Davidson appears to have conducted a determined attack and to have managed a skillful withdrawal, when outnumbered by about three to one.

292 This campaign is discussed by Hamilton Gardner, "Philip St. George Cooke and the Apache, 1854," *New Mexico Historical Review,* Vol. XXVIII (April, 1953), 115–32.

293 James H. Quinn was a merchant of Taos and Arroyo Hondo and, for a time, a trading partner of Lucien Maxwell. He is listed in the U.S. Manuscript Census for 1850 as a native of Maryland, 31 years of age, and a lawyer by occupation. He appears to have done a remarkably fine job as chief of scouts or spies for this expedition.

294 John Mostin, born in Illinois, was employed as Carson's interpreter from January, 1854, to October, 1859, when he died. Roster of Indian Agency Employees, National Archives, Washington, D. C. The name is Mostin in the manuscript, but Grant's edition renders it as Mastin, while Quaife's edition renders it as Martin. *The Register of Officers and Agents, Civil, Military, and Naval, in the Service of the United States,* for 1857, lists a John Martin, of New York, as Carson's interpreter as of September 30, 1857.

mals. Marched in the morning and in two days found the trail; followed it two days and overtook the Indians. They saw us approaching and retreated. They were pursued. Several Indians [were] killed and a number of horses and their camp equipage captured. There was one soldier killed and one wounded.

Captain Sykes, of the Infantry, deserves great praise for his conduct on this march.[295] He was in command of the Infantry. He had a horse with him but on which I do not think he mounted during the campaign. He would wade the streams, through mush ice and snow, often for the distance of ten miles. I really believe that by his conduct the courage of his men was kept up. I could not understand how men were able to undergo such hardships. The marches were generally long, over high mountains covered with snow, and not having a sufficiency of transportation. the troops were on half rations. They surely would have failed through fatigue and the want of provisions if they had not had an officer to command them as he did, willingly going through the hardships they all had to undergo, and being always in the advance.

When the Indians were seen, he and his company were in the advance of the troops, the spies being some distance ahead of him. But when the word Indians reached him, he and his men raised a run and entered the Indian village in company with the Dragoons. And from his Company the [one] man was killed and one wounded. The Indians were pursued through a deep canyon for about four miles. Many were not seen, but the number of Indians [killed] was seven, and a number wounded. It became dark. The command returned to where the Indians had been encamped and bivouacked for the night.

In the morning, the wounded man was sent back for the purpose of receiving medical aid.

295
Captain George Sykes, West Point, 1838, of the 3rd U.S. Infantry, had served in the Mexican War and later served in the Civil War. He died in 1880. Heitman, *Historical Register,* I, 941.

A corporal and a party of privates attended him, as an escort. The command now took the trail of the Indians, following them through deep cañons over high mountains covered with snow. They could not be again overtaken. They were broken up into small bands. Trails were leading in different directions, and trails would be followed and at night the command would nearly have returned to the place from which it marched in the morning. The Jicarilla Apache Indians are the worst that are to be pursued. They always, after having been attacked, retreat in small parties and have no baggage, and are capable of travelling several days without food [so] that it is impossible for any com[man]d of regular troops to overtake them, if they are aware of their being pursued. They were followed six days, and the comdg. officer, finding that they could not be overtaken, concluded to march to Abiquiu, a Mexican village situated on the Chama River, a tributary of the Del Norte, for the purpose of recruiting his animals.[296] Arrived about the 14 April.

296
Abiquiu was one of the larger settlements of the Río Arriba. It had a population of 3,557 in 1827, about the same as the population of Taos.

The party that had returned with the wounded man met on their march a Utah Indian, took him prisoner, depriving him of his arms and horse. He made his escape and joined his tribe. Col. Cooke, fearing that such treatment given a friendly [Indian] by men of his party might cause the tribe of which he was a member to join the Indians that were at war, I immediately departed for my agency at Taos, sent a man to the village of the Utahs, requesting their head men to come to the Agency, that I wanted to talk to them. In a short time after my arrival several came. I stated to them that the soldiers that took one of their tribe prisoner done so thinking that he was an Apache; that the Americans did not wish to do them any injury and I hoped that they would remain friendly, and for them to render no aid to the Indians that were at war. If they did, they would be treated as enemies. They promised not to render any assistance to the Apaches. I then returned to them the property captured, and they departed. I remained at the Agency.

Colonel Cooke, after remaining a few days at Abiquiu, marched in pursuit of the hostile Indians, followed them several days, was caught in a snow storm, and, the trail being many days old and the ground covered with snow, it was useless to attempt to proceed. He then returned to Rio Colorado.[297] A reinforcement of troops arrived under com[man]d of Major Brooks, 3rd Infantry.[298] As soon as the necessary preparations could be made, another campaign was to be made against the enemy.

Colonel Cooke took command of the troops that had been on the two previous campaign[s] and marched to Taos. The men of his command were much worn down by the hardships through which they had gone [and] his animals knocked up. All men and horses required repose. I can say of Colonel Cooke that he is as efficient an officer to make campaigns against Indians as I ever accompanied—that he is brave and gallant all know.

The Indians, by his persevering pursuit, lost many by hardship and the severe cold, and, if they had not been so fortunate as to have kept the American horse they captured in their fight with Lieut. Davidson, they would not have been as able to elude him, and if they had been caught they would have been chastised in such a manner that war with *that* tribe would never again occur.

Major Brooks and command marched against the Indians, followed their trail for several days, arrived in the Utah country.[299] Finding that the country was entirely cut up with trails and [it] being impossible to designate the one of the enemy, he was compelled to give up the pursuit

297
The Río Colorado refers to the Red River settlement north of Taos, which is now known as Questa, New Mexico.

298
Major William T. H. Brooks, West Point, 1837, of the 3rd U.S. Infantry, was a native of Ohio. He served in both the Mexican War and the Civil War and died in 1870. Heitman, *Historical Register,* I, 249.

299
The Utah country refers to the San Luis Valley in southern Colorado and to the mountains surrounding it.

and return to Taos. He arrived about the 15 May. Had been in the field some 10 or 15 days and had not the fortune to meet any of the enemy. Done no execution.

Maj. Carleton, 1st Drag[oon]s, was encamped in Taos making preparations for a campaign. About the 23 May, everything was ready. He marched in pursuit of the enemy. I accompanied him as principal guide. We marched north to Fort Massachusetts, then the spies under com[man]d of Captain Quinn marched to west of the White mountains, and thence, along its base, to the Mosco Pass, through on to the Huerfano, his object being to discover the trail from the place [where] Maj. Brooks gave up the pursuit.[300] It was evident that the Indians were making for the Mosco Pass. The command marched through the Sangre de Cristo Pass, was to join with Captain Quinn on the Huerfano in three days. Both parties joined on the Huerfano. I discovered a trail of three Indians in the Pass, followed it till I came to the main trail near the Huerfano. Quinn discovered, at the entrance of the Mosco Pass, an old encampment of the Indians. They had passed through the Pass as [had been] predicted. The main trail was now taken and followed six days, when the Indians were discovered. We marched over very rugged country—mountains, cañons, ravines had to be passed —but we overtook the Indians at last. The Indians were encamped in the east side of Fisher's Peak in the Raton mountains.[301]

The troops charged in on the village. The Indians run. Some were killed and about 40 head of horses were captured. They were followed till dark. There was a party of men under command of Lt. R. Johnston, 1st Drag[oon]s, left at the village. Captain Quinn and three of his spies were with him. They concealed themselves in the brush near the village. One of the spies knew the call to be made by those Indians when scat-

300
Fort Massachusetts was established in 1852 and maintained until 1858, when it was abandoned in favor of Fort Garland. It was located on Ute Creek, between six and seven miles north of present Fort Garland, Colorado. The White Mountains refer to Old Baldy and Sierra Blanca, two peaks of over 14,000 feet rising just north of the fort. Quinn and his party skirted the base of the latter mountain until they reached Mosca Pass (9,713 feet). Meanwhile, Carson guided Carleton over Sangre de Cristo Pass, to the east of the fort, and met Quinn on the upper Huerfano River.

301
The Raton Mountains lie directly south of Trinidad, Colorado, with Fisher's Peak the most prominent one visible from that city. The Indians were found east of Raton Pass, near the Colorado–New Mexico line.

*Carson wearing a beaver hat*, circa *1854*. (Courtesy of Kit Carson Museum) *See page 234*.

tered, sounded it, and shortly two Indians and two squaws made their appearance, were fired upon by the spies and one was killed, an Indian. Nothing more could be done. The Indians were made aware of the party being near them by the firing of the gun and the yells of the Indians that made their escape. In the vicinity of the village the brush was thick and, there being many places of concealment, I have no doubt [by] hiding in such places the Indians saved themselves.

The command marched back for a few miles and encamped for the night. It was entirely owing to the good management of Major Carleton that the Indians were discovered. He directed the spies to keep the trail. The troops followed, but keeping as much concealed as possible by marching through the brush and timber. In the morning of the day that we overtook the Indians, I saw a trail that was fresh, informed the Major that, if we met with no accident, that the Indians would be found by two o'clock. He told me that if such would be the case that he would present to me one of the finest hats that could be procured in New York. The Indians were found at the hour I had predicted. The Major fulfilled his promise, presenting to me a hat [which] he directed to be made in New York, and a fine one it was.

The command now commenced its return for Taos, travelling to the head waters of the Canadian and its tributaries.[302] Passed over beautiful though mountainous country and arrived at Taos in June. I did not accompany any other campaign for the remainder of the year.

Major Blake, 1st Drag[oon]s, made a campaign in July. He was absent some time but did not find any of the Indians. In August, I departed from the Agency to visit the Utahs for the purpose of collecting them to meet the Superintendent at Abiquiu in October.[303] I had to travel about 200 miles, passing in the vicinity of

302
The Canadian River heads in the Sangre de Cristo Mountains, northeast of Taos, and flows into the Arkansas River in eastern Oklahoma.

303
The superintendent of Indian Affairs at this time was David Meriwether, who was also governor of New Mexico Territory, 1853–57. He was born in Louisa County, Virginia, October 30, 1800. The family moved to Kentucky when he was a small child. As a young man he had been an Indian trader on the Missouri River and had been imprisoned in Santa Fe in 1820. Prior to his appointment in the Southwest, he had been a senator from Kentucky. His autobiography, dictated when he was eighty-five, ends in 1856. He died in Kentucky in 1892. See David Meriwether, *My Life in the Mountains and on the Plains,* edited by Robert A. Griffen (Norman, 1966).

Major George Alexander Hamilton Blake, a Pennsylvanian, obtained a commission in the Dragoons in 1836, served in the Mexican and Civil Wars, and retired in 1870. He was wounded at Gaines Mill in 1862 and brevetted Brigadier General after Gettysburg. He died October 27, 1874. See Heitman, *Historical Register*, I, 15; II, 223.

304
According to Governor Meriwether, the meeting which considered the problem of the murder of a Ute Indian by a Mexican was held at the home of "Mr. Head." Lafayette Head, afterward lieutenant governor of Colorado, was a resident of Taos at the time but was interested in colonizing the San Luis Valley. See Meriwether, *My Life,* 199–202.

a village of Apaches. Passed unperceived by them and arrived at the Utah village. Gave them the notice that the Superintendent wished to see them in October. They agreed to go see him. I then departed for the Agency, arrived in a few days.

In October, I proceeded to the Council.[304] The Indians attended as promised. Presents were given to them and they appeared friendly. Previous to the Council, some Mexicans had killed a Utah Indian for the purpose of getting the coat he wore. The Indians were much dissatisfied, requesting animals in payment of the death of the Indian. Animals would not be paid them, but it was promised that the murderers would be arrested and punished according to law. One of the murderers was even apprehended but, in a very short time, made his escape, and nothing more was attempted to be done to render justice to the Indians.

On their way to their hunting grounds, the small pox broke out among them. The leading men of the band of Muache Utahs died. They came to the conclusion that the Superintendent was the cause of the disease being among them, that he had collected them for the purpose of injuring [them], that to the head man he gave each a blanket coat, and that every one that received a coat died. That the coats were the cause of the deaths the Indians firmly believed, and the murderer of the Indians being allowed to escape unpunished and they having but poor faith in anything the Superintendent promised them, they commenced preparing for war. Joined the Apaches and commenced committing depredations. They attacked the settlement of [the] Costilla, killed some men and drove off nearly all the stock, and stole and murdered citizens as they be found.[305]

The regular troops in the country were not of sufficient force to make a campaign against the

305
Colonists were sent by Charles Beaubien to the Costilla River in 1850. The settlement was located on the line between New Mexico and Colorado. See Edmond C. Van Diest, "Early History of Costilla County," *Colorado Magazine,* Vol. V (August, 1928), 142.

The Indians' belief that they had been deliberately infected with smallpox was also a cause of the massacre of the inhabitants of El Pueblo on the Arkansas River, on December 25, 1854, by Mohuache Utes and Jicarilla Apaches under the Ute Chief, Blanco.

306
Carson's criticisms of the governmental policy toward the Indians were well founded. As Indian agent, he was sympathetic toward the peaceful Indians and helpful with their problems. Although handicapped by his illiteracy and his inability to keep accounts, he was a successful agent. See Marshall D. Moody, "Kit Carson, Agent to the Indians in New Mexico, 1853–1861," *New Mexico Historical Review,* Vol. XXVIII (January, 1953), 1–20.

307
Céran St. Vrain was born on May 5, 1802, at Spanish Lake, near St. Louis, Missouri. He first came to New Mexico in 1823. After several years as a trapper, he became the partner of the Bent Brothers until the firm was dissolved after the death of Charles Bent. He commanded the company of New Mexico Volunteers raised to help cope with the Taos Rebellion in 1847. He was a leading citizen of Taos and was listed by the Census of 1850 as holding real estate worth

Utahs, when joined with the Apaches. The Governor issued a proclamation calling for six companies of volunteers. It was immediately responded to. The companies were organized, several companies having offered their service more than was called for, showing the willingness of the people to enter military service when called upon to punish their enemies. And if the chastisement of the Indians of this country was left to the citizens, I have no doubt but that in a short period they would bring them to subjection. As it is at present, the Indians are master of the country. They commit depredations when they please. Perhaps a command of troops will be sent after them. They will be overtaken, some of the property they stole recovered, and they make their escape unpunished. The superintendent will then call them in to have a grand talk. Presents are given, promises are made, but only to be broken when convenient.[306] I can say that this country will always remain in its improverished state as long as them mountain Indians are permitted to run at large, and the only remedy is [to] compel them to live in settlements, cultivate the soil, and learn to gain their maintenance independent of the general government.

After the organization of the volunteers, the Governor appointed Captain Ceran St. Vrain, of Taos, as their Commander.[307] He was a gentleman in every manner qualified for such office, the greater part of his life having been passed in the mountains and this Territory. And when the people became aware of the Governor having chosen a man so competent to fulfill the duties of an office of such importance there was great rejoicing, for all knew the Captain to be a gentleman and the bravest of soldiers. And now [they] were confident that, under the command of such a man, that the Indians would be punished in such a manner that it would be long before they would again commence hostilities.

$25,000. He received a large land grant in southern Colorado, title to a fraction of which was finally confirmed. His home was in Taos but he died in Mora, New Mexico, where he suffered a paralytic stroke while sitting on the porch of his store smoking a cigar, and died several weeks later, on October 28, 1870. See Paul A. St. Vrain, *Genealogy of the Family of De Lassus and St. Vrain* (Kirksville, 1943). Also, F. W. Cragin Papers, Notebook VI, 11, 12, 13. Cragin's informant was St. Vrain's son, Felix, at Huerfano Butte, Colorado, December 9, 1907. The best biographical sketch is Harold H. Dunham, "Céran St. Vrain," *Mountain Men* (ed. by Hafen), V, 297–316.

308
Colonel Thomas Turner Fauntleroy, of the 2nd Dragoons, began his army service in 1836. He was ordered from Fort Union to Taos expressly for this campaign. A native of Virginia, he served in the Confederate Army during the Civil War. He died in 1883.

309
Lucien Stewart, a native of Vermont, is said to have come to New Mexico about 1842. He settled in Taos and was employed as an Indian trader by Céran St. Vrain. He died in the late 1890's. See F. W. Cragin Papers, Notebook XII, 32–33. Cragin's informant was Captain Smith H. Simpson, who participated in this campaign and later served as Carson's secretary, in an interview at Taos, New Mexico, on January 13, 1908.

310
Saguache Pass, in the words of Carson's biographer, Dr. Peters, who took part in this campaign, is "the

In fact, it was the only appointment of the Governor that met the approbation of the people. Many were surprised at his sound judgment in making such a noble choice.

In Feb. 1855, Colonel T. T. Fauntleroy, 1st Dragoons, arrived at Taos, commenced making preparations to take the field.[308] He had under his command four companies of Volunteers commanded by Colonel St. Vrain, two companies of Dragoons, one of Artillery, and one of spies, commanded by Lucien Stewart of this place, a gentleman that has passed a great deal of his life in the mountains and, having had a great deal of experience in Indian warfare, he was well qualified to perform the duties for which he was employed.[309]

The command took up its march the fore part of March, travelled north to Fort Massachusetts, thence to the Rio Del Norte, up it to where it leaves the mountain, thence north to the Saguachi Pass, where the Indians were found in force.[310] They were attacked, defeated, losing a number in killed and wounded.[311] The artillery was left, after the fight at Saguachi, in charge of the train of provisions, Lieut. Lloyd Beall, 2d Art[iller]y being in command.[312] It was [a] very important position and required an officer of judgment and one that did not fear danger to be entrusted with such a duty, and he was the one chosen, and the duty was performed to the satisfaction of the Colonel.

The command now marched in pursuit of the Indians, followed them a few days, and on the head waters of the Arkansas a large party was discovered.[313] They were immediately charged upon and defeated. Some were killed and many horses were taken. Marched on for Fort Massachusetts, passed through the Mosco Pass, and arrived the last of March.[314] The country passed over to Saguachi was level, covered with snow, and during the time there were as cold days as

great natural opening in the mountains that bound on the west the valley of San Luis." Peters, *Life and Adventures,* 498. Apparently the term was used to designate the eastern approach to Cochetopa Pass (10,032 ft.), which at that time was applied to the higher portions of the pass and to the approach from Cochetopa Creek on the Western Slope. The old Ute Trail traversed it, following the track of the buffalo. Modern pronunciation does not sound the final letter of Saguache but it was customarily sounded in the 1850's. The name is from a Ute word meaning *blue water* or, less probably, *blue earth.*

311
The site of the battle was a little west of present Saguache, Colorado. Captain Smith W. Simpson said that Lucien Stewart saved the day at the battle of Saguache when, after five charges by the Indians had the troops hard pressed, he made an unexpected flanking attack that confused the Indians and put them to flight. F. W. Cragin Papers, Notebook XII, 33–34.

For an able recent account of the battle and of Fauntleroy's entire campaign, based upon letters of Dr. Peters, see Morris F. Taylor, "Action at Fort Massachusetts: The Indian Campaign of 1855," *Colorado Magazine,* Vol. XLII (Fall, 1965), 292–310.

312
Lieutenant Lloyd Beall, of the 2nd U.S. Artillery, was a native of Washington, D. C. He served in the Confederate Army during the Civil War. Heitman, *Historical Register,* I, 202.

Beall was instructed to meet Fauntleroy in the Wet Mountain Valley. This involved recrossing San Luis

ever I experienced. The remainder of the march was over high mountains covered with snow.

I returned to Taos; the command was distributed in the several settlements so that forage could be procured for the animals, they being in a very reduced condition. Remained till the middle of April and started on campaign. I did not accompany this expedition. Colonel T. T. Fauntlery took a direction the same as on the previous campaign, and travelled to the Puncha Pass, where the Indians were found.[315] Many [of them] were killed, a number of animals and camp equipage captured. The Indians were entirely routed. Colonel St. Vrain marched through the Sangre de Cristo [Pass] and on to the Purgatoire River, where the Indians were discovered, attacked, completely routed, animals and baggage captured.[316] He followed on their trail, had men in pursuit of Indians in every direction. Indians were killed daily, women taken prisoners. On that campaign, the Apaches received chastisement for their many depredations that they thought could never have been given them. The commands returned to Taos.

Fauntleroy did not again take the field. The Volunteers had but a short period to serve, but St. Vrain did not allow them to be idle. He immediately again took the field, and kept in pursuit of Indians till a few days before the expiration of service. If the Vol[unteer]s had continued in the service three months and had [been] under the command and sole direction of Colonel St. Vrain, there would never again have [been] need [of] any troops in this country. The Indians would be entirely subjected and, in all probability, but a few of them would be left to be of any trouble. But such was not the case. Those in power considered the Indians sufficiently punished; the Indians asked for peace, it was granted them.

The Superintendent made, in August, treaties

Valley and then crossing the Sangre de Cristo Mountains by way of Mosca Pass (9,713 feet).

313
The battle of Saguache was on March 19, 1855. The pursuit over Poncha Pass was swift, and this second encounter took place on March 21 at present Salida, Colorado. See Rafael Chacon, "Campaign against the Utes and Apaches in Southern Colorado, 1855," *Colorado Magazine,* Vol. XI (May, 1934), 109. Carson used the term "headwaters of the Arkansas" to refer to the Arkansas River anywhere above the Royal Gorge.

314
They went down the Arkansas to Texas Creek and ascended that stream into the Wet Mountain Valley and crossed the Sangre de Cristo Range at Mosca Pass.

315
Poncha Pass (9,011 feet) separates the Río Grande drainage basin from that of the Arkansas. The location of Fauntleroy's encounter with the Utes on April 28, 1855, was farther up the Arkansas than the fight of March 21. Dr. Peters says that none of the guides had been that far north. He also says that it was at a place where they could look up a pass and see vapor rising from hot springs. See Morris F. Taylor, "Action at Fort Massachusetts . . . ," *Colorado Magazine,* Vol. XLII, 300, which quotes from a letter of Dr. Peters. Carson, of course, was familiar with the whole course of the upper Arkansas but he was not with this expedition. A letter from Colonel Fauntleroy headed "Camp, Head of Valley, April 30, 1855" says "I have the honor to report that on the night of the 28th

with the Indians that had not been at war.[317] In September the hostile Indians came in, received presents, and promised future friendship.

The Apaches did not all come in at the time of the treaty. They were committing depredations. The fact was reported to the Superintendent but would [not] be believed. Treaty should not have been made with the Apaches. No faith can be placed in their promises.[318]

The Indians were promised certain sums yearly; in case they wished to settle on some stream and commence farming, they had their choice of country. The Superintendent went to Washington with his treaties, which were laid before the Senate and [are] as yet not confirmed.[319] They should not be. Such treaties were not of a character to suit the people. The Apaches are now daily committing depredations. They go unp[un]ished and, in my opinion, ere long they may again commence hostilities. The other tribes with whom the treaties were made I think will comply with their demands, and will not again be hostile if the Government does not stop their supplies of provisions during such times as they cannot hunt.

I frequently visit the Indians, speak to them of the advantages of peace, and use my influence with them to keep them satisfied with the proceedings of those placed in power over them. I attended September 4th, 1856, at the assembly of Indians at Abiquiu held by the Superintendent for the purpose of giving them presents.[320] They appeared to be content, then there was a disturbance the next day. A Tabaguachi Utah tore up the blanket given him. It was old, had been worn, and he was dissatisfied. He wished to kill the Superintendent but was hindered by the other Indians.

I cannot see how the Superintendent can expect Indians to depart satisfied that he has called to see him from a distance of two or three hun-

instant, about twenty miles from Punche Pass, up the Arkansas River, I came upon a camp of Utahs, consisting of twenty-six lodges . . . ." See *Annual Report of the Secretary of War, 1855,* 64. These combined pieces of information determine the location with precision. It was at the confluence of Chalk Creek with the Arkansas, and the vapor arose from Mt. Princeton Hot Springs, about five miles up Chalk Creek.

316
Although he does not say so, Carson may have accompanied the early stages of St. Vrain's campaign. Rafael Chacon, of the New Mexico Volunteers, stated in his recollections that Carson did. See Sabin, *Kit Carson Days* (1914), 389–90. However, if Kit was with this expedition at all, he had returned to Taos before the campaign was concluded. See the letter of F. E. Kavanaugh to Carson, May 5, 1855, in Letters received from or relating to Kit Carson, 1854–1860, The National Archives, Washington, D.C. Carson forwarded this letter, reporting the successful end of the campaign, to Governor Meriwether.

317
See Meriwether, *My Life*, 226, in which Griffen quotes a letter from the Superintendent to Carson, dated August 26, 1855.

318
Carson did not have the same opinion of the Utes; there are many instances of his confidence in their good faith.

319
The treaty with the Apaches and several other treaties, besides, were not confirmed by the Senate. Meriwether, *My Life,* 214.

320
This meeting with the Indians was the scene of an altercation between Carson and Governor Meriwether. The Governor's version is presented in Meriwether, *My Life,* 226–32. It does not mention the attempt upon his life by the disgrunted Tabeguache Ute. The Governor placed Carson under arrest, suspended him as Indian agent, and charged him with disobedience, insubordination, disrespect, and cowardice. Using Judge Joab Houghton as intermediary, Carson apologized and was reinstated as agent. The charges were dropped.

Bearing in mind that Meriwether's account was dictated thirty years later and that it represents only his side of the quarrel, it still seems fairly evident that Carson was probably guilty on the first charges. The last charge, that of cowardice, rests upon Meriwether's statement that Carson hid under a bank of the river during the demonstration made by the Indians. This is a prejudiced interpretation. Carson took the Indian disturbance seriously, and advised the Governor to keep out of their way. When Meriwether refused to follow this advice, Carson simply disassociated himself from the Governor and any course he might pursue. Indians acting in a wild and uncontrolled manner were unpredictable, and the fact that they subsided does not prove Carson's judgment to have been unfounded. Caution is not equivalent to cowardice. The fact that Carson acknowledged that he had been wrong speaks very well for him. It is difficult to imagine the Governor ever making such an acknowledgment under any circumstances. Meriwether's belief that Carson had been spoiled by his great publicity was also an unwarranted conclusion. Carson simply had strong opinions about Indian policy and his views were different from the opinions of Meriwether. Unfortunately for Kit, the Governor was also the superintendent of Indian affairs and was not inclined to listen to his subordinates.

321
Carson was undoubtedly right in his opinion that the agency headquarters should have been located within the Indian country. He continued as agent until 1861.

322
In the introduction to his edition of Carson's autobiography, Dr. Milo M. Quaife relates the story of how the manuscript was found by Clinton Peters, a son of Dr. D. C. Peters, in a trunk containing papers left by his brother William, who died in Paris, in 1905. He also details the subsequent history of the manuscript until it came to rest in the Newberry Library, in Chicago, Illinois. Dr. Quaife then attempts to solve the identity of the person to whom Carson dictated his memoirs. He shows conclusively that it was neither Dr. Peters nor Mrs. Peters. He then makes the assumption that the writer was Jesse B. Turley, to whom the manuscript was assigned by Carson.

Jesse B. Turley was a brother of Simeon Turley, the distiller of "Taos lightnin' " killed at Arroyo Hondo when his mill was attacked by supporters of the Taos Rebellion in January, 1847. Jesse B. Turley had engaged in the Santa Fe trade prior to this time but had continued to reside in Missouri, at Arrow Rock, where he had a wife and children. However, in the process of settling his brother's estate he came to reside in Taos, where he lived for a time

dred miles, compelled to go several days without anything to eat, unless they have carried it with them. They are given a meal by the Superintendent, then the presents are given. Some get a blanket; those that get none are given a knife or hatchet or some vermillion, a piece of red or blue cloth, some sugar, and perhaps a few more trinkets. They could more than earn the quantity they receive in one day's hunt, if left in their country. They could procure skins and furs and traders could furnish the same articles to them and they would be saved the necessity of coming such a distance, thereby not causing their animals to be fatigued and themselves have to travel without food. If presents are given them it should be taken to their country. They should not be allowed to come into the settlements, for every visit an Indian makes to a town, it is of more or less injury to him.

I am now living in Taos, N. M., in the discharge of my official duties as Indian Agent. Am daily visited by the Indians, give to them presents, as directed by the Superintendent. I am opposed to the policy of having Indians come to the settlements, but as there are no agency buildings allowed to be built in the country of the Indians, necessity compels them to come to the towns.[321]

The foregoing I hereby transfer to Mr. Jesse B. Turley[322] to be used as he may deem proper for our Joint benefit.

C. Carson

with Ignacia Bent, widow of Governor Charles Bent and older sister of Mrs. Carson. He is known to have been a principal financier of Dick Wootton's sheep drive in 1852. He was a good business man, but drank and gambled heavily. He died at Mora, New Mexico, in 1861. See F. W. Cragin Papers, Notebook VIII, 59. Cragin's informant was Jesse Nelson, at Smith's Canyon Ranch, Colorado, July 9, 1908.

That Jesse B. Turley received the manuscript from Carson and that he acted as a literary agent in endeavoring to promote its publication is shown by a letter from Washington Irving to Turley, dated Nov. 9, 1857, in which Irving says that he has no intention of writing a life of Carson; and by an announcement in the *Liberty Weekly Tribune,* December 19, 1856, to the effect that Turley himself was writing a life of Carson. The first is among the Turley Papers in the Missouri Historical Society, St. Louis, Missouri; the second is from the index of the *Liberty Weekly Tribune,* State Historical Society of Missouri, Columbia, Missouri. Further, a letter from Lester F. Turley, El Monte, California, to Bernice Blackwelder, dated July 8, 1962, states that Jesse Turley entered into an agreement with Dr. Peters to write the life of Carson, with the profits, if any, to be divided equally by Peters, Turley, and Carson.

This explains how the manuscript came into the hands of Dr. Peters and was used by him and his collaborator, C. Hatch Smith, as the basis for the biography which appeared in 1858, with Peters as the author of record. Although Dr. Peters is reputed to have made $20,000 from the book, it is not believed that any of the money went to Turley or Carson.

Nevertheless, it does not appear that Jesse B. Turley actually wrote down Carson's story, for the very good reason that the manuscript is not in his handwriting, samples of which are available and have been compared with the writing of the manuscript. Carson's life is written in a more firm and flowing and less irregular hand than Turley employed. Despite this fact, it seems probable that Turley helped to persuade Carson to dictate his memoirs.

The scribe who wrote Carson's memoirs as he related them was certainly someone who was accustomed to taking dictation. The manuscript was written smoothly and rapidly, for there are few corrections in the hand of the original writer. There is no evidence of any attempt by the writer to elicit information from Carson beyond what he volunteered. If corrections were made in Carson's mode of speech, they were made smoothly and automatically, as if by one accustomed to doing it.

All of these things point to one of the men employed by Carson to handle his correspondence during his years as Indian agent. These men were John W. Dunn, Charles Williams, John Mostin, and John Martin. To this group may possibly be added Smith H. Simpson, on the strength of his own statement.

"Letters received from and relating to Kit Carson, 1854–1860" have been preserved among the field office records of the New Mexico Superintendency of Indian Affairs. Among these is a document prepared and signed by John W. Dunn, in a much larger and bolder hand than that of the writer of the Carson memoirs. So Dunn must be ruled out as a possible scribe. John Martin may be excluded on the grounds that he did not work for Carson before 1857 and the memoirs were almost certainly completed in the fall of 1856. Charles Williams was the enumerator of the Census of 1850 for Taos County. A comparison of his handwriting, as found in the Census schedules, with that of the memoirs makes it clear that he was not the writer. Smith H. Simpson may be eliminated on the ground that he was interviewed by E. L. Sabin concerning Carson, and if he had written the memoirs, he would certainly have claimed the credit for having done so. Many letters among those preserved by the New Mexico Superintendency are in the same handwriting as the memoirs. Although none of them is signed by John Mostin, they were almost certainly written by him for Carson. Mostin was employed from 1854 to 1859. The letters are found to be within this period and none in this hand are after August, 1859. Mostin died in October, 1859. See also Note 294, above.

The conclusion that John Mostin was the amanuensis employed by Carson to write his memoirs is confirmed by a holograph letter of Mostin's dated September 24, 1856, a reproduction of which was kindly furnished by Dale L. Morgan, Bancroft Library, Berkeley. The handwriting in this letter is identical to that of the Newberry Library's original of the memoirs, except for being less hurried and neater. The letter, written at Taos, mentions James H. Quinn, whose name is coupled with that of Mostin in the memoirs. Morgan informs me that the Bancroft Library has four other letters written by Mostin, between June 4 and October 14, 1859. The question of who recorded Carson's story for him is answered.

# III. The Closing Years, 1857-1868

When Kit Carson completed the dictation of the story of his life in 1856, he was not yet forty-seven years old. He had less than twelve years of life remaining, but being in vigorous health, he could not imagine that his time was running short. He was also at the height of his fame, or so it seemed, and could not have expected that he would have an opportunity to add more luster to his already tremendous reputation. Yet he was able to do so, in the relatively few years that remained to him.

In 1855, Kit's older half-brother, Moses Carson, showed up at the home of his niece, Susan, daughter of Kit's full brother, Robert. Big Mose had been a trapper, who had gone to California with Ewing Young's second expedition in 1831. He remained there till 1854 when, having accumulated a little money as foreman of a ranch in the Russian River country, he returned to St. Louis and had a brief and unsuccessful fling at matrimony. Now he tried to do a little trapping in Colorado with Jesse Nelson, Susan's husband, but gave it up. After visiting Kit in Taos, he moved on to Santa Fe, where he ran up bills in Kit's name to the amount of about $700. Kit paid the bills after Mose drifted farther on into the southwest.[1]

Flintlock Pistols

In 1856, Carson had been happily married for thirteen years. Josefa, his wife, was twenty-eight years old and had borne three children, two of whom, a boy and a girl, were living. Their first child, Charles, was born in 1849 and died two years later.[2] William,[3] called Julian by his mother and her people, was born in the fall of 1852 and Teresina, the eldest daughter, in the summer of 1855.[4] Both were born in Taos, and were now toddling around the adobe house at the northeast corner of the Taos plaza that was the Carson home during this period.[5]

Kit's earlier years as Indian agent were disrupted by campaigns against the hostile Mohuache Utes and Jicarilla Apaches, in which he frequently served as guide to the soldiers whose task it was to control such hostilities. While he was away, affairs of the agency were conducted by John W. Dunn, his interpreter and clerk. By 1856 the Indians had been defeated and Carson was able to spend more time in Taos, where he was regularly visited by Indians, whether they had business with him or not. It was his custom to meet them out of doors in front of his home, where he talked with them and fed them.

In some respects, Carson was an ideal Indian agent. The Indians respected him and he knew their customs and was willing to conform to them. He was also friendly and sympathetic to their problems and absolutely fair in his dealings with them. However, the fact that he was illiterate was a handicap in the operation of his office.[6] He had trouble keeping his accounts, and although he learned to dictate letters and reports, he could not do so to the satisfaction of Governor David Meriwether, the superintendent of Indian affairs, who was unwilling to allow adequate expenditures for clerical help. Kit did not need an interpreter, as most agents did. But since this was considered to be a legitimate expense, whereas the employment of a clerk or secretary was

1 See Harvey L. Carter, "Moses Carson," *Mountain Men* (ed. by Hafen), II, 75–79. Moses Carson died in or near El Paso, Texas, a few months before Kit's death in 1868.

2 Charles Carson, so named in honor of Charles Bent, was born May 1, 1849, and died May 21, 1851. McClung, *Carson-Bent-Boggs,* 75.

3 William Carson was born October 1, 1852, and died January 19, 1889. McClung, *Carson-Bent-Boggs,* 75–76. For his attempted education at the hands of General William Tecumseh Sherman, see Robert G. Athearn, "The Education of Kit Carson's Son," *New Mexico Historical Review,* Vol. XXXI (April, 1956), 133–39. He married Pasqualita, daughter of the mountain man, Tom Tobin. Their descendants live chiefly in Colorado. William Carson's death occurred accidentally. He was wearing a pistol and his horse kicked him, striking the pistol and causing it to fire. He was killed by the shot, not by the kick. The *Independent Journal,* Alamosa, Colorado, January 24, 1889, reported "Carson was shot by his horse on the previous Friday."

4 Teresina Carson was born June 23, 1855, and died April 6, 1916. She married De Witt Fulton Allen in 1871. They lived chiefly at Raton and at Wagon Mound, New Mexico. All their children died young.

not, Carson was forced to list his assistants as interpreters in order to avoid paying for clerical assistance out of his own pocket.

From January 1, 1854, until his death in October, 1859, John Mostin took care of Carson's paper work at the agency, although he seems to have been aided at times by John Martin and by Charles Williams, a brother-in-law of Dick Wootton. After the death of Mostin, J. P. Esmay (or Esonay) served from October, 1859, to March 31, 1860.[7]

Carson's first appointment as Indian agent expired in April, 1857, and he was reappointed until the adjournment of the current session of the United States Senate. The fact that Governor Meriwether had been replaced as superintendent of Indian affairs by James L. Collins, about three weeks earlier, undoubtedly made it easier for Kit to accept his reappointment. His salary as Indian Agent was about $1,500 a year. His "interpreter" received $500 annually. Ordinarily he was allowed about $3,600 a year for presents and provisions for the Indians. His second term of appointment ran out in March, 1858, and he was immediately reappointed.

During the Utah War, 1857–58, the federal government was apprehensive that the Utes might be persuaded to aid the Mormons. Carson was instructed to prevent this development and worked successfully to that end. He was also employed in keeping peace between the Utes and their enemies of the plains, the Cheyennes and Arapahoes, who were on the warpath in 1858. The Navahos also became troublesome in that year, and Carson was able to enlist about twenty Ute scouts to aid the army detachments sent against them. In December, 1858, he was entrusted, along with Captain Bonneville, with the task of conducting peace negotiations with the Navahos. When this was accomplished a new problem arose. In 1859, the Pikes Peak gold rush

5
The house is still in existence and is an object of interest to many people visiting Taos. It was somewhat more commodious than the average house in Taos during the period that Carson lived there, and served as his headquarters while he was Indian agent.

6
Carson was able to sign his own name and perhaps to laboriously trace other words in copy-book fashion. His letters as Indian agent were written by a number of different people, but were usually signed by him. His two most able biographers have considered him literate, but there is no satisfactory evidence that he was able to read or to write. He asked others to read to him and enjoyed hearing them do so, but if he had ever learned to read at all, he had forgotten how by the time he had occasion to employ such a skill in his work.

7
It was, without doubt, one of these clerks who served as Carson's amanuensis for his recording his memoirs in 1856. It was not John W. Dunn, whose writing can be identified. Unfortunately, none of the others signed or otherwise indicated their connection with the script of any of Carson's letters. A considerable number of agency letters appear to be by the same hand as the memoirs. The most probable chirographer was John Mostin, since none of the letters appear in this hand after his death and he served Carson more regularly than did John Martin or Charles Williams. See footnotes 294 and 322 in Chapter II, above.

brought several thousand white prospectors into South Park, which was the best hunting ground of the Mohuache Utes. Carson's problem was eased by the failure to find large quantities of gold in the area at that time, but it was clear that a long shadow had been cast over future Indian relations with the whites.[8]

The leading chief of the Mohuache Utes—who numbered about 350 men and 400 women, according to Carson's estimate—was Ka-ni-ache.[9] With this chief, Carson had very friendly relations. On one occasion, probably in 1859, when Ka-ni-ache was at Carson's house some other Mohuaches arrived, including Blanco, their leader in the Pueblo Massacre of Christmas Day, 1854, and in the campaigns of 1855. The Indians with him dismounted and engaged in the usual amenities, but Blanco remained seated on his horse, glowering at the company. When he finally drew his gun and aimed it at Carson, Ka-ni-ache bounded on him and took the gun from him before he could fire. Kit felt that this prompt action saved his life.[10] Of Blanco, Kit had reported in a letter of January 7, 1855, to Governor Meriwether " . . . nor does he often come about our settlements unless he intends mischief."

During his years as Indian agent, Carson liked to make a hunt in October. He often had both white and Indian companions and usually went into the mountains of the Ute country that lay northwest of Taos. He was not able to spare the time for a fall hunt every year, but he did so in 1857 and again in 1860. However, in the latter year he had a bad fall while leading his horse on a steep mountainside somewhere in the San Juan Mountains of Colorado. It was the horse that fell and rolled, but Kit was entangled in the rope and dragged for some distance over very rough ground.[11] He recovered gradually from the effects of this accident, but he may have had in-

8 "Letters received from or relating to Kit Carson, 1854–1860," the originals of which are in the field office records of the New Mexico Superintendency of Indian Affairs have been microfilmed by The National Archives, Washington, D. C. Many of these letters substantiate Carson's account of the Indian campaigns of 1854–56, as given in his memoirs. Marshall D. Moody, 'Kit Carson, Agent to the Indians in New Mexico, 1853–1861," *New Mexico Historical Review,* Vol. XXVIII (January, 1953), 1–20, a study based on these letters, concludes that Carson was one of the great Indian agents.

According to Dr. C. M. Clarke, a fifty-niner, who arrived on that date, Carson was in Denver on June 6, 1859. Whether or not it was Indian agency business that took him there, is is impossible to say. See C. M. Clarke, M.D., *A Trip to Pike's Peak and Notes by the Way* (San Jose, 1958; original edition, 1861), 70.

9 See Morris F. Taylor, "Ka-ni-ache," *Colorado Magazine,* Vol. XLIII (Fall, 1966), 275–302, for an able delineation of this chief and a perceptive account of the difficulties of the Mohuache Utes at this time.

10 The F. W. Cragin Papers, The Pioneer's Museum, Colorado Springs, Colorado, Notebook VIII, 67. Jesse Nelson was Cragin's informant.

11 The source of our knowledge of this accident is the letter dated January 7, 1874, from Colonel Henry R. Tilton, the army surgeon who attended

*Carson*, circa *1860*. (Courtesy of State Historical Society of Colorado)
*See page 235.*

ternal injuries from it that grew worse with the passage of time.

His family was increased by the birth of a son in the summer of 1858. The boy was named Christopher and called Cristobal by his mother's people, but in later life he was always known as Kit Carson II.[12]

Carson retained the Ute agency until June, 1861, at which time he resigned in order to become lieutenant colonel of the First New Mexico Volunteers, organized in defense of the Territory as a result of the outbreak of the Civil War. The Indian agency was thereupon transferred from Taos to Maxwell's Ranch.

Although a Kentuckian by birth and a Missourian in his youth, Kit never wavered in his devotion to the Union.[13] In September, 1861, when Céran St. Vrain resigned as colonel because of poor health, Carson succeeded him. The example of both St. Vrain and Carson was important in securing the loyalty of the citizens of New Mexico. With good cause, both of them protested the withdrawal of regular army units from the Territory. The Arizona portion of the Territory had declared for the Confederacy, all the Indian tribes were restless, and a threatened invasion from Texas was rapidly being prepared.

Colonel Carson's first activities were confined to the drilling of his regiment of volunteers. He was stationed at Albuquerque and his wife and children came to live there in the officers' quarters for a time. Another son was born there during the summer of 1861. He was called Charles in memory of their first child, who had died.[14] At the end of January, 1862, Carson was ordered to join other forces that were being concentrated at Fort Craig under General Edward R. S. Canby. Josefa and the children returned to Taos at this time.[15]

Fort Craig was located on the Río Grande about thirty-five miles below Socorro, at the be-

Carson in his last illness, to John S. C. Abbott, author of *Christopher Carson, Known as Kit Carson* (New York, 1873). This letter Abbott published in his book as a sort of appendix, 343–48.

12 Christopher Carson II was born June 13, 1858, in Taos, and died February 9, 1929, at La Junta, Colorado. He was married in 1890 to Maria Guadalupe Richards and they have numerous descendants residing chiefly in Colorado. McClung, *Carson-Bent-Boggs*, 79–81.

13 When the news of Lincoln's election reached Taos, Carson and seven other men hoisted the flag in the Taos plaza and kept it flying despite opposition. See Edwin L. Sabin, *Kit Carson Days* (New York, 1914), 394. Captain Smith H. Simpson, one of the participants, was Sabin's informant.

14 Charles Carson was born August 2, 1861, and died at La Junta, Colorado, September 20, 1938. In 1912 he married Mary Alice Gallegher and they have numerous descendants living in Colorado.

15 Blackwelder, *Great Westerner*, 303; Estergreen, *Kit Carson*, 231.

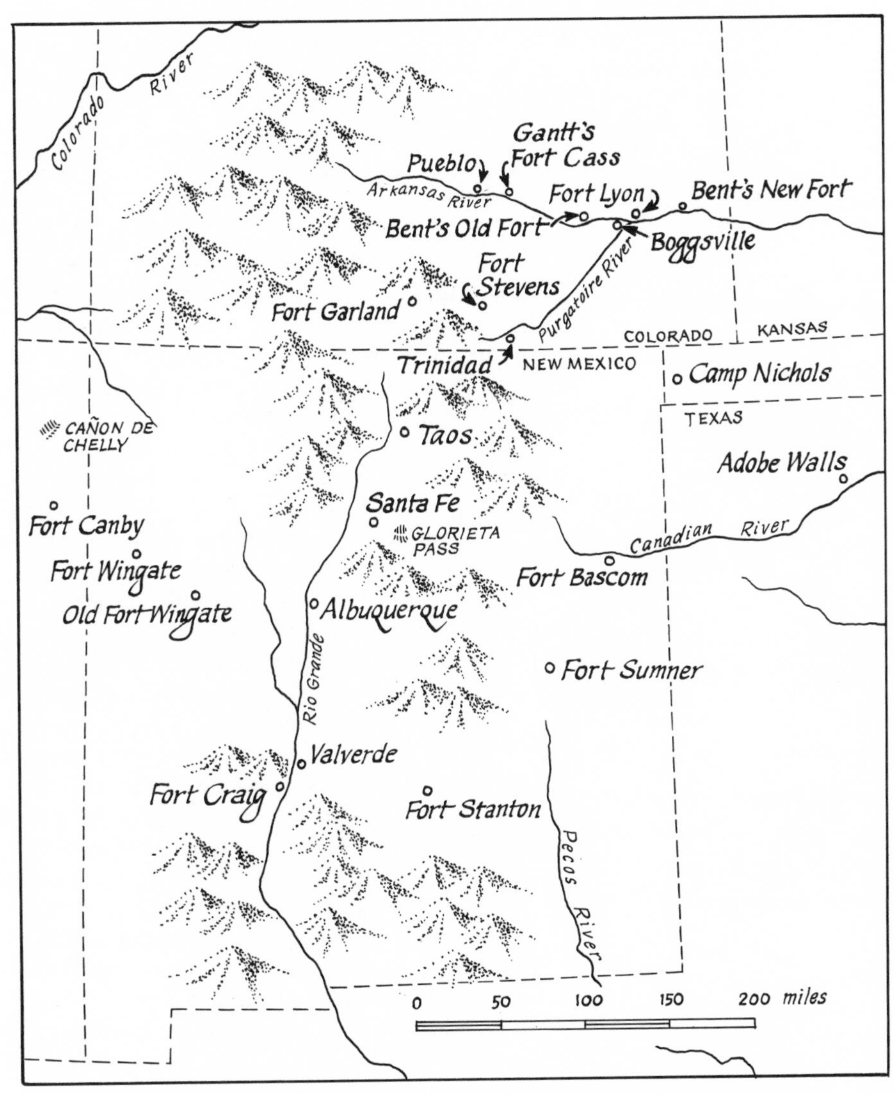


Region of Civil War and Indian Wars Campaigns

ginning of the eighty-mile stretch of desert known as La Journada del Muerto. Canby had replaced Colonel W. W. Loring, who had resigned in order to join the Confederacy, and was preparing to resist an invasion by General Henry Hopkins Sibley, coming north from El Paso and Messilla with some two thousand men. Canby had thirty-eight hundred men at his disposal, but they were largely militia and volunteers.

Sibley crossed to the east side of the river at Valverde in an attempt to bypass Fort Craig, but Canby sent Colonel B. S. Roberts to attack him on the morning of February 21, 1862. Carson knew that his regiment of volunteers would do better if they were not committed too early in the fight. Canby agreed, and ordered him to take a position on the left of Roberts, where he might keep a watch on the Confederate right. This they did from 9 A.M. till 1 P.M., without engaging the enemy. At the latter hour, General Canby ordered Carson to cross the river and carry the fight to the enemy. He did this with initial success and was preparing to try to clear the enemy from some woods when the order came for him to retreat and recross the river, which he was able to do in good order.

Thus, from Carson's limited point of view, the battle was going well. But Canby had perceived that McRae's battery was the focal point and had been unable to save it from capture by a fierce charge of nearly a thousand dismounted Texans. Finding that his New Mexico militia was useless, he decided to withdraw from the field and return to Fort Craig. The Union losses amounted to 68 killed, 160 wounded, and 35 captured; the Confederate losses were 40 killed and 200 wounded.[16]

Sibley was able to occupy Albuquerque and Santa Fe, but his forces were defeated thereafter at Apache Cañon and Glorieta Pass, and he was forced to retire as he had come. In these events

16 The most detailed account of the battle of Valverde is probably that of Sabin, *Kit Carson Days* (1914), 394–408. See also Max L. Heyman, Jr., *Prudent Soldier: A Biography of Major General E. R. S. Canby, 1817–1873* (Glendale, 1959), 162–70, with map, 171.

Carson had no part, and when Canby took the field to hurry Sibley from the Territory, he left Carson in charge of Fort Craig. Meanwhile, General James H. Carleton, an old friend of Carson's, had marched overland from California to New Mexico with about twenty-five hundred men, and in August, 1862, when Canby was ordered to report to Washington, D. C., Carleton was placed in charge of New Mexico. Under Carleton, during the next four years, Kit Carson was to have an opportunity to serve his country as an Indian fighter once more—which was what he was best qualified to do, after all.

Toward the end of September, 1862, Carleton ordered Carson and five companies of his First New Mexico Volunteers to Fort Stanton, a post a little more than a hundred miles almost directly east of Fort Craig. From this fort Kit supervised a swift and successful campaign against the Mescalero Apaches. Their leaders were sent to Santa Fe to make such terms as they could with General Carleton. That energetic commander was already establishing Fort Sumner at the Bosque Redondo in east central New Mexico, and he ordered that all the Mescaleros be rounded up there. What he had in mind was a sort of colonization scheme, by which the Indians would be transformed into farmers and ranchers.[17]

In March, 1863, Carson obtained a short leave and returned to Taos for a visit to his family. He was not permitted to remain with them very long, because General Carleton already had plans to send him westward into the Navaho country.

It is perhaps not generally known that the Navaho tribe was the one most feared in New Mexico. They had been almost constantly at war with the inhabitants of the Territory from the time of the outbreak of the Mexican War. The campaign against them required considerable

17
Sabin, *Kit Carson Days* (1914), 409–17, a pioneering work on Carson's later career, is still probably the best reference on these matters.

planning and preparation. Carson's part in this was to secure the services of some good Mexican guides and some Ute Indians to be used as scouts. Carson's old friend, Chief Ka-ni-ache, was persuaded to take charge of a few of his braves in the latter capacity. They performed very well for a time, but the army regulations did not conform to their own ideas of warfare, and they left before the campaign was concluded.[18]

In late June, 1863, Carson marched, with more than seven hundred men in his command, from Albuquerque to Fort Wingate, where he stopped for a few days to get organized for his push into the Navaho country. While in Albuquerque, he took a sutler to task for selling whiskey to the troops, contrary to regulations. The sutler showed him a stack of authorizations, all signed by Carson himself. He had been signing requests without bothering to have them read to him![19]

General Carleton had asked the Navahos to surrender peaceably, before July 20, 1863, and be transported to the Bosque Redondo. Some of them did, but not a large number. The remainder were divided into small bands and prepared to make war in their own fashion. There was no large body of them to strike. One band raided across the Territory in the vicinity of Fort Sumner, and another band stole horses from Carson at Fort Canby, from which he directed operations.[20] Carleton's orders were to kill all Navaho men able to bear arms and take the women and children as prisoners. For months the war consisted of raids and forays by each side into the territory of the other. Carson applied several times for leave, but was refused each time. General Carleton was giving him an education in the ways of the army. When the Navahos showed a disposition to make peace after a few months, Carleton would accept only an unconditional surrender. So the war dragged on.

Finally, Carleton ordered Carson to make an

18 See Taylor, "Ka-ni-ache," *Colorado Magazine,* Vol. XLIII (Fall, 1966), 288–89. The Utes were not allowed to keep women, children, or livestock that they captured.

19 Sabin, *Kit Carson Days* (1914), 425–26.

20 Carson's orders were to build Fort Canby at the Pueblo Colorado, the site of present Ganado, Arizona. He found this location to be unsuitable and rebuilt Fort Defiance, 28 miles northeast of Ganado, which had been abandoned two years earlier. This rebuilt fort was officially known as Fort Canby. See Lawrence C. Kelly, "Where was Fort Canby?" *New Mexico Historical Review,* Vol. XLII (January, 1967), 49–62.

inroad to the Cañon de Chelly, a thirty-mile gorge through which ran a small stream. Some Navahos lived in the canyon and they regarded it as a place of refuge. Carson set out in January, 1864, from Fort Canby, heading for the west entrance to the Cañon but detached Captain Albert H. Pfeiffer with about a hundred men to go through the Cañon, entering on the east and emerging from the west opening. Pfeiffer succeeded in traversing the Cañon, killing three Indians and capturing nineteen women and children. On January 23, 1864, Carson reported the results of his expedition as follows: "Killed, 23; captured, 34; voluntarily surrendered, 200; captured 200 head of sheep."[21]

In later editions of Dr. Peters' well known biography of Carson, the absurd statement is made that "Carson succeeded in getting the enemy into a bed or ravine, and had his own forces so disposed as to command every approach, and in doing this compelled the surrender of ten thousand Indians, being the largest single capture of Indians ever known." Although corrected by Jacob P. Dunn in his fine account, published twelve years after Peters' revised edition of Carson's life, this statement or modifications of it have continued to be credited down to the present time.[22]

The actual event was far less spectacular than is generally believed. Carson ably applied General Carleton's strategy, which may best be described as a scorched earth policy. After the Cañon de Chelly expedition, the Navahos surrendered in small bands, but in increasing numbers. Eventually about nine thousand were taken to Fort Sumner. Carleton's attempt to force them to become farmers there was a total failure and in 1867, after much suffering, the seven thousand who survived were permitted to return to their own country. They were never thereafter the warlike people they had been before, but per-

21
Jacob Piatt Dunn, *Massacres of the Mountains* (New York, 1886), 447–76, contains an excellent account of the Navaho campaign based upon Carson's Reports, which are reproduced in Sabin, *Kit Carson Days* (1914), 561–603. Sabin's account, *Kit Carson Days* (1914), 418–39, is also very reliable. Raymond E. Lindgren, "A Diary of Kit Carson's Navajo Campaign, 1863–1864," *New Mexico Historical Review*, Vol. XXI (July, 1946), 226–46, is of considerable interest.

22
DeWitt C. Peters, *The Story of Kit Carson's Life and Adventures* (Hartford, 1874), 553.

Two college textbooks (both of which I have used for several years) LeRoy R. Hafen and Carl C. Rister, *Western America* (New York, 1941) and Ray Allen Billington, *Westward Expansion* (New York, 1949) have accepted this version of Carson's Navaho campaign, only reducing the number of Navahos corraled from ten thousand to seven thousand.

haps a fourth of them never surrendered or left their homeland at all.[23]

Now, at last, Carson was given leave to visit his family in Taos. In the spring of 1864 Josefa gave birth to a second daughter, but Kit had probably returned to duty shortly before the event occurred. However, the child was called Rebecca, in compliance with his wish, that having been his mother's name.[24] He was back at Fort Canby from mid-April to mid-July, 1864, after which he was made acting superintendent of the Indian reservation at the Bosque Redondo. He remained there until November, 1864, when he was ordered to Fort Bascom. Carleton had decided to make use of his talents as an Indian fighter once more.

The object of the expedition now entrusted to Colonel Carson was to strike a blow at the Plains Indians of the Texas panhandle, especially the Kiowas. Fort Bascom was located on the Canadian River in northeast New Mexico and furnished a convenient place from which to operate. The troops assigned to the expedition had been assembled at Fort Bascom, with provisions sufficient for a campaign of forty-five days, and were awaiting the arrival of their commander. Carson and seventy-five Mohuache Utes under Chief Ka-ni-ache, who were to act as scouts, arrived on November 10, 1864. This tribe, so well known to Carson from his years as their agent, was in dire straits for food. The warriors agreed to go on the expedition only if their families would be fed at Maxwell's Ranch while they were away.

Two days after his arrival, Carson moved eastward out of Fort Bascom, with a command of 335 officers and men, not counting his Utes. He was headed for the abandoned Bent trading post of Adobe Walls, which he expected to be able to use as a base. There were twenty-seven wagons carrying provisions and one wagon fitted out for

23 Estergren, *Kit Carson,* 250–52.

24 Rebecca Carson was born at Taos April 13, 1864, and died April 15, 1885, by her own hand. She was married to John Lewis in 1883, but was divorced from him and left no children.

*Colonel Carson, 1865.* (Courtesy of State Historical Society of Colorado)
*See page 235.*

use as an ambulance. There were also two twelve-pound howitzers, in charge of Lieutenant George H. Pettis.

On the fourth day of their march they passed the spot where, fifteen years earlier, the Apache captors of Mrs. White had been surprised. This well-known episode of the frontier had also occured in November and the weather was snowy, as it had been on the earlier occasion. Carson related the events, as he recalled them from seeing the ground once more, to an interested group of younger officers.[25] In mid-afternoon on the twelfth day out they made camp at Mule Spring, about thirty miles west of Adobe Walls, and awaited the return of some Ute scouts. The Utes in camp spotted the returning spies long before anyone else noticed them. They brought news that an enemy village had been found.

The march was resumed till midnight, by which time the command had traveled fifteen miles. At dawn on November 25 the march was resumed again, and in a short time they encountered and put to flight an Indian outpost at a ford of the Canadian River. They advanced rapidly and came to a village about three miles from Adobe Walls at about 9 A.M. The village had been hurriedly deserted, but the warriors reassembled and made several charges on the approaching vanguard. They were repulsed and then scattered by a few shots from the howitzers.

By 10 A.M. the command had pushed on to Adobe Walls, near which they saw a larger village.[26] There was another sharp conflict, and again the Indians disappeared after the fourth shot from the artillery. Carson was inclined to think that there would be no renewal of the fight and allowed his men to eat. However, he kept his spy-glass active and soon was aware of at least a thousand mounted Indians on all sides of his command. The battle now began in earnest, and continued most of the afternoon. Several

25
For this detail and for much other information on this campaign, the source is George H. Pettis, *Kit Carson's Fight with the Comanche and Kiowa Indians* (Santa Fe, 1908), an extremely interesting and valuable account by the officer who had charge of the indispensable howitzers.

26
Carson's estimate of the number of lodges in the first village was 150 and in the second village at least 350 lodges. Pettis reported the first village as consisting of 170 lodges and the second one, 500 lodges. The second was a Kiowa encampment, but there is some question about the first one. It may have been peopled mainly by Apaches.

more villages could be seen within a distance of ten miles down the Canadian valley, and from these villages the Indian forces constantly received reinforcements until the total may have been as high as three thousand warriors.

The Indians were chiefly Kiowas, but there were also many Comanches and Apaches and, Carson thought, some Arapahoes. Carson's officers wished to advance and destroy the large village just ahead, but Kit was aware of the fact that only the howitzers had kept his army from being overwhelmed by sheer numbers. About 4 P.M., therefore, he began a retreat, intending to destroy the village through which they had come. The Indians discerned his purpose and endeavored to prevent it, but it was accomplished. The Indians then set fire to the prairie and Carson countered with a backfire and drew off, with the two howitzers in the rear so that these dreaded weapons might be used to cover the retreat if necessary. The Indians followed for two days but did not dare to attack.

Such was the battle of Adobe Walls, in which two soldiers and one of the Ute scouts were killed and about twenty-five men were wounded. The number of the enemy dead Carson estimated at sixty, but all other estimates are a hundred or more.[27] Against the wishes of his officers, Carson decided to return to Fort Bascom. He knew that by leaving the Indians in possession of the field he had suffered a technical defeat. But he also knew that when the Indians counted their dead and faced the fact that their favorite winter campground had been penetrated by an army upon which they had inflicted no damage, they would consider it a defeat and be very discouraged. Carson's judgment in concluding the campaign was undoubtedly correct. Only George Custer, in 1876, ever faced as large an aggregation of Indian braves. It is doubtful that the number on the Little Bighorn was quite as

27
Carson's official report on the Adobe Walls campaign is reprinted in Sabin, *Kit Carson Days* (1914), 604–10. Sabin's account of the campaign, a very good one, is found in *Kit Carson Days* (1914), 440–66.

large as that at Adobe Walls. The contrast between the two campaigns is marked. Fortunately, Carson was no Custer; but if he had acted as many of his officers wished him to he might very well have anticipated Custer's fate by a dozen years.

Early in 1865 Carson was given an extended leave and spent nearly four months at home. General Carleton was very much pleased with his services and also with his assurance that he would not resign his commission as long as Carleton remained in New Mexico. In March, Carson was brevetted Brigadier General of Volunteers for important services in New Mexico, and his conduct at Valverde was specifically commended. However, official notification and documents of this promotion did not arrive until December, 1865. In a letter dated January 2, 1866, Carson wrote to Secretary of War Stanton, regarding his promotion, "though unsolicited by me, I accept with grateful pleasure, as a memento that during the late rebellion, the exertions of the New Mexican Volunteers, though restricted in its sphere of influence to its own territory, have not been overlooked by the United States Government." On January 4, he took the required oath.[28] Thus the man who once had been refused a lieutenant's commission was commissioned a general without ever having been a lieutenant.[29]

Meanwhile, in May, 1865, Kit was sent to take charge of Camp Nichols, located on the Cimarron Cut-off of the Santa Fe Trail, where he was expected to further pacify the Kiowas, Comanches, and other Plains Indians he had recently fought.[30] During his stay at Camp Nichols he made a trip to Fort Lyon, on the Arkansas River, to make a statement regarding the Sand Creek Massacre, which was then under investigation. This affair had occurred November 29, 1864, on the Cheyenne Reservation, north of the Arkan-

28 "Letters received from or relating to Kit Carson, 1854–60," The National Archives, Washington, D. C. Although seemingly out of place, Carson's commission and letter of acceptance are among his letters as Indian agent.

29 The lieutenant's commission he had been refused, of course, was in the regular army, whereas his general's commission was not.

30 Camp Nichols was actually in the Oklahoma panhandle. It was about sixteen miles west of present Boise City, in Cimarron County, Oklahoma. See Albert W. Thompson, "Kit Carson's Camp Nichols in No Man's Land," *Colorado Magazine,* Vol. XI (September, 1934), 179–86.

*Brigadier General Carson, 1866.* (Courtesy of Kit Carson Museum)
*See page 236.*

sas, while Carson was engaged in his Adobe Walls campaign. His deposition was in the nature of expert opinion, since he did not possess firsthand knowledge of the event, and merely stated his thoughts on general Indian policy.[31] Carson did not remain at Camp Nichols even for the full duration of its short existence, but returned to Fort Union before the camp was closed in the early fall.

From Fort Union he traveled again to Fort Lyon, where he served on the President's special commission which concluded a treaty with the Cheyennes and Arapahoes in an effort to atone for Sand Creek. Then, in the fall of 1865, he made an extended trip starting from Fort Lyon. He went first to Fort Leavenworth, thence to visit his relatives in Missouri, then to St. Louis, where he called on General William T. Sherman, and finally to Washington, D. C., where he was photographed by the Civil War photographer, Mathew B. Brady. Just what business he transacted is hard to say, but probably his call on General Sherman had to do with Carson's request for an appointment and explains his assignment to command Fort Garland the following year.[32]

During the early part of 1866, Carson was undoubtedly at home. But so much of his life had been spent in the saddle that he was not content to stay inactive for long. It is not surprising, then, to find him making trips to Santa Fe, to Fort Union, and to Maxwell's Ranch. His old friend, Lucien Maxwell, had secured title to the huge Beaubien and Miranda Land Grant and had built a fine establishment near the spot where Carson had tried farming for a few months long ago. Carson continued to have some business dealings with Maxwell as long as he lived. He seems to have been at Maxwell's on several occasions during this period, enjoying the company of travelers who stopped there, because it

31 Carson's deposition is reprinted in Sabin, *Kit Carson Days* (1914), 610–14.

32 Details of this trip are obscure. Blackwelder, *Great Westerner,* 344, states that he was ordered to report to St. Louis, which may have been the case. However, she says that he returned to take charge of Fort Union on December 8, 1865. I have been unable to verify that he ever commanded at Fort Union. Estergreen, *Kit Carson,* 268, says that he went on to Washington and New York. I can find no evidence of his having gone to New York, but it is difficult to find any other time when the Brady photograph could have been made, so I am inclined to believe that he did go to Washington. General Carleton had proposed that he become the chief sutler at Fort Union, but Carson correctly felt that he did not have a head for business. He was concerned about his future, however, and I believe that he probably discussed his problem with General Sherman. Sherman was unable to do anything to help him at the time, so Carson may have gone on to Washington.

33 Henry Inman, *The Old Santa Fe Trail* (New York and London, 1898), 375. Colonel Inman speaks of meeting Carson there and seeing him play seven up with Maxwell.

was Maxwell's custom to offer hospitality to all comers.[33]

In early August, 1866, Carson was at Fort Union, where John W. Davidson, whom he had known since Kearny's march to California, was now in command.[34] A matter of army business had taken Carson north of Maxwell's Ranch and perhaps now took him back to Fort Union. In July, 1866, the decision was made in Santa Fe to establish a new fort, called Fort Stevens, somewhere south of the Arkansas River.[35] Carson and Céran St. Vrain were asked to select the location. They chose a plateau at the foot of the Spanish Peaks, and there the fort was built and Captain Andrew J. Alexander placed in charge of a small garrison. On returning to Santa Fe, Carson learned of his appointment to the command of Fort Garland, just over La Veta Pass, on the other side of the Sangre de Cristo Mountains from Fort Stevens.[36] He went there to take charge at once. At the same time, his rank was to be reduced to that of lieutenant colonel, in line with the general policy prevailing, now that the Civil War was over.

Carson retained his post at Fort Garland only for about a year. He requested the appointment of sutler, but this was refused because of a new regulation which prevented army officers from engaging in selling supplies.[37] Probably this was the most compelling reason for Carson's decision to give up a position he had sought and for which he was well qualified. His family was increased in the winter of 1866 by the birth of another daughter, Estefana, usually called Stella in later years.[38]

Another reason may have been his failing health. It was while he was at Fort Garland that he began to notice the pain in his chest and the racking cough that were to lead to his death. He found it difficult to travel on horseback because of this. But it is probable that economic consid-

34
James F. Meline, *Two Thousand Miles on Horseback* (New York, 1868), 246–51. Colonel Meline tells of meeting Carson in Santa Fe at this time and of enjoying his conversations with Kit.

35
See Taylor, "Ka-ni-ache," *Colorado Magazine,* Vol. XLIII (Fall, 1966), 295. See also, "Fort Stevens," *Colorado Magazine,* Vol. XLIII (Fall, 1966), 303–307. Fort Stevens had a very short existence, being discontinued September 26, 1866, only three months after it was organized.

36
General John Pope was actually at Santa Fe when Carson was there in early August and his letter recommending Carson's appointment to General Sherman was written at Fort Union, August 11, 1866. It is difficult to avoid the conclusion that Sherman had planned it all in advance. He had been a Carson admirer for a long time.

37
Blackwelder, *Great Westerner,* 351.

38
McClung, *Carson-Bent-Boggs,* 82–83. Estefana Carson was born December 23, 1866, either at Taos or at Fort Garland, depending on when Josefa and the children joined Carson at the fort. She married Spear Erasmus Wood in 1884, and there are descendants of the marriage. She died October 1, 1899.

erations were primary. When General Sherman visited Fort Garland, he discussed with Carson his responsibility to his growing children. Kit admitted that he was concerned about their education and welfare. The result was that Sherman promised to do what he could for the eldest son, William. This promise he carried out after Kit's death, largely at his own expense, but William was not sufficiently prepared to profit from an education and failed to pass the examinations required for an officer's commission.[39] It also resulted in Kit's application for the Superintendency of Indian Affairs either in New Mexico or in Colorado Territory, a post for which Sherman recommended him. It was apparent, however, that even if this application were successful, it would be some time before it could become a reality. So during his time at Fort Garland, Carson divided his time between his duties and his plans for the future.

General Sherman visited Fort Garland in September, 1866, not long after Carson was installed there. While he was there, important meetings were being held with the Southern Utes. Carson knew the Indian protocol and Sherman was tremendously impressed by his ability to handle the Indians.[40] It was clear that the head chief, Ouray, a very influential man among his people, was on very good terms with Carson and much guided by his opinions. Carson's old friend Ka-ni-ache, whose Mohuache band was reduced nearly to starvation, caused trouble on the eastern side of the mountains in October, 1866, and Carson was drawn into the final stages of the uproar and helped to bring about a settlement in Taos.[41]

Carson's tenure at Fort Garland seems to have been quite successful and in view of its location overlooking the San Luis Valley, proximity to Taos, and Carson's ability to deal with the Utes, it seems to have been the ideal spot for him. In response to inquiries about Fort Garland, Car-

39 See Athearn, "The Education of Kit Carson's Son," *New Mexico Historical Review,* Vol. XXXI (April, 1956), 133–39.

40 Edward S. Ellis, *Life of Kit Carson* (New York, 1889), 248–52, prints a letter from Sherman to the author written at St. Louis, June 25, 1884. See also James F. Rusling, *Across America* (New York, 1874), 135–39.

41 See Taylor, "Ka-ni-ache," *Colorado Magazine,* Vol. XLIII (Fall, 1966), 297–302.

*Crayon portrait of Brigadier General Carson, 1866.* (Courtesy of Kit Carson Museum) *See page 236.*

son signed a report dated June 10, 1866, in which he spoke highly of its situation and function.[42] At Fort Garland, too, his family seems to have been happy. Josefa had been accustomed to Indians visiting her home in Taos when Kit ran the Ute agency there. The children were able to play unmolested and had the opportunity of seeing that their father was much respected by the Indians.[43]

Despite the attractions of Fort Garland, Kit had decided as early as November, 1866, to settle on the Purgatoire, near its confluence with the Arkansas and only a few miles from Fort Lyon. There were several reasons for this decision. His old friend William Bent lived in that vicinity, where he still had some influence among both settlers and Indians. He might be able to help Kit get the Colorado Indian superintendency. Tom Boggs, another old friend, had married Josefa's niece, Rumalda Luna, and was farming there, and so was Jesse Nelson, who had married Kit's niece, Susan Carson. Furthermore, there might exist an opportunity for Carson to acquire considerable land in that locality.[44]

In July, 1867, Carson submitted his resignation from military service, giving ill health as the reason. He then moved his family to the Purgatoire, where the new settlement was known as Boggsville. Probably he remained technically in charge of Fort Garland until he was officially mustered out in November, 1867. Meanwhile, he endeavored to get his own affairs into better order, traveling to Denver and to Maxwell's Ranch on business. In a suit by the heirs of Charles Bent against Maxwell, Carson testified for the Bent faction.[45] However, he and Maxwell remained friends and continued to have business dealings.

In January, 1868, the appointment Carson had sought as superintendent of Indian affairs in Colorado was assured to him through General J. C. McFerran's influence with General U. S.

42 See "Report on Fort Garland by Kit Carson to Major Robert James, June 10, 1866," edited by Gene M. Gressley, *Colorado Magazine,* Vol. XXXII (July, 1955), 215–24. The editor is mistaken concerning the name of the officer to whom the report was sent. It was Major Roger Jones. See Heitman, *Historical Register,* 582. The language of the report makes it clear that Carson did not simply dictate it. It was composed by someone else and signed by Carson, but undoubtedly it embodied some of his information and opinions.

43 See A. B. Sanford, "Reminiscences of Kit Carson, Jr.," *Colorado Magazine,* Vol. VI (September, 1929), 179–84. For a general history of both Fort Massachusetts and Fort Garland, see Duane Vandenbusche, "Life at a Frontier Post: Fort Garland," *Colorado Magazine,* Vol. XLIII (Spring, 1966, 132–48.

44 According to Kit Carson, Jr., in Sanford, "Reminiscences of Kit Carson, Jr.," *Colorado Magazine,* Vol. VI (September, 1929), 183, Josefa had a claim to some land there. If so, this claim must have stemmed from her cousin, Donaciano Vigil, who succeeded Charles Bent as territorial governor of New Mexico. The area at the mouth of the Purgatoire was within the grant made to Cornelio Vigil and Céran St. Vrain in 1843. They subsequently allotted shares to Charles Bent, Donaciano Vigil, Manuel Armijo, and Eugene Leitensdorfer. In 1869, a claim was filed on behalf of the Carson heirs. See LeRoy R. Hafen, "Mexican Land Grants in Colorado," *Colorado Maga-*

*Oil painting of Carson, 1867.* (Courtesy of State Historical Society of Colorado)
*See page 236.*

Grant.[46] In February, the Ute Indians were asked to send a delegation to Washington, D. C., to negotiate directly with the commissioner of Indian affairs in drawing up a treaty. Carson was urgently requested to be present as a special commissioner. He scarcely felt able to make the trip, but he felt that it was his duty to do so, in fairness to the Utes and because of his recent appointment to a position of responsibility for the Indians of Colorado Territory. Entertaining the hope that Eastern medical men might be able to improve his health, he took the stagecoach from Fort Lyon to Fort Hays. From there, he took the railroad train to St. Louis, where he was joined by the other special commissioner, Colonel Albert Gallatin Boone, a grandson of Daniel Boone, who, like Carson, had been a trapper and an Indian agent. They journeyed together by train to the capital city.[47]

By March 2, the Utes had agreed to a treaty whereby they would confine themselves to a reservation of some fifteen million acres beyond the Continental Divide, in western Colorado. Carson was much lionized and photographed, but he was in desperately bad health. The photographs bear witness to the fact that he had lost much weight, and his cheeks were hollow and sunken where once they had been full. He was able to visit with both General Frémont and General Carleton, the two men with whom he had been most intimately associated. Frémont was so concerned about Carson's health that he sent for his wife to come to Washington and do what she could to help him. Jessie Frémont came, and was unable to do much for him, but she left a moving account of her contact with Kit at this time. She wrote:

> I had been written to from Washington that Carson was there, ill and depressed; that he had not consulted a physician yet, but thought he had the heart injured in an accident; that if I would

*zine,* Vol. IV (May, 1927), 88. Blackwelder, *Great Westerner,* 356, says that Carson bought two tracts from Céran St. Vrain. John M. Boggs told F. W. Cragin in an interview of July 5, 1908, at Las Animas, Colorado, that William Bent had been promised 6,000 acres on the Purgatoire (no doubt by St. Vrain) and that he gave Kit Carson and Tom Boggs half of it. See F. W. Cragin Papers, Notebook VIII, 80, 82.

45 The Bent heirs won a judgment of $18,000 against Maxwell in 1866.

Lucien Maxwell, son of Hugh B. Maxwell and Odille Menard Maxwell, was born at Kaskaskia, Illinois, September 14, 1818. He married Maria de la Luz Beaubien in 1844. The validity of the Beaubien and Miranda Land Grant was confirmed in 1860 and by 1865 Maxwell had gained sole control by buying out all other heirs. Known as the Maxwell grant, its 1,750,000 acres made him the largest landholder in the United States until he sold it in 1870. His last years were spent on a ranch near Fort Sumner, New Mexico, where he died July 25, 1875. See Harold H. Dunham, "Lucien Maxwell: Frontiersman and Businessman," *Denver Westerners Brand Book,* V (March, 1949), 1–22.

For the events of the summer of 1867, see Sabin, *Kit Carson Days* (1914), 485–87; Blackwelder, *Great Westerner*, 357–59.

46 Blackwelder, *Great Westerner,* 360.

47 Sabin, *Kit Carson Days* (1914), 488–89.

urge him to come to me and be well nursed and see a physician, something might yet be done although his condition seemed very serious.

... I saw, for the last time, one of the few who had not changed from that old time of youth, and health and friends, and a complete home.

But Carson was only troubled by my emotion, and told me, with his own simplicity of courage, that he had seen Doctor Sayre, who has told him that he might live to reach his home ... but that he might also die at any moment, as the heart was fatally injured ... His open-air and absolutely temperate life delayed the inevitable end.

His only wish now was to get home and not let his wife have the shock of hearing of his death.

"Yesterday I thought I was gone," he told me. The Indian chief who was with him in his room told him what he had said—he himself only knew that all at once he had felt the bed rise with him and with that "a drowning feeling," but with a new strange element which made him cry out, "Lord Jesus, have mercy."

The chief had taken him from the bed and carried him to an open window. "I noticed he was crying. 'What's that for,' I asked him. 'Because you looked dead and you called Lord Jesus.' "[48]

Despite such seizures as just described, Carson traveled to Philadelphia, New York, and Boston, expressly to consult other medical men. But their opinions were the same as that of the Washington physician. In Boston, his last photograph was taken. Then he started the long journey home by way of Chicago and Council Bluffs. Over the Union Pacific, he was able to travel as far as Cheyenne.

From there he took the stagecoach for Denver. At Namaqua, just west of present Loveland, Colorado, he stayed overnight at the home of Mariano Medina, a Mexican trapper and squaw man who remembered Carson from his own boyhood in Taos and who was very impressed, now, to be able to give lodging to the famous

48
This unsigned account appeared originally in the *New York Ledger.* It was reprinted in *The Prairie Farmer,* February 27, 1875, and a clipping from this magazine was kindly furnished to me by Dr. LeRoy R. Hafen. Obviously, Jessie Frémont was the author.

49
See Lucas Brandt, "Pioneer Days on the Big Thompson," *Colorado Magazine,* Vol. VII (September, 1930), 180; also F. W. Cragin Papers, Notebook XXVII, 93. Those who saw him at Medina's remembered that he was ill and coughing a great deal.

50
Josephine Carson, born at Boggsville, *Colorado,* April 13, 1868, died October 10, 1892. McClung, *Carson-Bent-Boggs,* 83. She was married first to James Howard and second to William Squires. Both marriages were unfortunate. F. W. Cragin Papers, Notebook XII, 19, 20, 21. Her sister Teresina Carson Allen was Dr. Cragin's informant at Raton, New Mexico, March 18, 1908.

scout, in his black suit and silk hat.[49] Carson's weakened condition forced him to stop over in Denver for two days, but on April 11 he reached La Junta, Colorado, where his wife met him with a team and carriage.

Two days later, Josefa gave birth to a girl baby, who was called Josefita, or Josephine.[50] Ten days later, the mother died, on April 27, 1868.

Josefa's sudden death was a severe blow to Kit, all the more so because of his own enfeebled condition. He got a letter off to Aloys Scheurich, in Taos, who had married his niece, Teresina Bent, begging him to come and bring his wife and her mother to help him care for his family.[51] They responded to his plea, but when they arrived on May 15 they learned that on the preceding day Tom Boggs had taken Kit to the army post at Fort Lyon, where he could have medical care.

The day after his arrival at Fort Lyon, Kit made his will, naming Tom Boggs as his executor and guardian of his children.[52] His estate, when finally settled, amounted to about $9,000. It consisted mainly of money owed to him by Lucien Maxwell, Ferdinand Meyer, and others, about two hundred head of cattle, some small pieces of land near Taos, and the house and furniture at Taos.

When Dr. H. R. Tilton, assistant army surgeon, explained to Carson that he might die by suffocation or that more probably the aneurysm would burst and cause death by hemorrhage, Kit expressed the hope that it would be the latter.[53] He was well aware that his time was short. Aloys Scheurich came to be with him and stayed with him both night and day. That his condition was deteriorating was apparent from the fact that he was coughing up blood. He had been forbidden to smoke and could take little nourishment. About all the surgeon could do was to allay his pain somewhat by administering chloroform.

On the afternoon of May 23, he asked Scheu-

51 Estergreen, *Kit Carson,* 274–75, reproduces this letter. In it, Carson refers to Ignacia Bent as "the old lady" and says that no one can look after his children like she can. Ignacia was fifteen years older than Josefa but two years younger than Kit.

Josefa was forty at the time of her death. Dr. Tilton described her as retaining remnants of former beauty at this time. She seems never to have been photographed. L. H. Garrard, who saw her in 1847, when she was nineteen and had been married four years, was much taken by her rather haughty type of beauty. See Lewis Hector Garrard, *Wah-to-yah and the Taos Trail* (Norman, 1955), 181.

52 See Estergreen, *Kit Carson,* 275–77, for a reproduction of the will.

53 See Abbott, *Christopher Carson,* 341–48, for Dr. Tilton's letter describing Carson's last illness.

54 See Estergreen, *Kit Carson,* 277–79; Sabin, *Kit Carson Days* (1914), 494–97. Medical opinion holds it unlikely that an aneurysm of the aorta would be traceable to the fall that Carson suffered in 1860, from which he felt his trouble stemmed. However, none of the more usual causes for this condition are known to have existed in Carson's case. Today such damage can be successfully repaired by the installation of a dacron tube to replace the weakened section of the great artery, and some people live for years after having had such an operation performed.

*Painting of Carson by Charles S. Stobie, 1867.* (Courtesy of State Historical Society of Colorado) *See page 236.*

rich to cook him a buffalo steak. He ate it with enjoyment and drank coffee with the meal. Then he asked for his old clay pipe and had a smoke, conversing with Dr. Tilton and Scheurich while he enjoyed his pipe, as he had been accustomed to do at the close of a day's journey at so many campfires. Suddenly there was a change. Kit called out "Good bye, Doctor." and to Scheurich, "Adios, *Compadre*." A strong gush of blood came from his mouth and he was dead. It was 4:25 P.M.[54]

Immediately word was sent to his family and friends at Boggsville. He was given a military funeral conducted by the post chaplain, the Reverend Gamaliel Collins, at 10 A.M. the next day. The army wives at the post detached the paper flowers from their hats to serve as flowers for his casket. His body was conveyed to Boggsville and buried there beside that of his wife.

The following year the remains of both Carson and his wife were taken to Taos and buried in the cemetery there. Kit had been a member of the Masonic Lodge in Santa Fe since 1854.[55] In 1908, the Masons of Taos erected a simple headstone on his grave, and Kit, Jr., and Charles provided one for their mother. Since then, many people have stopped to see the spot where one of the best-known and best-loved Americans lies at rest after having traveled the last of his many trails.

55
He later transferred to the Taos Lodge, in 1859, when it was organized, but back to the Santa Fe Lodge in 1865, when the one at Taos temporarily ceased to function.

Captain Smith H. Simpson was responsible for removing the remains to Taos. Burial there was in accordance with Carson's wish and that of his wife.

Steckmesser, *The Western Hero,* 18, says "Carson . . . renounced his Catholicism and became a Mason." Although Carson's Catholicism was perhaps somewhat of a formality, I have found no evidence that he renounced it. It is not true that Masons will not accept Catholics as members—or at least that was the statement of Albert Pike, the great Masonic scholar, who had once been a trapper in New Mexico as Carson had been. Pike was Grand Commander of the Scottish Rite, Southern Jurisdiction, from 1859 to 1891. I suspect Dr. Steckmesser of having accepted a legend and, by applying it to Carson, of having created one.

# IV. Carson the Man: A New Appraisal

When the average American thinks of the pioneers who crossed the Appalachians and fought the Indians for the rich lands of the earlier west, he thinks of Daniel Boone. When his thoughts turn to the frontiersmen who penetrated the Rocky Mountains and found their way to the Pacific, Kit Carson is the name that comes to his mind. Historians may point out that others were in Kentucky before Boone and that Carson was by no means the first to explore the Far West as often as they please without reducing the popular esteem in which Boone and Carson are held. Their place is secure and nothing will ever change it. I find this to my liking for this reason: although both men owe their preeminent position in popular esteem to the fact that their careers were more successfully publicized than the careers of others with whom they were associated, it can be said truthfully that neither Boone nor Carson consciously sought to achieve such a position. Moreover, both men accepted acclaim without alteration of their personalities or of their lives. It is this characteristic that has endeared them to the American people in such an enduring way. To reach the topmost pinnacle of fame and still remain the same person, pursuing the same course of action

Conestoga Freighting Wagon

and retaining the same outlook on life, is not given to everyone upon whom fortune bestows her lavish favors. Yet that is what Boone and Carson did, and that is why so few critics are found to say that they were undeserving of lasting renown.

Neither man possessed, in any marked degree, the characteristic of leadership, although Carson showed some development of this capacity in later life. Both men exhibited a far greater tendency to act for the good of others than to act for their own advancement regardless of the effect on other people. Although they were individualists in most respects, they never showed the extreme aggressiveness so often thought to be an essential characteristic of individualism. Carson, indeed, to a much greater extent than Boone, was inclined toward sociability and the companionship of other people. Although Boone was the more impressive man in his physical attributes, clearly he was no more fully equipped, physically or in any other way, to master a wilderness environment than was Carson. The true key to the character of both men lay in their simplicity, in the best and most admirable sense of that word. Some future Plutarch may write the parallel lives of these two pioneers, for there are many remarkable parallels to be drawn. It is sufficient here merely to call attention to the fact that the best comparison with Carson is to be found in the older pioneer, Daniel Boone.

*Sketch of Kit Carson.* (National Archives, U.S. Signal Corps Collection) *See page 237.*

Comparisons of Carson with other Mountain Men, his contemporaries and his peers, are likely to raise the question of whether or not one or more of them deserved the accolade of historical renown more than Carson did. Kit was not a shrewd and sharp trader, as his friend, Lucien Maxwell was; he was not an aggressive, acquisitive, dominating, businessman, as both Charles and William Bent were; he was not an enterprising, farsighted, economic innovator, like his old employer Ewing Young. He was just a hard-working free trapper, more competent and experienced than most of his kind, but perfectly content to work for someone else. Maxwell, Young, and the Bents were all empire builders in their way. Carson had no inclination even in this direction.

Nor did he possess any of the aggressive, ambitious drive that marked such rising young men as Jedediah Smith, Thomas Fitzpatrick, and William Sublette, all of whom, if they had lived longer, would have been drawn to politics if I read the indications aright. They had the qualities of leadership that Carson lacked. They also did things which Carson, under no circumstances, would have done. Fitzpatrick started a rumor that Gantt and Blackwell were bankrupt in order to hire their men away from them and lessen his competition. William Sublette forced his own brother to go back on his agreement to purchase goods from Nathaniel Wyeth. Jedediah Smith, whom recent historians have extolled as a rival to Carson's pre-eminent position, lost ten men to the Mohave Indians, lost nearly his whole party to the Umpquas, and lost his own life on the Santa Fe Trail. Carson was just one of the Rocky Mountain boys when these men had their own company; but he defended his life, and the lives of others, better than Smith, and maintained his reputation for honor and honesty better than Sublette or Fitzpatrick.

Carson was not a vivid "personality," like Joe Meek, John L. Hatcher, and Jim Bridger. He was not inclined to be a great talker; he did not have the instinct for dramatization that these men had. There was nothing of the showman in Carson. Meek entertained and impressed Mrs. Victor with tales of the same life that Carson led, and she has shared his experiences with posterity. Carson's memoirs are dull and plodding compared with Meek's vivid recollections of some of the same events. John Hatcher has come down to us as a master wit and storyteller through the pages of Lewis Garrard. Even Bridger, with his reputation for tall stories, finally impressed Grenville Dodge so much that he wrote a lively characterization of Bridger as he was in his later years. Carson enjoyed hearing such master raconteurs around the campfire, but he could not compete with them. An extremely skilled conversationalist might have drawn something more than a straight story from him, but Carson had no flair for it.

Certainly he was not a colorful eccentric like Old Bill Williams or Peg Leg Smith or Mark Head. Carson not only talked in a straightforward sensible way but he behaved that way as well. Meek and Bridger and Hatcher acted sensibly enough, but their talk was sufficiently embellished to set them apart from the common run of their fellows. Old Bill and Peg Leg and Mark Head were set apart by the peculiarities of their actions. Old Bill, flinging his dry goods by the bolt into the streets; Peg Leg, stealing horses from California and boasting about it in saloons in later life; Mark Head, going into a plum thicket to fight a wounded grizzly bear in order to win a bet—these are idiosyncrasies that Carson would never have imagined. Of course, he was not a heavy drinker like Old Bill and Peg-Leg were—and Head doubtless took more liquor than the bears he fought. But drunk or sober, there was nothing eccentric about Carson.

Comparisons with other Mountain Men have given us a measure of what Carson was not. Let us now examine the man himself in order to determine what traits account for his long lasting and universal popularity. First of all, let us consider his outward appearance. His appearance was by no means as impressive as his reputation, but it may be of more importance than at first it seems to be, because there is something gratify-

*Equestrian statue of Carson by Lukeman and Roth, Trinidad, Colorado.*
(Courtesy of State Historical Society) *See page 237.*

ing to the average man in the knowledge that a man of very ordinary appearance, habits, and language has risen to an extraordinary place through extraordinary adventures.

There are a number of descriptions of Carson that exhibit general agreement. None of the descriptions apply to his trapping days. The earliest comment that we have on Carson's appearance is that of John C. Frémont at the time of their first meeting, when Kit was thirty-two years old. Frémont wrote, "I was pleased with him and his manner of address at this first meeting. He was a man of medium height, broad-shouldered and deep chested, with a clear steady blue eye and frank speech and address; quiet and unassuming."[1]

In his *Memoirs*, William Tecumseh Sherman described Carson as he remembered having seen him for the first time, nearly forty years earlier, when Carson brought the first overland mail into Los Angeles. Sherman wrote, "I cannot express my surprise at beholding a small, stoop-shouldered man, with reddish hair, freckled face, soft blue eyes, and nothing to indicate extraordinary courage or daring."[2] Sherman, of course, was ramrod-straight himself, so he may have slightly exaggerated Carson's slouch, and it must be remembered that Carson was weary from a long ride. Still, it cannot be denied that Carson was somewhat stoop-shouldered. Another description from about this time said "Carson was a small man, very wiry, and about as ready an appearing man as I ever saw. He looked as if he would know exactly what to do, if awakened suddenly in the night, ready for anything that might turn up at any moment."[3] Another description is that of Lieutenant G. D. Brewerton, dating from 1848. He wrote, "The *real* Kit Carson I found to be a plain, simple, unostentatious man; rather below the medium height, with brown, curling hair, little or no

1 Frémont, *Memoirs,* 74.

2 William T. Sherman, *Memoirs* (2 vols., New York, 1886), I, 46–47.

3 J. H. Widber, (Untitled Manuscript, The Bancroft Library, Berkeley, California).

beard, and a voice as soft and gentle as a woman's."[4]

A newspaper correspondent wrote from Santa Fe, in 1851:

> The world-renowned Kit Carson has been here for some days past. You would not suppose from a glance at the man that he was the hero of so many border exploits—the terror of the wild nomad, the far-famed Kit Carson. I was disappointed at first sight of the man, and so perhaps would any one be, who had heard merely of the character and exploits of the man, without having seen a minute description of his contour. It was only when I came closely to analyze his features that I detected the real *Kit*. He was not dressed in the outlandish habiliments with which fancy, since the time of Boone, instinctively invests the hunter and the trapper, but in genteel American costume . . . Carson is rather under the medium height, but his frame exceedingly well knit, muscular, symmetrically proportioned. His hair, a light auburn, and worn long, falls back from a forehead high, broad and indicating more than a common share of intellect. The general contour of his face is not handsome, and yet not unpleasing. But that which at once arrests and almost monopolizes your attention is the eye—such an eye! gray, searching, piercing, as if with every glance he would reach the well-springs of thought, and read your very silent imaginings.[5]

The author of this description went on to describe John L. Hatcher, whom he also saw at the same time, and said, "His eye is quick and piercing but not steady and penetrating like that of Carson."

Elias Brevoort, whose acquaintance with Carson dated from about the same time, has left his impression of Kit in these words:

> Personally he was mild, rather effeminate voice, but when he spoke his voice was one that would draw the attention of all, everybody would stop to listen.
>
> His head was large, forehead high and full, face

4
George D. Brewerston, "A Ride With Kit Carson," *Harper's Magazine,* Vol. VIII (August, 1853), 308.

5
*Arkansas Gazette and Democrat,* June 13, 1851. The author of this interesting description, which I obtained through the kindness of Dr. LeRoy R. Hafen, is identified only as a correspondent of the *National Era.*

broad, and long straight hair down to his neck but not on his shoulders; thin firm lips, a good Grecian nose, clear, strong, bold, unflinching eye; face tapered a little to chin, which was well shaped.[6]

Two interesting descriptions of Carson were made in 1859.[7] Dr. C. M. Clarke, who arrived in Denver on June 6, 1859, saw Carson there and wrote:

> The old mountaineer, Kit Carson, was in Denver, at the time we reached there; but to see him, with his full, good natured face, and dressed in a suit of sober black, one would scarcely conceive him to be the sturdy, invincible Kit Carson, the pathfinder of the Rocky Mountains and the terror of the Indian. We expected to find him a man of hard, stern features and dressed in fringed buckskin from head to toe, after the manner of most mountaineers. His home is in New Mexico, where he has the agency of the Ute Indians, receiving a salary from the Government.

Albert D. Richardson, a well-known newspaper reporter of the period, was also in Denver at this time, but he does not mention seeing Carson there. However, Richardson rode with Carson from Santa Fe to Taos in October, 1859. Of their meeting, in Santa Fe, he wrote, "At the hotel supper table I noticed a stout middle-aged man, with straight brown hair, mild eye and kindly face. He wore a suit of grey, and looked like an Illinois farmer; but when he took off his hat the face and head indicated character.

James F. Rusling, who saw him in the fall of 1866 at Fort Garland, described him as stoutish, florid, and talkative. He mentioned Kit's mild blue eyes and especially remarked on his voice which was as soft and gentle as a woman's. He thought Carson seemed about forty-five, but corrected this statement later to fifty-five, which was about Kit's actual age.[8]

A young officer, who met Carson a year later and spent two weeks with him, wrote:

6
Elias Brevoort, "The Santa Fe Trail" (Manuscript, The Bancroft Library, Berkeley, California) (1884).

7
Clarke, *A Trip to Pike's Peak*, 70; Albert D. Richardson, *Beyond the Mississippi* (Hartford, 1869), 256.

8
James F. Rusling, *Across America* (New York, 1874), 135–36.

> A man old in years but erect and strong on his feet came toward me and extended his hand and told me I was welcome. The man was Kit Carson, who guided John C. Fremont on his pathfinding journey across the mountains and plains of what was then an unknown territory of the United States. Carson was the one man that was thought of by white men living east of the Mississippi River as knowing more about the Indian of the West and Southwest than any other man alive up to that date. To describe him physically is easy. A small, compact, well-proportioned body, weighing about one hundred and thirty five pounds; five feet six inches in height; gray eyes that looked into yours with honesty and strength—a characteristic of the man. My impression was that I had met my master, one who could teach me what I wanted to know; and so it proved.... To me he was a friend never to be forgotten.[9]

Such were the impressions of Kit Carson at various stages of his adult life, as recorded by those who knew him. It will be noted that some observers said his eyes were blue and others said they were gray. We shall have to compromise and call them blue-gray. All who mentioned his hair agreed that he wore it rather long, and since most of them said it was straight, we shall have to interpret Brewerton's statement that it was curly as meaning only that it tended to curl up at the ends. The color of his hair was light brown with a reddish glint in the sunlight. His complexion was fair, and, since Carson was an outdoorsman, it was slightly freckled. He was not over five and a half feet tall; all are agreed that he was sturdily built. He was soft-spoken and unobtrusive in his manner, and tended to grow more talkative as he got older. At the age of fifty, he had become rather stout and he retained this plump figure until about 1866, when his illness began to cause him to lose weight.

The photographs that we have of Carson bear out this description well. He was rather full in

9
Charles A. Montgomery, as quoted by Blanche C. Grant in her edition of Carson's memoirs (*Kit Carson's Own Story . . .* , Taos, 1926), 130, citing an article in *Sunset Magazine* (March, 1911).

the face until his last two years of life. His lips were rather compressed, giving him a look of determination. The mustache that he wore in later years added distinction to his appearance. His stoop became much more evident during the last year or two that he lived, and his face was furrowed and his cheeks hollow in the pictures made a few months before his death. Until those last two years, probably he looked a bit younger than his actual age.

No one became well acquainted with Kit Carson without coming to the realization that he was illiterate, or so nearly so as to make no practical difference. Sherman said that he could write only his name and that he learned to do that much only in later years.[10] Richardson said he read with difficulty and could write little beyond his own name.[11] That he could write no more than his signature is beyond question. He learned to do this when he became Indian agent in 1854 and needed to sign letters. Before this time there are no examples of his signature. While Carson was with Frémont he signed many vouchers for his salary, and these are all signed with his mark.[12] It is probable that he learned to write his signature by copying his name from a model furnished by someone else. The letters are formed without much connection between them, the pen stroke is firm and heavy and indicates that uniform pressure was applied, as by a slow and unpracticed hand. He wrote only "C. Carson," never spelling out his first name. No letters in his handwriting have been seen, although there are a few cases where "Yours etc," preceding Carson, appears to have been written by him, probably by way of practice in learning to write more, a project apparently soon abandoned.

Carson's inability to read is almost as firmly established. He is thought to have had only a few months of schooling. His own statement, to Jes-

10
Edward S. Ellis, *The Life of Kit Carson* (New York, 1889), 248–52, wherein a letter from Sherman, dated June 25, 1884, is reproduced.

11
Richardson, *Beyond the Mississippi,* 260.

12
This information was kindly furnished to me by Donald Jackson, who is preparing an edition of Frémont's papers.

In a letter of Superintendent James L. Collins, Santa Fe, June 26, 1857, to the Commissioner of Indian Affairs, Collins, who was Carson's superior, wrote, "I have known Mr. Carson for many years, he is an illiterate man, but can both read and write, tho' not sufficiently well to do the business of his office without the assistance of a clerk." National Archives, New Mexico Superintendency, Letters Received (Microfilm). This statement, I believe, supports the position I have taken regarding Carson's illiteracy. His ability to decipher words by reading or to form them by writing was so limited that he must be regarded as illiterate.

*Equestrian statue of Carson by MacMonnies, surmounting the Pioneer's Monument in the Civic Center, Denver, Colorado.* (Courtesy of Denver Public Library) *See page 237.*

sie Benton Frémont, was that at the cry of "Indians" he had thrown down his books and never returned to school.[13] The statement of his sister, Mary Ann, to the effect that Kit was a smart little fellow at his books and that his father intended to make a lawyer of him is more of a reflection on his small size in comparison to other members of his family than anything else.[14] At the most it might indicate that he learned to repeat

> A was an Archer, who shot at a frog
> B was a butcher, who kept a big dog

and that his father was pleased with him.

Nor do we need to take his request to Mrs. Frémont to read a poem to him, because she could read it so much faster than he could, as proof that he could read. The request was obviously that of a person who had been puzzling over a picture, and whose interest was aroused to know more about it. The truth is that Carson was ashamed of his inability to read, and did not want to confess outright to a woman that he could not do it. Mrs. Frémont was kind enough not only to read to him, but also to preserve his face-saving pretense that he could read slowly. Similarly, he told Albert Richardson that he had looked into his biography by Peters here and there, but had not read it.[15]

Literacy is not a measure of intelligence, and Carson's comments to Mrs. Frémont upon the things she read to him indicate an active and thoughtful mind. "The stag at eve had drunk his fill" evoked pleasant memories in a hunter like Carson; "Mazeppa's Ride" had great appeal to a man, who had spent most of his life on horseback. He responded with approval to the equalitarian sentiment of "a man's a man for a' that," as might have been expected.[16] His pleasure in listening to a reader is convincing proof that he could not read for himself without being

13 Quoted in Blackwelder, *Great Westerner,* 15.

14 Estergren, *Kit Carson,* 21. Both Blackwelder and Estergren credit Carson with more literacy than I have been able to find evidence to support. There is too much testimony to the contrary from those who knew him in adult life. The necessity of employing a clerk proves he could not write, and if he ever had learned to read, which is doubtful, he had forgotten how from long disuse.

15 Richardson, *Beyond the Mississippi.*

16 Jessie Benton Frémont, *The Will and the Way Stories* (Boston, 1891).

overwhelmed by words he could not recognize, which took all the pleasure out of it.

His oft-quoted comment on his biography by Dr. Peters, to the effect that Peters had "laid it on a leetle thick," is an indication that he had had parts of it, at least, read to him. Colonel Henry Inman's story of his having shown Carson a magazine, on the cover of which Kit was depicted in the act of saving a swooning female from an Indian attacker while dealing out death to her assailant, has a ring of truth to it. He said that Carson studied the picture intently (making no attempt to read it) and then handed it back with the comment, "That thar may be true but I haint got no recollection of it."[17]

This brings us to the question of Carson's mode of speech. Edgar L. Hewett wrote, on the authority of an interview with Jesse Nelson, who knew Carson well, that he spoke the everyday language that most westerners use today, and not the vernacular ascribed to frontiersmen by writers who never saw one.[18] Now it is undoubtedly true that by the time Nelson got to know Kit, which was about 1850, he no longer used the peculiar slang of the Mountain Men—that delightful idiom reported in the works of Garrard and Ruxton. The day of the trapper was past, and Kit had learned a few phrases of the typical army officer's vocabulary from his association with Frémont, Beale, and many others. This source of new words is plainly evident in his memoirs, where he uses words like "impracticable" and "execution" and speaks of "gallant" and "noble-souled" officers.

Nevertheless, I believe Hewett misunderstood Nelson's meaning, which I take to be that Kit talked much like Nelson did himself. Both men were born in Madison County, Kentucky, and I think there is little doubt that they spoke in the vernacular of the southern backwoods country people. They said "thar" and "whar" and "hyar"

17
Henry Inman, *The Old Santa Fe Trail* (New York and London, 1898), 301.

18
Estergreen, *Kit Carson,* xviii. Hewett contributed the introduction to this biography.

and "baar." They said "fit" for fought and "done" for did. For my part, I feel it is regrettable that Carson's amanuensis did not write his memoirs just as he spoke. It would have made an interesting document, with a mingled vocabulary and with Kit, no doubt, floundering around and correcting himself now and then. It is somewhat ungrammatical and involved as it stands, but the writer was a good speller and was rapid enough in his writing so that, with Kit's slow speech, he was able to clarify expression, to some extent, as he went along.

We are told that about 1850 "his language was forcible, slow, and pointed, using the fewest words possible. He talked but little, was very quiet, and seldom used immoral or profane language; sometimes when greatly excited he would swear, but not generally . . . ."[19]

Tom Tobin told Edgar Hewett, "Kit never swore more'n was necessary,"[20] which was putting it admirably and accurately. James F. Rusling gave an account of Kit's expression of opinion about the Sand Creek Massacre of 1864, which he heard Carson deliver at Fort Garland two years after the event. It is an interesting sample of his language as well as his feelings. One can almost hear him saying it:

> To think of that dog Chivington, and his hounds, up thar at Sand Creek! Whoever heerd of sich doings among Christians! The pore Injuns had our flag flyin' over 'em, that same old stars and stripes that we all love and honor, and they'd bin told down to Denver, that so long as they kept that flyin' they'd be safe. Well, then here come along that durned Chivington and his cusses. They'd bin out huntin' hostile Injuns, and couldn't find none no whar, and if they had, they'd run from them, you bet! So they just pitched into these friendlies, and massa-*creed* them—yes, sir, literally massa-*creed* them in cold blood, in spite of our flag thar—women and little children even. . . . And ye call

19 Elias Brevoort, "The Santa Fe Trail" (Manuscript, The Bancroft Library, Berkeley, California) (1884).

20 Estergren, *Kit Carson,* xx.

> *these* civilized men—Christians; and the Injuns savages, du ye?
>
> I tell ye what; I don't like a hostile Red Skin any better than you du. And when they are hostile, I've fit 'em—fout em'—as hard as any man. But I never yit drew a bead on a squaw or papoose, and I loathe and hate the man who would. 'Taint nateral for brave men to kill women and little children, and no one but a coward or a dog would do it. Of course, when we white men du sich awful things, why, these pore ignorant critters don't know no better, than to follow suit. Pore things! I've seen as much of 'em as any white man livin', and I can't help but pity 'em. They'll all soon be gone, anyhow.[21]

Rusling may not have been able to reproduce Carson's exact words as they were spoken, but I think there can be no doubt that he came close to it. Rusling differs from most others who knew Kit in saying that he had expected to find him reticent and found him talkative. Carson may have become more talkative with increasing years, or he may have felt more at home at Fort Garland, entertaining Sherman, with whom he felt at ease, or being in command of the post may have given him added confidence.

It is clear that he did not customarily relate his own experiences, especially to strangers. Richardson, who was a skilled interviewer, managed to get a few stories of his trapping days from Kit in 1859, as they ate and smoked cigars halfway between Santa Fe and Taos. James F. Meline, who spent three days with him in Santa Fe in 1866, said that he had to be drawn out, but once he was persuaded to talk, Meline found him delightful. One of the stories he got from Carson was one that Richardson had heard from him, too. He told how he had been fooled by an Indian at whom the dogs had barked because he saw the Indian snap at the dog like a wolf. The thing that convinced him was that he heard the

21 Rusling, *Across America*, 137–38.

click of the teeth in the snap. But the wolf impersonator produced this effect with a pair of buffalo rib-bones which he clicked together.[22]

22 James F. Meline, *Two Thousand Miles on Horseback* (New York, 1867), 246–51; Richardson, *Beyond the Mississippi,* 258. Meline reported the story with greater accuracy.

We may conclude that Carson was a slow talker and not a ready one, but that when the circumstances were right he could be very good company. Carson was acutely aware of his lack of education, and this made him reluctant to talk until he was certain that his lack of polish made no difference to his listener.

A subject related to Carson's use of the English language is his ability to speak other languages. He came to New Mexico when he was young enough to learn Spanish as it was spoken there, using it with greater facility than most of the older trappers and traders. This accounts for his employment as an interpreter after a little more than a year of residence. Of course his wife spoke in Spanish, and it was natural for him to adopt it as the preferred language within his family circle. Since he had somewhat more occasion to use it in Taos than he had opportunity to use English, he actually became more fluent in Spanish than in his native tongue. He sometimes used Spanish terms when speaking English.

It is a matter of record that he knew several Indian languages also. This does not mean that he knew any of them extensively. It means that he had a working vocabulary in the Navaho, Apache, Comanche, Cheyenne, Arapaho, Crow, Blackfoot, Shoshone, Piute, and Ute languages, which, when combined with the universal sign language known to the trappers and used by all the Indians, enabled him to converse with these tribes very readily. He probably knew at least some words of other tribal tongues, although it is doubtful whether he knew much of the speech of the Sioux. This accomplishment enabled him to understand that the Cheyennes were planning to kill him on one occasion. They did not recognize him and talked about it among themselves, not realizing that he could understand them. This knowledge of languages was a great asset to him as an Indian agent, of course, and a convenience at all times on his many journeys, to say the least.[23]

Somewhat related, too, is the fact that he had a retentive and reliable memory. I have found that his memoirs are more accurate than most reminiscences. It is true that he confined himself to essential facts and did not stray off the subject or get lost in a maze of detail. It is true also that not as much time had elapsed since the occurrences he was narrating as was the case with many other persons. But it should also be remembered that since he was illiterate, he had nothing to depend upon except his memory. I believe that his honesty supplemented his memory, for he seldom deviated to any great degree in the way he related events.[24]

Carson did make some mistakes in chronology. The worst of these occur in the years 1835–40. It will be noted that they occur right after he finished relating the story of his duel. We are told, on good authority, that he could never tell this story without getting very angry all over again.[25] I believe, therefore, that it was his emotional state that confused his narration of the five years following the duel. Some of the events that he remembered later, after his thinking straightened out a little, he dated 1839 instead of 1835. It is almost as if he realized that he had made some mistakes, but did not want to trouble his writer to make corrections. He may have thought that it would not make any difference, since few people could say whether it was accurate or not.

Aside from this, his memory was excellent. In several cases, he errs a few days in giving an exact date, but often he is precise. His ability to recall the name and rank of the many officers with whom he served is nothing short of amaz-

23
Rusling, *Across America*, 137, and Richardson, *Beyond the Mississippi*, 260, both speak of his language abilities.

24
This point can be verified by comparing the events of his 1847 reminiscence, as given in Appendix B, with the same events as they are related in his memoirs in 1856.

25
Both Mrs. Fremont and Smith H. Simpson observed that this was true.

ing. There is no instance where I have found him in error; he always gave the rank correctly for the period in which he knew the officer.

In recalling his trapping days, he sometimes refers to an associate whose name he has forgotten. In general, he does not mention many of the trappers, except for those who were his employers or leaders. It is my belief that he did not realize the interest people had, and still have, in the activities of the fur traders, and did not think it was especially important to supply names. What a pity it is that he did not have someone taking down his story who would have questioned him and jogged his memory, as Mrs. Victor did with Joe Meek. As General Meline observed, Carson needed to be drawn out.

In two instances Kit remembered to settle a score in his memoirs. One of them he had kept in mind for five years; the other was of very recent origin. In the first case, Carson said very plainly what he thought of Colonel Edwin V. Sumner for failing to send aid to him, against a threatened attack by the Cheyennes, in response to his urgent request. Incidentally, he displayed a talent for sarcasm while, at the same time, he neatly exposed Sumner's motive in sending aid after others had already done so. In the other instance, Carson did not mention his target by name, but he directed some well-aimed shafts at Governor David Meriwether, who had suspended him as Indian agent in 1856. Upon thinking it over, Kit evidently felt that he had been out of line and had apologized to the Governor and been reinstated. Consequently, there is nothing personal in his memoirs about the Governor, who, while he was superintendent of Indian affairs in New Mexico, was Kit's superior. However, Kit had not changed the views about Indian policy which had caused his arrest and suspension, so he took the opportunity to state his own ideas about the proper treatment of the

Powder Horn

Indians rather fully, and to criticize those of Meriwether.

Jessie Frémont said that she remembered hearing Kit say, concerning some unnamed person, "If I ever have a chance, I will do him an *honest* injury."[26] She liked the expression, and it seems to me that in these two instances he was able to act upon this principle. He also told her that he had waited three years to get even with the Blackfoot Indians for stealing a cache of his furs. Like Mrs. Frémont, I think it is a good principle; if some people did not follow it, those whose nature it is to take advantage of others would be entirely undeterred. Carson never took unfair advantage of anyone, so it was quite natural for him to resent such treatment at the hands of other people.

If we broaden our view of this principle of retaliation, we will find that it applies to Carson as an Indian fighter. All his fighting was against Indians who were on the warpath or were impeding his own course of action by some agressive action of their own. At least, that was the way he looked at the matter. Blackfeet, who prevented his trapping, Crows, who stole his horses, Diggers, who killed his companions, Klamaths, who attacked him by night, all had to be punished for their actions or they would do it again. Carson extended the principle for the benefit of others. He was willing to recover stolen property for them or fight a punitive war in their behalf against Indians who were hostile, or, in a few cases, against those whom he believed to have hostile intentions. If the fact that the white man was the original aggressor in his invasion of Indian territory is overlooked—and all whites of Carson's time did conveniently overlook it—then Carson's Indian fighting can be interpreted as defensive, retributory, and occasionally preventive, action. This was the way he interpreted it himself.

26
*The Prairie Farmer* (February 27, 1875).

He was not an Indian hater, as he is so often represented to have been.[27] His own statement regarding Chivington and Sand Creek makes this clear. To peaceable Indians, he was an understanding and sympathetic friend. The Indians themselves understood this. They considered it a fair attitude which made him a good Agent, in their estimation. He did not agree with General Carleton's plan to transplant the Navahos to the Bosque Redondo, nor did he fully approve or fully carry out the orders to kill all Navaho males able to bear arms. His attitude toward Indians was much the same as it was toward anyone else. He never started a fight with them and never failed to take up a fight that they had started.[28] The world would be a better place if all human beings were so constituted.

27 Lucius Beebe and Charles Clegg, *The American West* (New York, 1955), 11–13, begin their popular picture book with the statement that "Kit was a notable hater of Indians . . . Nothing made the day for Carson like killing an Indian or two before breakfast and he did it regularly." A picture is captioned, "Kit Carson admired an Indian for breakfast any time." Nothing could be farther from the truth. These writers may be notable for their mishandling of that precious commodity, but the opinion of Carson they present is a rather common one.

28 The sole exception was his duel with Shunar, and even there, a general challenge had been issued and Carson took it up. He referred to it as the only fight he ever engaged in on his own account.

Carson was essentially a man of action. Few people have lived such a strenuous life as he did from start to finish. To be sure, he enjoyed some repose now and then, and he was not insensible to the comforts of home. He appreciated the fact that his first Indian wife always had a kettle of warm water ready for him to soak his feet in, when he came in from a hunt. He played contentedly with his children, and called Josefa, his Mexican wife, by the pet name of Chipita. But a sedentary life had no great appeal for him, even in his later years. If there was any action going on, he got into it. A break in the action was welcome, and he chafed when—as in the long Navaho campaign—he could not get it. But after a few days at home, the idleness began to seem less attractive, and he was restless for action again.

Few people, even among the Mountain Men or the army officers of his day, ever spent more time on horseback (or muleback) than Carson. The miles he traveled are impossible to compute. The travel he engaged in was not only strenuous but also often fraught with danger. His fights were skirmishes, for the most part, but they were innumerable, and often the action was hand to hand.

Carson told Albert Richardson in 1859 that as a young man he had been reckless and daring, but that he had learned to exercise great vigilance because he had seen so many men killed through their own carelessness.[29] No truer statement could be made. Kit was naturally inclined to be hot-headed in a fight. This is evident from his memoirs, where his inclination is always for immediate action in the early days. " I proposed to charge them" is a phrase he uses more than once. Even during his years with Frémont, when he had learned caution so well that he condemned Godey for needlessly risking his life by stepping into the firelight, sometimes he reverted to his former impetuous disregard of such considerations. Shortly after his criticism of Godey, he led a charge across a stream against an Indian village, that might have ended disastrously had Frémont not come up with the rest of the party. What is more, he was so excited by this battle that he failed to recognize his mistake. In recounting it in his memoirs, he says that Frémont came up only after the action was finished.

Frémont describes Carson as "of great courage, quick and complete perception, evaluating chances of victory or defeat." But the record will show that his perception, though quick, was not always complete. Significantly, Frémont describes both Godey and Owens in somewhat different terms. Godey was "insensible to danger, had perfect coolness, and stubborn resolution." Owens was "equal in courage to both, and in coolness to Godey." It is notable that Frémont does not apply the word "coolness" to Carson.[30] Kit was not cool; he was excitable in the heat of battle, and, until he learned better, it affected his judgment.

This may have been the reason that Frémont made Owens captain of the First Company of

29
Richardson, *Beyond the Mississippi,* 258.

30
Frémont, *Memoirs,* 427.

the California Battalion and Godey his first lieutenant. Another reason may have been Carson's illiteracy. At any rate, Carson remained a private, although Frémont said that under Napoleon all three men would have become marshalls. This remark may tell us more about Frémont than about Carson, indicating, as it does, that Frémont thought of himself as a Napoleon. But we may conclude that Frémont considered Carson the Marshal Ney of his officers, "the bravest of the brave," but no strategist, and not even a very good tactician.

The fact is that there was no guile in Kit. He learned to guard against deception in others, but he never practiced it himself. He was as honest and straightforward in his fighting as he was in everything else.

Eventually, Kit did learn caution, if not coolness. Brewerton lays great stress upon his caution on the trail and in making camp. The culmination of his caution was at the battle of Adobe Walls, where his refusal to follow the wishes of his officers and resume the offensive probably saved his whole command from destruction. So great did his caution appear in later years that he was sometimes accused of cowardice. Such accusations were entirely untrue. Carson himself would have admitted that there had been an element of luck in his self-preservation and that he had decided, in later years, not to press his luck, but to be guided by common sense and experience.[31]

The one quality that seems to set Carson apart from most of the men with whom he was associated might be called his sense of duty. Even more than that, he was always willing to volunteer for things that were beyond the call of duty. Had he lived a century later, he would have been an Eagle Scout, and had he taught a Sunday School class, he would have called it the Willing Workers. Doing his best was a strong character-

31 Brevoort, "The Santa Fe Trail," (Manuscript, The Bancroft Library, Berkeley, California) (1884), tells us that Carson was superstitious about some things and mentions that he did not like to start any enterprise on a Friday. This was probably one more precaution taken because of his conviction that he had been lucky.

istic of Carson's, and he retained it all his life. The remarkable thing about it was that he seemed to have none of the self-complacency and priggishness that accompany this trait in most people. It was more noticeable after he began to work for Frémont, but since he was frequently among the vanguard of the trappers in their fights with the Blackfeet, I think it safe to say that it was an aspect of his character which developed very early. It is not strongly evident in other men of his family, nor among the trappers as a class.

Among Frémont's men, it was always Carson who was willing to ride to the head of the buffalo herd to pick off the best animals; it was Carson who would ride out to scout approaching Indians; it was Carson who rode to Fort Hall for food and brought it back to Salt Lake. When Frémont asked for volunteers to recover cattle which had been stolen from Mexicans by Indians, only Godey and Carson responded. Kit expected there would be others, but there were not, and he did not criticize those who held back.

It was Carson who was chosen for the arduous task of carrying the overland mail, and when, on his second trip, he learned that his commission had not been confirmed by the Senate, his sense of duty held him to the job. Campaigning with Philip St. George Cooke, the dragoons had to swim their horses back through the icy waters of the Río Grande to help the infantry get across, but Carson crossed and recrossed the rocky river twenty times. At San Pasqual, it was Carson, the scout who had no particular responsibility to be there, who was in the vanguard of the charge. The fact that he was thrown when his horse stumbled probably saved him from death or serious wounds at the hands of the Mexican lancers. But he was unharmed, and volunteered to accompany Beale when he crept through the enemy lines and walked thirty miles for rein-

Double Ox Yoke

forcements. The list of such actions could be extended; let us add only his last journey, when he was desperately ill, made largely out of a sense of responsibility for the Utes.

It was good Puritan doctrine, still much preached in the nineteenth century, that hard work was the sure road to success. Probably most men believed it, but most acted upon it only when they were working for themselves. Carson worked all his life for employers, public or private, in return for wages or a salary. Yet he worked harder than many men worked for themselves. That he was not simply bucking for a lieutenancy in the army, which he failed to get, is shown by the fact that he acted on this principle throughout his life, even when there was no visible advantage to be gained. We must conclude that it was simply not in his nature to be a slacker or shirker. Something inside him prompted him to give the best that he had to give.

There may be some significance in the fact that Carson lost his father when he was less than nine years old and that he ran away from home when he was fifteen. A psychologist might say that he ran away in search of his father.[32] A certain amount of support for such a view might be found in the fact that he definitely was not a rebel against society, as many runaways are said to be. His desire toward conformity was rather strong. Particularly, he seems to have wished to earn the approval and good opinion of those in authority. This desire is evident throughout his life, and may explain his readiness to perform beyond the ordinary standards that most men set for themselves. It certainly explains his marked success in all his connections with military officers.

Other Mountain Men served as scouts, but no others displayed the aptitude for this work that Carson did. Antoine Leroux, John L. Hatcher,

32 His mother had remarried and it was doubtless his stepfather who made the arrangement to apprentice Kit to the saddler. Kit gave his dislike of saddle-making and the lure of the West as his reasons for running away, and there is no reason to doubt his statement. The weakness in any psychological analysis lies in the long period between the time of his father's death and his own decision to leave home.

Antoine Robidoux, Thomas Fitzpatrick, Joseph Walker, Alexis Godey, Richard Owens, and Robert Fisher all did scouting that was satisfactory to the officers for whom they worked. However, none of them seems to have enjoyed it as much as Carson did, or to have stayed with it as long. None of them found in it an avenue to a later military career, even though some of them had a better start in that direction than Carson did.

Carson was connected, at certain points in his career, with several individuals from whom he learned a great deal. First among these was Ewing Young—at least fifteen years older than Kit— a man who always directed any company with which he was connected. From Young, Kit learned his first lessons of survival among the Indians, especially that Indians must never be allowed to get away unpunished for an attack on white trappers. Young, on his part, recognized Carson, the youngest member of his party, as the most trustworthy man that he had.[33]

Next, Carson certainly learned something from Jim Bridger, a man about five years his senior, who had directed large parties of trappers successfully for many years. Bridger possessed naturally that caution which Carson had to acquire. Perhaps Carson did not pattern himself after Bridger during his young manhood, but his experience as one of that astute leader's men stood him in good stead later, when he worked for Frémont.

Frémont was three years younger than Carson, but he possessed military authority. He was the boss with whom Kit could argue over what should be done and when, without its being resented. Sometimes Carson's advice was accepted, and when it was not, Kit did not resent it. Frémont represented a world with which Carson had no acquaintance. He liked Kit and appreciated his good qualities, and he let Kit know it.

33
Kenneth L. Holmes, *Ewing Young: Master Trapper* (Portland, 1967) is a fine biography of one of the greatest leaders of the fur trade, who has hitherto not received the attention he deserves.

He recognized that Kit was complete master of an environment that the government was trying to penetrate and understand. Frémont opened the way for Carson to bridge the gap between the West, where he was so much at ease, and the East, of which he had no knowledge. Without Frémont's aid, probably Carson could never have done this. With the aid of Frémont's favorable publicity, he was able to gain some recognition from that alien world of the East, with a minimum of adjustment on his own part. The East was ready to accept him for what Frémont said he was, which meant almost on his own terms.

Finally, there was General James H. Carleton, also about three years younger than Carson. Carleton was not only a man of military authority, but also an authoritarian personality. He was a sincere admirer of Carson, however, and he determined to make use of Carson's abilities as an Indian fighter while, at the same time, he undertook to mold him into an acceptable military officer. Such a program might have had unfortunate results, but because of the respect the two men had for each other, it worked out very well. Kit learned the essentials of military discipline under Carleton's firm but friendly hand when he was past the age of fifty. Carleton was a more difficult master than Frémont; he required that Kit conform to the values set by the army.[34] It is a measure of Carson's adaptability, as well as his desire for approval, that he came through the ordeal surprisingly well.

A very amusing story has been preserved which illustrates Carson's desire to conform to the standards of the world of polite society, of which he knew himself to be woefully ignorant. During his tour of inspection in 1866, General John Pope had with him an artist of the popular Hudson River school, Worthington Whitredge, who shared a room with Carson during Pope's

34 See Clarence G. Clendenen, "General James Henry Carleton," *New Mexico Historical Review*, Vol. XXX (January, 1955), 23–43, for an excellent analysis of Carleton and his relations with Carson.

stay in Santa Fe and recorded the story in these words:

> A great ball was to be given in honor of General Pope and his staff, and Carson was uneasy to know whether he should attempt to go there without a pair of pumps, an article he had heard of but didn't know what they were. He hated to ask any of the officers as to how he should dress and, finally applied to me, asking me to step aside for a little conversation. I told him that pumps were a sort of low shoe but that no army officer would think of wearing pumps at a ball, and that he must go in his boots. He was still so uncertain about it that he asked me if I would not go with him to a certain store in Santa Fe, where they kept everything, he said, and see if we could not find the desired article. I had little faith in finding pumps at any place in Santa Fe at that time, but I consented to go with him and after explaining to the storekeeper what pumps were, he ransacked the store and finally brought a pair of ladies's [sic] slippers, which he said had got into his stock by mistake. They were tried on, and fitted Carson perfectly, and he bought them at a high price. That evening when we all went to the ball Carson took me aside before starting and told me that he had the pumps with him and if he found when he got there, that the officers kept their boots on, he would not use them; if they all changed their boots, he would have his pumps ready to put on. The officers did not change their boots, but for a moment it was difficult for me to see where in the world in his tight fitting uniform, he had managed to secrete his slippers. On close inspection it was evident that he had buttoned one on each side of his breast until his figure was not unlike the figure of many of the handsome 'senoras' whirling in the waltz.[35]

35
"The Autobiography of Worthington Whitredge," edited by John I. H. Baur, *Brooklyn Museum Journal* (Brooklyn, 1942), 48–49.

Evidently Carson was strongly conscious of his lack of knowledge of the ways of society on the occasion of his first visit to Washington. It is also evident that he did not intend to be embarrassed by being out of keeping with the oc-

36 Victor, *River*, 439.

casion and prepared himself as well as possible to meet the situation.

Joe Meek's solution to the same problem was quite different from Carson's. Meek, on being sent to Washington as an emissary for the Oregon settlers, was troubled by the realization that he was an uncouth Mountain Man, who would be out of place in the capital. He resolved to make a virtue of necessity and to brazen it out, calling attention to the oddity of his manners and appearance in every way possible. "Joe Meek you are and Joe Meek you will remain," he told himself,"Go it, Joe Meek."[36] Meek's solution was satisfactory for him; he enjoyed attracting attention to himself as a curiosity from the West. Carson never even thought of such a solution. He wanted to be as inconspicuous as possible, to blend with the crowd and be no different from anyone else.

Many people have considered Carson a natural leader, but it is against all the facts to do so. He came to leadership only gradually, and only because others—notably Frémont and Carleton—trusted him with important assignments and he was not the man to let them down. He frequently referred to his trapping days as the happiest days of his life. This was because they were carefree days, with no responsibility of leadership.

It cannot be too strongly emphasized that Carson was never a leader among the trappers. He did not command the men among whom he fought the Blackfeet, as Dr. Peters wrote in his biography. He never had his own band of trappers, as so many writers, following the tales of Oliver Wiggins, have assured us that he did. Frémont was entirely correct when he wrote, on the occasion of his selecting Carson to carry dispatches to Washington, "Going off, at the head of his own party with *carte blanche* for expenses and the prospect of novel pleasure and honor at the end was a culminating point in Carson's life."[37] It was the first time Carson had commanded a party of his own, and as such, it was the culminating point in 1847. Actually it was only the beginning, for Carson had many commands of his own after that time.

It cannot be said that Carson shrank from leadership or that he ever failed to live up to expectations in that respect. But he did not avidly seek it, he was not a natural leader, and he found the responsibility wearisome enough that he was glad to look back on his trapping days as the happiest time of his career.

This brings us to what I consider to be Carson's outstanding trait and his greatest asset, namely, his simplicity and modesty. Meek could make a display of himself because it was natural for him. For Carson, it would have been completely foreign to his nature.

Meline, talking to Carson in Santa Fe in 1866, was struck by his simplicity and his candor. If he did not know the answer to a question, he said so. He freely admitted that a good many of the Ute Indians were better rifle shots than he was. He told stories of how he had been deceived by the Indians more often than he told stories that demonstrated his own prowess. He said he had killed a grizzly weighing twelve hundred pounds, but that Lieutenant Beale had told him of a much larger one.[38]

Carson disliked loud-mouthed boasters and braggarts. He himself was given to understatement in talking about his own adventures. Richardson said of him, "He is a gentleman by instinct; upright, pure, and simple-hearted, beloved alike by Indians, Mexicans, and Americans."[39]

Carson admired simple bravery in others. In his memoirs, he praised the unnamed Mexican, who proposed that Carson should leave him alone to face a party of Indians. Carson stayed with him and they faced the Indians together.

37
Frémont, *Memoirs,* 567.

38
Meline, *Two Thousand Miles,* 247–49.

39
Richardson, *Beyond the Mississippi,* 261. The good will of Indians, Mexicans, and Americans was held by very few men. Possibly William Bent and Céran St. Vrain could qualify for such a compliment, but, I think, not to the extent that Carson could.

Of one California Indian he said, "He was a brave man and deserved a better fate but he took the wrong path." In glowing terms he stated his admiration for Captain Sykes of the Infantry, who shared all the hardships of his men. Even though Philip St. George Cooke had testified against Frémont at the court-martial, Carson recognized in that officer a real soldier, when he scouted for him later, and he said so.[40]

It is perhaps a remarkable thing that Carson seems to have been absolutely unspoiled by the national publicity and adulation he received.[41] Few people can be so much in the public eye without becoming self-important. It may be that his illiteracy saved him; had he been able to read all that was said about him, he might have begun to believe it. But I think that his own inherent modesty probably counteracted the heady wine of public acclaim. After all, he was aware of the fact that he had become a national hero, even if he could not read all about it in detail. He seemed simply to accept it as a fact, and not to let it make any particular difference in his life.

I find the most revealing example of this to be the record of his feelings about the attempted rescue of Mrs. White, which failed, through no fault of his own. He felt that Mrs. White had been expecting him to come to her aid because she was aware of his reputation. He accepted it as perfectly natural that this should have been the case, and his only regret was that he had been unable to justify her supposed expectations. There is something truly fine in Carson's simple acceptance of the responsibility of living up to the reputation with which he had been endowed in the public mind. It is strongly reminiscent of the story told of Louis de Crillon, the simple and illiterate but inordinately brave soldier of sixteenth-century France, who, upon hearing the events of the Passion of Jesus related in church, sprang to his feet with tears streaming down his

40 Colonel Cooke also thought highly of Carson and wrote of him in these words, "Kit Carson, who has been in the mountains for 30 years and who is justly celebrated as being the best tracker among the white men in the *world,* says that in all his experience he never saw such wonderful trailing in his life as was made on this campaign by Captain Quinn and his Mexican and Indian spies and he willingly admitted that these men had kept on the track when he himself would have given up. . . ." Quoted in Hamilton Gardner, "Philip St. George Cook and the Apache, 1854," *New Mexico Historical Review,* Vol. XXVIII (April, 1953), 115–32.

41 Describing Frémont's men as they rode through the streets of Monterey, after the Americans had taken over the California capital, a British naval officer wrote, "Kit Carson is as well known there [on the prairies] as the Duke is in Europe." The Hon. Frederick Walpole, R. N., *Four Years in the Pacific in Her Majesties Ship Collingwood, 1844–1848,* II (London, 1849), 216. It is fairly safe to say that neither of the famous men mentioned in this remark had ever heard of the other, so probably neither Carson or Wellington would have been flattered by the comparison.

Another young Englishman recently settled in the United States, John Minto, was on his way to Oregon on August 30, 1844, when he met a stranger near Fort Bridger, whom he afterward identified, "from photos," as Kit Carson. Minto's imagination was working overtime, since Carson was in Taos, at this date, having recently returned from Frémont's second expedition. No photographs

face and sword unsheathed and cried out, "Where were you when you were needed, brave Crillon, where were you when they nailed Him to the cross?"

It is, without much question, Carson's simplicity and modesty that have kept him a national hero beyond his own time. Frémont, as Emerson noted upon reading his *Reports*, was very concerned about "the picture" that he made —or, as the wordmongers of a later day would have said, "his image." Emerson thought the real problems of survival in the Far West ought to have been enough to suppress "this eternal vanity of how we look."[42] Carson would have agreed with Emerson. He would have said that it is not what a man seems to be but what he is that matters.

Two questions arise with reference to Carson. First, was he typical of his kind; and second, was he overrated? The answer to both of these questions has to be both yes and no.

In one sense, Carson was typical of the Mountain Men—of the frontiersmen of his time. He was typical in the sense that he spent his life on the frontier as most of them did; he mastered that difficult environment as many of them did; he had the experiences common to most of them. If we are to choose someone to represent these men, as a class, he is as typical a man as could be found, although no more so than a dozen others.[43]

On the other hand, Carson was far from typical in his inner attributes. In some aspects of his character, as noted above, he was almost unique. Also, he was not typical of the Mountain Men because he displayed greater adaptability to the changes brought by the passing of the fur trade than did most of his associates.

It must be admitted that Carson was overrated in some respects. No one could have been the superman that the novelists represented him

of Carson existed at the time, so Minto's conclusion was reached some years after the event. Minto also saw a part-Indian woman packing goods on two fine mules and concluded that this was Carson's Mexican wife. The final absurdity was that they were buying plow irons, so Minto reasoned that they had come to Fort Bridger for that purpose, and were preparing to return to "Toas." His story is repeated here as an illustration of the power of Carson's fame upon the imagination of others, and because, despite its absurdity, it has been accepted as true by some writers. See John Minto, "Reminiscences," *Oregon Historical Quarterly*, II (1901), 165–66.

42
Quoted in Bernard DeVoto, *The Year of Decision, 1846* (Boston, 1943), 196.

43
Allan Nevins, "Kit Carson Bayard of the Plains," *The American Scholar*, Vol. VIII (Summer, 1939), 333–49, says that Boone and Carson have been singled out not because they were greater, but because they were more typical.

to be. Even his biographers tended to make him out to be better than he was. He was overrated, too, in the sense that he received nearly all the public attention, to the exclusion of many other frontiersmen who had notable careers and deserved a measure of fame.[44]

In respect to his actual exploits and his actual character, however, Carson was not overrated. If history has to single out one person from among the Mountain Men to receive the admiration of later generations, Carson is the best choice. He had more of the good qualities and fewer of the bad qualities than anyone else in that varied lot of individuals who possessed in common their following of the fur trade as a way of life. There are many men whose deeds could be compared with his, but there are none who could have worn their laurels so lightly, so gracefully, and so well.

It is difficult to point out any very grievous faults in Carson's life or defects in his character. He fought Indians on a retaliatory principle, but he did so in the belief that this was necessary in order to ensure the safety of white men traveling in the Indian country. This belief was commonly held at the time and it is hard for later generations to contradict it. Carson was caught napping at Klamath Lake, but it was Frémont's responsibility to post a guard and he failed to do so. Carson was condemned, even by friends, for shooting three Mexican prisoners south of Sonoma, but his explanation that he did it upon Frémont's orders has not been disproved; in fact, it was substantiated by an eyewitness account of the incident. In the same way, Carson has been blamed for the Navaho campaign, but he was merely carrying out General Carleton's orders. He acted in an insubordinate manner to Governor Meriwether, but apologized for it next day, and the Governor's charge of cowardice would have been unbelievable to most people.

44
A. J. Noyes, *In the Land of the Chinook* (Helena, 1917), 88, quotes a Montana pioneer, Bill Bent, as having concluded that Carson was overrated. Incidentally, it is doubtful that this Bent was the son of William Bent, of Bent's Fort, as he claimed, and even if he was, Carson was not his "Uncle Kit."

45
"Reminiscences of Kit Carson, Jr.," edited by A. B. Sanford, *Colorado Magazine,* Vol. VI (September, 1929), 180–81. The boy was called Juan Carson. A picture of him is in the Colorado State Historical Society Library, Denver, Colorado.

*Carson house and museum, Taos, New Mexico.* (Courtesy of Kit Carson Museum) *See page 237.*

Carson sold an Indian boy to Sutter at the rendezvous of 1838, and bought one at Utah Lake when he was returning on Frémont's second expedition. We do not know what circumstances these slaves were in before he acquired them, however, and it is possible that he saved them from death or, at least, from a less desirable existence. Moreover Negro slavery was legal in the United States at the time, and Carson had a slave-state background. When Josefa traded a horse to the Utes for a Navaho captive because they threatened to kill him, Kit gave him his own name and provided for him until his marriage to a Mexican girl.[45]

Carson gave little thought to making provision for his family until it was too late. But he had always earned a good living for them. It is doubtful that he had enough business ability to have done any better financially for himself and his family than he did by his military and government service. He was unfortunate in not receiving a regular army commission, which would have entitled him to retirement pay.

His personal habits were better than those of most men in his walk of life. He drank very little and gambled at poker and seven-up only for small stakes. All in all, Carson must be given a pretty clean slate.

One more question must be dealt with in evaluating Kit Carson. Some readers will be willing to accord him a place as a national hero but will deny that he had any great historical importance. It seems to me that only by taking a narrow view of history can such a position be maintained. Certainly Carson was never a policy maker, a man whose decisions swayed the fate of nations. In history as the record of politics and diplomacy, he had no part. But in the realm of action, his part was considerable. Though his roles were minor and subordinate ones, he played them well, and the drama in which he participated was the great one of national expansion. He came into contact with the great men of his time —the principal actors in the drama—and not only did he impress most of them favorably, but his own fame has outshone theirs.

If a bill of particulars is necessary, it can be produced. Although Carson was never a leader in the fur trade, he was a member of the vanguard of whites in the Far West, a notable thing in itself. If Frémont's mapping of the Far West was a notable contribution to human knowledge, it is well to remember that Carson guided him over the country that was mapped. If Frémont's presence in California at the outbreak of the Mexican War had historical significance, then Carson had his share in that significance. If it was important for the government to know what was taking place in California, then the dispatch bearer who kept them informed had some importance of his own. If the preservation of New

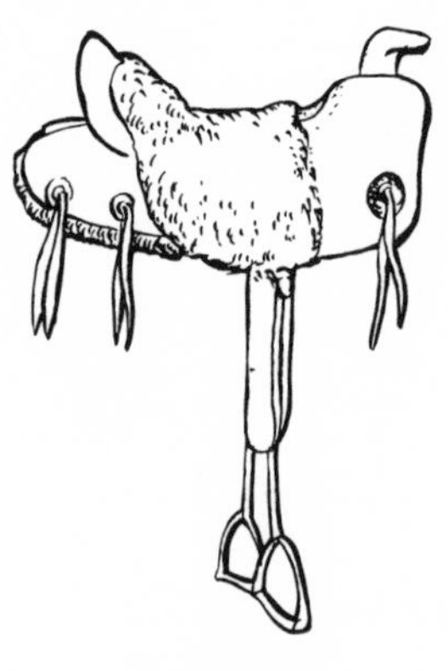

Saddle

Mexico to the Union during the Civil War was valuable, then Carson deserves a share of the credit for preserving it. If the issue of dealing with the Indians of the West was a vital one, then Carson was one of the most vital agents in that policy, whether in peace or in war. Finally, if the whole concept known as Manifest Destiny had any validity, Kit Carson was perhaps the best exemplar of it, all the more so because he was not a conscious but an unconscious agent of the concept.

It is not surprising to find Carson's name perpetuated on the map of the United States, in view of his extensive travels in the Far West. A pass in California, a river, a lake, and a sink in Nevada, as well as that state's capital city; a county in Colorado; and a national forest in New Mexico bear his name.[46] Fort Carson, a large army post near Colorado Springs, Colorado, was named in his honor at the time of World War II, in which, as in the first World War, some of his descendants participated.[47]

Two fine equestrian statues commemorate Carson's fame. The first of these stands in Trinidad, Colorado. Lukeman and Roth were the sculptors. The second, by MacMonnies, graces the pedestal of a large pioneer monument in the Civic Center of Denver, Colorado. There is a Kit Carson Museum in Taos.

Will Rogers said that he never met a man he didn't like. It could be said of Kit Carson that he never met a man who did not like him. This may be a slight exaggeration, but certainly those who disliked him were very few. Other frontiersmen may not have understood why Carson became so famous. They were often asked whether or not they knew him. They always said they knew him well, but they seldom told anything about him. None spoke in disparagement of Kit; they just resumed the story of their own adventures. It is my belief that they considered him to be

46
The list could be extended and is not meant to be inclusive.

47
In 1956, I heard Zebulon Pike, Jr., relate that he and Kit Carson were both in training at Camp Carson (now Fort Carson) and that they began to enjoy themselves when they discovered that certain officers thought they were trying to be provoking when they gave their true names—only to find out later that the names were perfectly in order. There were two Kit Carsons in World War II, one the grandson and the other the great-grandson of the original Kit. The latter did not survive the war.

The only Carson descendant whom I have had the pleasure of knowing is Kit Carson, eldest son of the original Kit's eldest son William, and father of the Kit who died in World War II. He bears some resemblance in face, voice, and temperament to his famous grandfather, although he is slighter in build. Several years ago he gave a talk to the Historical Society of the Pikes Peak Region, but when I invited him to speak to my college class in western history, he courteously refused, saying that a person of no education like himself had no business speaking in a college. He is still living in Alamosa, Colorado, at the age of eighty-four, as this is written.

just a very ordinary nice guy, and that they never quite figured out how he rose to the top. Nice guys are supposed to finish last, whether in the cutthroat world of the fur trade or of the modern corporation or university.

Bill Bent was a hard-driving business man, as Carson was not. Bent had little love for the federal government and its regulations, whereas Carson had worked for it, regulations, and all, for a good part of his life. One evening, in 1864 or 1865, Carson rode up to Bent's ranch on the Purgatoire, with some Indians. An eyewitness recalled that "Bill Bent pulled Kit off his horse and they hugged and kissed like a couple of children."[48]

Frémont, with his love for French history, called Carson "the Bayard of the Plains." It was a high compliment and not altogether inappropriate. Frémont said on one occasion, "Mounted on a fine horse, without a saddle, and scouring bareheaded over the prairies, Kit was one of the finest pictures of a horseman I have ever seen."[49] On another occasion, he said, "With me, Carson and Truth are one." In calling Kit "the Bayard of the Plains" he was really combining his two observations by comparing him with the famous French Chevalier, who was said to have been "without fear and without reproach."

The title of "The Nestor of the Rocky Mountains" used by Peters in the title of the original edition of Carson's biography was less appropriate. There were a good many older frontiersmen than Kit and a good many that were more talkative and inclined to give advice. It may have been justified in the circumstances under which Peters knew Carson, but it can more properly be applied to Old Bill Williams.

Brewerton called Kit "one of Dame Nature's gentlemen." Rusling thought him "as simple as a child but as brave as a lion." Sherman said, "These redskins think Kit twice as big a man as

48 F. W. Cragin Papers, Notebook XXVII, 22. Cragin's informant was Asa F. Middaugh in an interview at Denver, Colorado, in November, 1903. Middaugh placed the incident in 1864, but it was more probably in 1865, when Carson is known to have been in that vicinity.

49 Frémont, *Narrative,* 9. "A gentle knight was pricking on the plain" is the line that comes to mind.

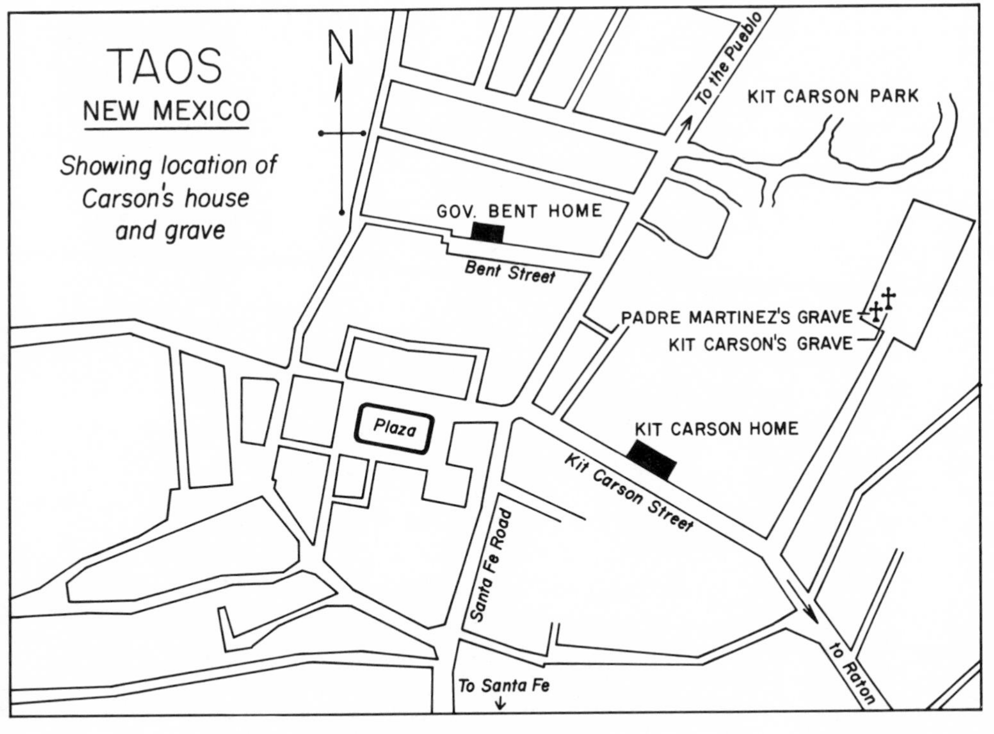


*Diagram of Taos, showing location of Carson house and grave.*
(Courtesy of Blair Galleries, Ltd.) *See page 238.*

me—why, his integrity is simply perfect." Edwin L. Sabin put it extremely well when he wrote, "Kit Carson was not a great man, nor a brilliant man. He was a great character; and if it was not his to scintillate, nevertheless he shone with a constant light."[50]

There were two persons who had known him very well who thought of his passing in a more personal way and expressed their feelings in almost poetic language. Edward Fitzgerald Beale, who had shared tremendous dangers and hardships with Carson, wrote in 1870, "Dear old Kit, O wise of counsel, strong of fame, brave of heart and gentle of nature."[51]

Jessie Benton Frémont liked Carson immensely and took the trouble to get a little closer to his thoughts than any one else. When Carson had his feelings hurt by a man of high position in Washington, he told her about it in these words. "Who would have thought it of him, such a fair looking gentleman, too. They are great men here—princes in their way—but when they come out to the plains, we are the princes; and they could not live without us."[52] It was the sentiment of an old-fashioned American, a self-reliant man.

Jessie Frémont felt Carson's passing from the scene no less keenly than Beale, and expressed herself fully as well. To her, let us give the last word. She wrote, in 1877, nearly ten years after his death, " . . . all who knew Carson best, when they hear him spoken of, will not think of him only as the brave man, or the great hunter, or the cool, sagacious, admirable guide, but first and tenderly as their 'Dear old Kit.' "[53]

50 Sabin, *Kit Carson Days* (1914), 503.

51 Quoted in W. J. Ghent, "Kit Carson," *Dictionary of American Biography,* III (New York, 1939), 530–32.

52 From an unsigned article entitled "Kit Carson," which appeared originally in the *New York Ledger* and was reprinted in *The Prairie Farmer* (February 27, 1875), from which this quotation is taken. Mrs. Frémont is clearly the author.

53 "Kit Carson," *The New York Ledger,* cited in *The Prairie Farmer* (February 27, 1875).

# Appendix A
## *A Chronology of Kit Carson's Life*

THIS CHRONOLOGY HAS BEEN PREPARED in order to enable the reader to follow more easily the revisions made where Carson's sequence of events is in error during his years as a trapper, and also to serve as a convenient reference for events of his entire life.

1809 Born in Madison County, Kentucky, December 24.

1811 Moved with his parents to Boon's Lick, Howard County, Missouri.

1818 Death of his father, Lindsey Carson.

1824 Apprenticed to David Workman, saddler, Old Franklin, Missouri.

1826 Ran away and joined a wagon train at Fort Osage, Missouri, headed for Santa Fe, in August.

1826–27 Wintered with Matthew Kinkead in Taos.

1827 Started to return home but met a party on the Arkansas River and returned with it to Santa Fe. Hired as teamster and went to El Paso and back to Taos

1827–28 Cooked for Ewing Young during the winter.

1828 Started home, but repeated action of previous year. Went with Philip Trammell, as interpreter, to Chihuahua. Worked for Robert McKnight at copper mines. Returned to Taos in August.

1829 Joined Ewing Young's trapping party in August. Trapped Arizona streams and then headed for California. Trapped San Joaquin Valley.

1830 Trapped Sacramento Valley and summered there, leaving September 1, for Los Angeles. Trapped Colorado River and Arizona streams during winter.

1831 Arrived back at Taos with Ewing Young in April. Joined Thomas Fitzpatrick in the fall and headed north. Wintered on Salmon River in Idaho.

1832 Trapped south to Green River with Fitzpatrick, starting in April. Left Fitzpatrick there and joined John Gantt in North Park.

1832–33 Wintered on Arkansas River near Pueblo, Colorado. Fought the Crows and recovered horses near Colorado Springs, in January.

1833 With Gantt to Laramie River in spring. Detached to chase thieving deserters to Arkansas River. Fought off Comanches south of the Arkansas. Rejoined Gantt in South Park. Left Gantt and trapped Colorado Mountains and returned to Taos in October. Joined Captain Richard Bland Lee and went to Fort Uinta.

1833–34 Wintered at Fort Uinta with Antoine Robidoux.

1834 In March, found Fitzpatrick on Little Snake River and worked for him one month. Became free trapper on Laramie River. Joined James Bridger and attended rendezvous on Green River. In September, went with Bridger to Three Forks of the Missouri

1834–35 Wintered on Snake River, November to February.

1835 Wounded in fight with Blackfeet in February. Spring hunt on Snake and Green Rivers with Bridger. Duel with Shunar at rendezvous on Green River. With Bridger to Henry's Fork on Snake River in September. Carson and thirteen other Bridger men joined Joseph Gale's party on Madison River and fought off Blackfeet. Returned to Snake River and joined Northwest (Hudson's Bay Company) for fall hunt on Malade and Raft Rivers.

1835–36 Wintered on Snake River near Fort Hall.

1836 With Alexis Godey, joined Thomas McKay of Hudson's Bay Company. Trapped down Humboldt River and returned, starving, to Fort Hall. Attended rendezvous on Green River. Married Waanibe? Rejoined Bridger for the fall hunt and trapped the Crow country.

1836–37 Wintered on Yellowstone at mouth of Clark's Fork. "Island fight" with Blackfeet and big fight averted on February 22.

1837 In spring, trapped Bighorn River and went through Crow and Bannock country to rendezvous on Green River. In fall, with large party under Lucien Fontenelle and Bridger, to Yellowstone River.

1837–38 Wintered on Powder River near Antonio Montero's Portuguese Houses, December, 1837 to April 1, 1838. Daughter Adaline born?

1838 Trapped up the Yellowstone and down the Gallatin with Fontenelle and Bridger. Crossed to Madison River and fought "prettiest fight" with Blackfeet June 3, despite smallpox among them. Crossed Teton and Wind River Mountains to rendezvous on Popo Agie. In fall, went to Brown's Hole. Joined Philip Thompson and Prewitt Sinclair on trading trip to Navahos.

1838–39 Hunter for Fort Davy Crockett during winter.

1839 Trapped Black Hills (Laramie Mountains) for three months with Richard Owens. Returned to rendezvous on Green River. Arrived with Owens at Fort Davy Crockett on September 1. Owens joined horse thieves; Carson did not.

1839–40 Wintered at Fort Davy Crockett. Birth of second daughter?

1840 In spring, with John Robertson to Antoine Robidoux at Fort Uintah. Probably returned to rendezvous on Green River, where Father De Smet was present. In fall, trapped Grand River.

1840–41 Wintered at Fort Davy Crockett. Death of Waa-nibe?

1841 Spring hunt in New Park and Utah country. Summer at Fort Uintah. In September, traveled with five companions to Bent's Fort on Arkansas River.

1841–42 Hunter for Bent's Fort, September, 1841 to April, 1842. Baptised by Padre Martinez at Taos, January 28, 1842. Second Indian wife, Making-Out-Road. Divorced and took up with Antonina Luna.

1842 Went home to Missouri with Bent wagon train starting in April. Left Adaline with relatives. Went to St. Louis and met John C. Frémont on Missouri river steamer. June 10 to September 3, guided Frémont's first expedition.

1843 Reached Bent's Fort in January. On February 6, married Josefa Jaramillo in Taos. In April, with Bent and St. Vrain wagon train as hunter, but returned to Taos with message for Governor Armijo. To Bent's Fort and then rejoined Frémont July 21 at Fort St. Vrain.

1843–44 From July 21, 1843, to July 4, 1844, guided Frémont's second expedition to Salt Lake, over Oregon Trail to the Dallas, south to Klamath Lake and Pyramid Lake, across Sierras via Carson Pass in winter to Sutter's Fort, south to Oak Creek Pass and Mojave River, northeast via Vega of Santa Clara to Utah Lake, east to Fort Uinta, Brown's Hole, and North Park, south to Middle and South Parks, and southeast to Bent's Fort.

1844–45 At Taos, till March, 1845.

1845 Farmed on Little Cimarron with Owens till August, 1845. Rejoined Frémont at Bent's Fort for third expedition. Went across Rockies via Arkansas, Eagle, and White Rivers, to Salt Lake and across Nevada desert to Humboldt River and Walker's Lake and across the Sierras at Truckee Pass to Sutter's Fort.

1846 Frémont ordered from California in January. To Lassen's Ranch and on to Klamath Lake area, fought Indians, returned to Lassen's Ranch May 24. At Sonoma June 24, at Monterey in July, at San Diego and Los Angeles in August. Sent with dispatches to Washington September 5, met General Kearny at Socorro, New Mexico, October 6, and guided him to California. Fought at San Pasqual, carried message to Stockton in December.

1847 Sent by Frémont to Washington with dispatches, leaving Los Angeles February 25. Arrived back in Los Angeles in October. Military duty.

1848 On May 4, with Lieutenant Brewerton, sent with dispatches to Washington; reached Taos June 19, on to Washington with news of gold discovery and returned to Taos by October. Trading expedition for Bent to Adobe Walls in fall.

1849 In January, Frémont arrived at Carson's home in Taos from disastrous attempt to cross Rockies in winter. In February and March, guided for Colonel Beall. In April, started farming at Rayado. In November, guided Major Grier in effort to recover Mrs. White and child.

1849–50 Wintered in Taos.

1850 May 4, started to Fort Laramie with Tim Goodale. Returned in July to Taos. Went to Rayado and acted as detective to apprehend Fox in robbery on Santa Fe Trail.

1850–51 Wintered at Rayado.

1851 In March, went to Kansas City for Maxwell with wagon train. On return trip, threatened by Cheyennes but arrived safely at Rayado and wintered there.

1852 In March, started with eighteen men and trapped the Colorado Rockies.

1853 In February, bought sheep in the Río Abajo. In early March drove them to Sacramento, arriving on September 5. Visited friends and relatives in Russian River Valley. Returned via Los Angeles with Maxwell, arriving in Taos, December 25.

1854 In March, began duties as Indian agent. In April, guided for Colonel Philip St. George Cooke. In May and June, guided for Major Carleton. In October, council meeting concerning Indians. At home, in Taos, for the winter.

1855 In February, guided for Colonel T. T. Fauntleroy. Fought Indians at Saguache and Poncha Pass. Reached home in April.

1856 Worked as Indian agent and dictated memoirs. In September, met Indians at Abiquiu and had altercation with Governor David Meriwether.

1857 Reappointed as Indian agent. Made a hunt in the fall.

1858 Continued as Indian agent. Also employed keeping peace with the Cheyenne and Arapaho tribes and negotiating with the Navahos.

1859 Blanco attempted to kill Carson at his home, but was prevented from succeeding by Ka-ni-ache.

1860 Injured by a fall while hunting in the San Juan Mountains in October.

1861 Resigned as Indian agent in June. Became Colonel of New Mexico Volunteer Regiment in September. Drilling at Albuquerque.

1862 Participated in the battle of Valverde in February. At Fort Craig until September. Directed, from Fort Stanton, a fall campaign against Mescalero Apaches.

1863 Prepared for Navaho campaign, March to June. Conducted Navaho campaign, June to December.

1864 Concluded Navaho campaign in January. Visited Taos and returned to Fort Canby in April. Ordered to Fort Bascom in November, for campaign against Plains Indians. Battle of Adobe Walls, November 25.

1865 At Taos until May. Brevetted brigadier general of volunteers in March. At Camp Nichols, May to September. In fall, made a trip to St. Louis and probably to Washington.

1866 At Taos, Santa Fe, and Maxwell's Ranch until August. Appointed to command at Fort Garland and took charge in August. Entertained General Sherman there in September.

1867 Resigned from the army in July and was mustered out in November. Moved to Boggsville, Colorado, in the summer.

1868 Appointed superintendent of Indian affairs for Colorado Territory in January. Spent February and March in Washington and other eastern cities, negotiating treaty for the Utes and consulting physicians about his health. Arrived home, April 11. Wife died, April 23. Carson died, May 23, at Fort Lyon, Colorado. Buried at Boggsville.

1869 In late spring, remains of Carson and wife were removed to Taos and reinterred in cemetery there.

# Appendix B
## *An Early Account of Kit Carson of the West*

The following account originally appeared in the *Washington Union*, during the summer of 1847, and was reprinted in the *Supplement to the Connecticut Courant*, July 3, 1847. It is from the latter source that it is reproduced herewith. Obviously based on an interview with Carson, it is the earliest account purporting to give the facts of his earlier years. As such, it affords an interesting comparison and a reliable check on the account of those years which Carson gave, nine years later, in his memoirs. Insofar as can be ascertained, this account has not been reprinted in its entirety since 1847.

Kit Carson of the West

This name, within a few years, has become quite familiar to the public, mainly through his connection with the expeditions of Fremont, one of the best of those noble and original characters that have from time to time sprung up on and beyond our frontier, retreating with it to the West, and drawing from association with uncultivated nature not the rudeness and sensualism of the savage, but genuine simplicity and truthfulness of disposition, and generosity, bravery, and single-heartedness to a degree rarely found in society. Although Kit has only become known to the reading people of "the States" and of Europe through Fremont's reports, he was long ago famous in a world as extended, if not as populous; famous for excelling in all the qualities that life in the trackless and vast West requires and develops. He has been celebrated (though now aged only about 37 years) as a hunter, trapper, guide or pilot of the prairies, and Indian fighter, uniting to the necessary characteristics of that adventurous and sturdy class a kindness of heart and gentleness of manner that relieve it of any possible harshness or asperity. He is now in "the States," having recently arrived with despatches from California; and I have taken the opportunity to extract from him a few incidents of his eventful life.—He is worthy of an honorable and more extended memoir; and were his adventures fully written out they would possess an interest equal to any personal narrative whatever.

Christopher Carson was born in Kentucky, in the year 1810 or 1811, his father having been one of the early settlers, and also a noted hunter and Indian fighter. In the year following Kit's birth, the family removed, for the sake of more elbow room than the advancing population of Kentucky left them, to the territory of Missouri. On this frontier, bred to border life, Kit remained at the age of fifteen, when he joined a trading party to Santa Fe. This was his introduction to those vast plains that stretch beyond the state of Missouri. Instead of returning home, Kit found his way, by various adventures, South, through New Mexico, to the copper mines of Chihuahua, where he was employed some months as a teamster.

When about seventeen years old he made his first expedition as a trapper. This was with a party which had been induced by favorable accounts of fresh trapping grounds on the Rio Colorado of California to an adventure; so that Kit's first exploits were in the same remote and romantic region where, during the last year, he and all his comrades, with their commander, have earned imperishable honor. The enterprise was successful, and Kit relates many interesting anecdotes of the hardships of the wilderness and of the encounters of his party with the Indians.

The Mexican authorities and settlers in California, were even at that time jealous of the Americans, and threatened to seize this inoffensive and roving party of beaver catchers. They made good their return, however, to Taos, in Mexico; whence, soon after, Kit joined a trapping party to the head waters of the Arkansas, (likewise a region embraced, since the last published expedition, in the surveys of Col. Fremont.)—Without recrossing the prairies, Kit went Northward to the region of the Rocky Mountains that gives rise to the Missouri and Columbia rivers, and there remained near eight years, engaged in the then important occupation of trapping. The great demand for the beaver, and the consequent high prices at that time paid for the peltries, gave an additional stimulus to the adventurous spirit of the young men of the West, and drew nearly all who preferred the excitements and hazards of life in the wilderness to quieter pursuits, into the recesses of the Rocky Mountains. Here a peculiar class was formed; the elements, the sturdy, uncurbed character of the frontier; the circumstances that influenced and formed it, nature in her wildest, roughest, and grandest aspects—savages, both as associates and foes, of every cast, from the wretched root diggers to the vindictive Blackfeet and the courageous and warlike Crows—and a vocation of constant labor, privation and peril in every shape, yet of gains of a nature and degree to give it somewhat of the characteristics of gambling.*

The decrease of the beaver before a pursuit of the poor animal so ruthless as was thus stimulated, and the substitution of other commodities for the beaver fur, have left trapping scarcely worth following as a vocation; and the race of trappers has nearly disappeared from the mountain gorges where they built their rude lodges, where they set their traps for the wily beaver, where were their frequent combats with the savages and with wild beasts not less formidable. In the school of men thus formed by hardship, exposure, peril and temptation, our hero acquired all their virtues and escaped their vices. He became noted through the extent of the trapping grounds, and on both sides of the Rocky Mountains as a successful trapper, an unfailing shot, an unerring guide, and for bravery, sagacity, and steadiness in all circumstances. He was chosen to lead in almost all enterprises of unusual danger, and in all attacks on the Indians. At one time, with a party of twelve, he tracked a band of sixty Crows, who had stolen some of the horses belonging to the trappers, cut loose the animals which were tied within ten feet of the strong fort of logs in which the Indians had taken shelter, attacked them, and made good his retreat with the recovered horses; an Indian of another tribe, who was with the trappers, bringing away a Crow scalp as a trophy.

In one combat with the Blackfeet, Carson received a rifle ball in his left shoulder, breaking it. Save this, he has escaped the manifold dangers to which he has been exposed, without serious bodily injury. Of course in so turbulent and unrestrained a life, there were not unfrequent personal encounters among the trappers themselves, nor could the most peaceably disposed always avoid them. These were most frequent and savage at the periods when the trappers went in the 'rendezvous' as were called the points where the companies kept their establishments for receiving the peltries and supplying the trappers. Here a few days of indulgence were commonly allowed himself by the trapper, and there was much drinking and gambling, and consequently fighting. Feuds, growing out of national feelings, would also, naturally enough, sometimes occur among the trappers—there being Canadians and Mexicans as well as Americans: all having pride of race and country.

*Six dollars was the price paid to the trapper, at that time, for a beaver skin; and a good backwoodsman would secure from four to seven of a night; so that, notwithstanding the exorbitant charges of the companies for every necessary or luxury furnished to the trappers, (for example, twenty dollars for a blanket, two dollars for a tin cup full of brown sugar, and the same for the same measure of coffee,) the trappers were still incited by the frequent receipt of such sums as gave additional zest and fascination to the pursuit.

On one occasion, a Frenchman who ranked as a bully had whipped a good many Canadians, and then began to insult the Americans, saying they were only worth being whipped with switches. At this Carson fired up and said, "He was the most trifling one among the Americans, and the Frenchman might begin with him."—After some little more talk, each went off and armed himself—Carson with a pistol, the Frenchman with a rifle—and both mounted for the fight. Riding up until their horses' heads touched, they fired almost at the same instant, Carson a little the quickest, and, his ball passing through the Frenchman's hand, made him jerk up his gun, and sent the ball which was intended for Carson's heart grazing by his left eye and singeing his hair.—This is the only serious personal quarrel of Carson's life, as he is, like most very brave men, of a peaceable and gentle temper.

Col. Fremont owed his good fortune in procuring Carson's services to an accidental meeting on the steamboat above St. Louis—neither having ever before heard of the other. It was at the commencement of Fremont's first expedition. Carson continued with it until, in its return, it had recrossed the mountains. His courage, fidelity and excellent character so far conciliated the good will of the commander that, in his second expedition, he gladly availed himself again of Kit's services, on meeting with him, as he chanced to do, on the confines of New Mexico. Kit again left the party after its arrival this side of the mountains—not, however, until Fremont had obtained a promise from him to join the third expedition, in case one should be organized.—Some incidents will be interesting connected with this latter expedition, which was interrupted in its purely scientific character by the treachery of the Mexican chief (Castro) compelling Fremont to change his peaceful employment, and which, owing to the continuance of the war with Mexico is not yet completed.

In the interim between Fremont's second and third expeditions, Carson had settled himself near Taos, and had begun to farm, preparing to lead a quiet life, when he received a note from Fremont, written at Bent's Fort, reminding him of his promise, and telling him he would wait there for him. On this occasion Carson showed his strong friendship for his old commander, and the generous and unselfish nature of his feelings. In four days from receiving the note Carson had joined the party, having sold house and farm for less than half the sum he had just expended upon it, and put his family under the protection of his friend, the late Governor Bent, until he should return from a certainly long and dangerous journey. This protection, unfortunately, was taken from them in the late massacre at Taos, when Carson's brother-in-law was one of the victims to the fury of the Mexicans against all connected with the Americans. Mrs. Carson saved her life by flight, leaving them to rob the house of everything. Kendall, and all others who have written of their adventures in New Mexico, ascribe the highest character to the women of that country for modesty, generosity, quick sympathy, and all feminine virtues. To this amiable class belongs the wife of Carson, who has paid so dearly for her affection for him.

The route of the third expedition led the party to the Southern and Western side of the great salt lake—a region entirely unexplored, and filled, according to the superstitions and tales current among the Indians and the trappers of the mountains, with all imaginable horrors. A vast desert, void of vegetation and fresh water, abounding in quicksands and in brackish pools and rivers, with only subterranean outlets. This was the reputed character of the country, justifying at least the apprehension of lack of those indispensables to the voyager of the wilderness—water and grass. In truth, the Southern border of the lake was found to be skirted with a salt plain of about 60 miles in width. Over this, as elsewhere, Carson, in his capacity of scout, was always with the advance party, to search for water and convenient places for camp—the usual signal of the prairies—a fire—serving by its column of smoke, to point out where the advance were halting.

The neighborhood of the Rio Colorado and the Sierra Nevada of California is infested with Indian tribes of hippophagi, or horse eaters, (as they may well be called) who keep the Northern parts of California in alarm by sweeping down into the settlement, and carrying off horses and mules, which they use for food. With these savages the expedition had several skirmishes; but, owing to the perpetual vigilance which was exercised, neither men nor animals fell into the hands of the savages.

When Fremont's party, in May, 1846, (not knowing of the existence of the war with Mexico,) retired from California, they proceeded North as far as the Tlamath lake, in Oregon proposing to explore a new route into the Willhameth valley.

A courier having overtaken Col. Fremont there, to say that Mr. Gillespie and five men were endeavoring to overtake him, he took two men and returned 60 miles with the courier; making all haste, in order to reach them before night, and prevent any attack which the Indians might be tempted to make on a small party. These Tlamath Indians, by nature brave and warlike, have now a new source of power in the iron arrow heads and axes furnished them by the British posts in that country. Their arrows can only be extracted from the flesh by the knife, as they are barbed, and of course are not to be drawn out. The events of that night and the days following illustrate so fully the nightly dangers of an Indian country, and the treacherous nature of savages, that I will give them in Carson's own words:

"Mr. Gillespie had brought the colonel letters from home—the first he had had since leaving the States the year before—and he was up, and kept a large fire burning until midnight; the rest of us were tired out, and all went to sleep. This was the only night in all our travels, except the one night on the island in the salt lake, that we failed to keep guard; and as the men were so tired, and we expected no attack now that we had sixteen in party, the colonel didn't like to ask it of them, but set up late himself. Owens and I were sleeping together, and we were waked at the same time by the licks of the axe that killed our men. At first I didn't know it was that; but I called to Basil, who was that side, 'What's the matter there?—what's that fuss about?' He never answered, for he was dead then, poor fellow; and he never knew what killed him—his head had been cut in, in his sleep; the other groaned a little as he died. The Delawares (we had four with us) were sleeping at that fire, and they sprang up as the Tlamaths charged them. One of them caught up a gun, which was unloaded; but, although he could do no execution, he kept them at bay, fighting like a soldier, and didn't give up until he was shot full of arrows—three entering his heart; he died bravely.

"As soon as I had called out, I saw it was Indians in the camp, and I and Owens cried out 'Indians.' There were no orders given; things went on too fast, and the colonel had men with him that didn't need to be told of their duty. The colonel and I, Maxwell, Owens, Godey, and Stepp, jumped together, we six, and ran to the assistance of our Delawares. I don't know who fired and who didn't; but I think it was Stepp's shot that killed the Tlamath chief; for it was at the crack of Stepp's gun that he fell. He had an English half-axe slung to his wrist by a cord, and there were forty arrows left in his quiver—the most beautiful and warlike arrows I ever saw. He must have been the bravest man among them, from the way he was armed, and judging by his cap. When the Tlamaths saw him fall, they ran; but we lay, every man with his rifle cocked, until daylight, expecting another attack.

"In the morning we found by the tracks that from fifteen to twenty of the Tlamaths had attacked us. They had killed three of our men and wounded one of the Delawares, who scalped the chief, whom we left where he fell. Our dead men we carried on mules; but after going about ten miles we found it impossible to get them any farther through the thick timber, and finding a secret place we buried them under logs and chunks, having no way to dig a grave. It was only a few days before this fight that some of these same Indians had come into our camp; and although we had only meat for two days, and felt sure that we should have to eat mules for ten or fifteen days to come, the colonel divided with them, and even had a mule unpacked to give them some tobacco and knives."

The party then retraced its way into California; and two days after this affair, they met a large village of Tlamaths—more than a hundred warriors. Carson was ahead with ten men, but one of them having been discovered, he could not follow his orders, which were to send back word and let Fremont come up with the rest in case they found Indians. But as they had been seen, it only remained to charge the village; which they did, killing many, and putting to flight the rest. The women and children, Carson says, "we didn't interfere with"; but they burnt the village, together with their canoes and fishing nets. In a subsequent encounter, the same day, Carson's life was imminently exposed.—As they galloped up, he was rather in advance, when he observed an Indian fixing his arrow to let fly at him. Carson levelled his rifle, but it snapped; and in an instant the arrow would have pierced him, had not Fremont, seeing the danger, dashed his horse on the Indian, and knocked him down. "I owe my life to them two," says Carson, "the colonel and Sacramento saved me." Sacramento is a noble Californian horse, which Capt. Sutter gave to Col. Fremont in 1844, and which has twice made the distance between Kentucky and his native valley, where he earned his name by swimming the river after which he is called, at the close of a long day's journey. Notwithstanding all his hardships, (for he has travelled everywhere with his master,) he is still the favorite horse of Col. Fremont.

The hostile and insulting course of Castro drew Fremont into retaliatory measures, and, aided by the American settlers, he pursued the Mexicans for some time; but, being unable to make them stand and fight, (they always flying before him,) the flag of independence was raised at Sonoma on the 5th of July, 1846. Learning soon after of the existence of the war, the American flag was promptly substituted, and the party proceeded to Monterey, where they found the fleet under Com. Sloat already in possession. Castro, with his forces, had retreated before Fremont; and, to prevent their escape into Sonora, Col. Fremont, with a hundred and sixty men, was offered the sloop of war "Cyane" to carry them down to San Diego and facilitate the pursuit, as he hoped by that means to intercept Castro at Puebla de los Angelos.

Then Carson, for the first time, saw the blue ocean, and the great vessels that, like white-winged birds, spread their sails above its waters. The vast prairies, whose immense green surface has been aptly likened to the sea, together with all objects ever seen upon it, were familiar to him, but it proved no preparation for actual salt water, and the pride and strength of the backwoodsmen were soon humbled by the customary tribute to Neptune. The forces were landed, and raised the flag at San Diego, and then they proceeded jointly to the capital, (Ciudad de los Angelos,) where, although from the detention at sea Castro had escaped, American authority was also established.

From this point, on the 1st of September, 1846, Carson, with 15 men, was despatched by Fremont with an account of the progress and state of affairs in that distant conquest. Carson was to make the journey from Pueblo to Washington City and back, in 140 days. He pushed ahead accordingly, not stopping even for game, but subsisting on his mules, of which they made food as the animals broke down in the rapidity of the journey. He had crossed the wilderness, as he expected, in 30 days, when, meeting with Gen. Kearney's company within a few miles of Santa Fe, he was turned back by that officer, to whose orders he believed himself subject, and with infinite reluctance resigned his despatches to another, and returned to guide Kearney's command in California.

Gen. Kearney entered California without molestation until the fight of San Pasqual, an official account of which has been published. In the charge made upon the Mexicans, Carson, as usual, was among the foremost, when, as he approached within bullet range of the enemy, who were drawn up in order of battle, his horse stumbled and fell, pitching him over his head, and breaking his rifle in twain. Seizing his knife, he advanced on foot until he found a killed dragoon, whose rifle he took, and was pressing on, when he met the mounted men returning from the charge, the Mexicans having galloped off.

At the instance of Carson, the American party then took possession of a small rocky hill, near the scene of the battle, as the strongest position in reach. Not being in a situation to go forward, they encamped here; and the enemy collecting in force they remained in a state of siege. There was little grass or water on the hill, and soon both animals and men began to suffer. The way so thickly beset by the enemy, that the commander doubted the propriety of attempting to cut a passage through, when, after four days' siege, Carson and Passed Midshipman Beale, of the navy, who had been sent to meet Kearney, with some thirty men as a complimentary escort to San Diego,) volunteered to go to Captain Stockton, at that place and bring a reinforcement.

This daring enterprise these intrepid and resolute young men, accompanied by a Delaware Indian, who was attached as a spy to General Kearney's command, successfully accomplished, but not without extreme suffering and peril. The distance between the camp and San Diego was but thirty miles; but, as they had to make long detours, they travelled nearer fifty. They left the camp in the night of the 9th of December, crawling in a horizontal position through the enemy's lines. Their shoes made some noise, for which cause they took them off, and during the night unfortunately lost them. Lying by all day to avoid the enemy, they succeeded by the end of the second night in reaching their destination, and procuring the necessary reinforcement. Their feet and flesh torn and bleeding from the rocks and thorny shrubs, haggard from hunger, thirst, anxiety and sleeplessness, they were again, nevertheless, in full performance of duty at the battles of the 8th and 9th of January.

When Fremont after meeting with and accepting the surrender of the Mexican forces, reached Los Angelos, Carson immediately returned to his command, and in the ensuing month was again selected to cross the desert, the wilderness, the mountains, and the prairies, to bring news of those far-off operations of its agents to the government in Washington. Leaving the frontier settlements of California on the 25th of February, Carson arrived in St. Louis about the middle of May—making the journey notwithstanding the inclemency of the season, and an unavoidable detention of ten days at Santa Fe, in a shorter time than it was ever before accomplished in.

The unsettled state of the country—the war with Mexico inciting the savage tribes to unusual license and daring—added much to the inevitable hazards and privations of the journey, rendering the most unceasing vigilance necessary night and day; while the speed with which the party travelled debarred them from the usual resource of travellers in uninhabited regions and they were fain to resort to the unsavory subsistence of those hippophagi of the Sierra Nevada; only converting the poor beasts to food, however, when they were travel worn and exhausted.

Fortunately, the journey was made in its extent without serious mishap, and Carson, Lieut. Beale, his comrade in the night march to San Diego, and Lieut. Talbot, the young gentleman who led the gallant retreat of the little party of ten through the enemy's midst, a distance of three hundred miles from Santa Barbara to Monterey, are all now in Washington.

Since Carson's arrival, he has received a commission of lieutenant in the rifle regiment of which Mr. Fremont is the Lieut. Colonel.

# Appendix C
## *Commentary on the Illustrations*

Frontispiece: The last photograph of Carson was made, according to Sabin, in Boston, on March 25, 1868; but Mr. Jack K. Boyer thinks that it may have been made in Washington, D.C. At any rate, it was taken during his last trip to the East and the effects of his illness are clearly apparent in the picture. Carson was also photographed in Washington, about this time, in company with other persons. Some of these photographs are reproduced in Sabin, opposite pages 484 and 490, and show his debilitated condition perhaps even more clearly. Unfortunately, this last photograph is frequently the only picture of Carson to be reproduced in books on western American history.

Page 13: *The Fighting Trapper or Carson to the Rescue* was a dime novel, the cover illustration of which is reproduced here. It is taken from Albert Johannsen, *The House of Beadle and Adams and its Dime and Nickel Novels* (Norman, 1950). The fictional Carson in action, as depicted here, agrees closely with the one described by Emerson Bennett in *The Prairie Flower*, from which I have quoted extensively in Chapter I.

Page 19: The drawing of Carson in buckskins and broad beaver hat, holding his long rifle, and standing beside his horse, I have captioned *The Legendary Carson*. It first appeared in the biography of Carson by Dr. Peters (1858), and was probably made expressly as an illustration for that book. Possibly Dr. Peters supplied some description of Carson to the artist, for the drawing bears considerable resemblance to Kit both in face and in figure. Peters said that the horse was Carson's favorite and was named Apache. This drawing probably is very close to the picture of Carson that most people have in their minds, for it was used later in Beadle's *Western Wilds* and in Triplett's *Conquering the Wilderness*, both widely read books.

Page 23: In this illustration, taken from Frémont's *Memoirs of My Life*, the mounted and bearded figure in the right foreground is Frémont and the horseman to his right probably is Carson. Carson appears to be pointing with his gun toward a buffalo he has selected for Frémont to shoot. The illustration probably was prepared from Frémont's description of a buffalo hunt that occurred during his first expedition.

Page 33: This illustration, also taken from Frémont's *Memoirs*, is signed by W. C. Jackson. It depicts the triumphant return of Carson and Godey to Frémont's camp in the Mojave River region on April 25, 1844. They are driving before them Andres Fuentes' stolen horses, which they had recovered from the Indians. Godey has the two Indian scalps attached to his rifle. Carson has risen in his stirrups to wave his hat to the other members of the party, thus announcing their victorious return. Frémont was greatly impressed by this event, and he was lavish in his praise of the two Indian fighters.

Page 59: The earliest likeness of Carson appeared in a book called *The Mexican War and its Heroes*, published anonymously in 1848. The picture was captioned Lieutenant Christopher Carson, which was an error, for Carson was not a commissioned officer at the time. A later edition (Philadelphia, 1860) refers to it as a zinc portrait. Sabin says it was a woodcut. Nothing further seems to be known about it.

However, the fact that Carson is given the rank and title of lieutenant is a clue to the time at which the sketch was made. It could have been done at no other time than June, 1847, after the interview with President Polk, in which he was told by the President that his nomination for a lieutenant's commission would be made.

It is possible that the publication of this sketch of Carson, dressed in the fashion affected by United States senators at that time, appearing in a book mainly devoted to officers of the regular army on the staff of General Scott, may have produced an adverse feeling toward Kit which had something to do with failure of the Senate to confirm his nomination for a lieutenant's commission. This is a speculation for which I have no evidence other than the picture itself.

Page 78: The sketch of Carson by Lieutenant George D. Brewerton was undoubtedly made during their association in 1848. Brewerton published "A Ride with Kit Carson" in *Harpers New Monthly Magazine* (August, 1853), with many line illustrations done by himself, but this sketch was not among them nor did it appear in his second western article (April, 1854). A third article, "In the Buffalo Country," was lost temporarily as a result of a fire in the Harper printing establishment. Later it was recovered and published (September, 1862). It was in this article that the sketch of Carson first appeared. Whether Carson signed the sketch when it was made or later, at Brewerton's request, is not known. Brewerton had considerable artistic ability and the sketch is the only likeness of Carson in profile. It was later used in Dunn's *Massacres of the Mountains.* A photograph of this sketch of Carson by Brewerton was used by Frémont as an illustration in his *Memoirs.*

Page 97: The daguerreotype of Kit Carson and John C. Frémont, reproduced on page 97 herein, can be dated rather precisely. It was made during the latter part of January, 1849, when Frémont was in Taos at Carson's house after the failure of his fourth expedition, or a few days later when Carson accompanied him to Santa Fe, where Frémont remained for three days before going on to California. The heavy cloak and full beard worn by Frémont, as well as his jaunty Alpine hat, are evidence of the fact that the picture was made in cold weather. Carson himself is wearing a heavy military coat. Frémont appears to be serene and relaxed, despite his recent disaster, but Carson seems stiff and ill at ease. There is a strong probability that this was the first time Carson had ever had his picture taken. If this is true, it would account for his uneasy posture.

The State Historical Society of Colorado has a letter dated March 20, 1945, from Mrs. Katherine S. Baker, Newark, New York, to Kit Carson's grandson of the same name, Alamosa, Colorado, in which she offers him a copy of this daguerreotype, which she describes as being a likeness of Carson and her grandmother's cousin, Ed Perrin, who served under Carson in the southwest. Edwin O. Perrin, the person in question, was "born December 3, 1822, in Springfield, Ohio . . . . In 1861 he was dispatched by Secretary Cameron to New Mexico . . . where he served with the command of . . . Kit Carson . . . In 1868 he was elected Clerk of the Court of Appeals (of New York State), and was appointed to the same position by the Court in 1870." This information is from Paul A. Chadbourne, editor, *Public Service of the State of New York*, III (Boston, 1882), 68, and was kindly furnished to me by Mr. Jonas Olsoff, assistant librarian of the New York State Library, Albany, New York, who also provided a photograph of Edwin O. Perrin.

The man in the picture with Carson bears a great resemblance to other pictures of Frémont. He also bears some resemblance to the photograph of

Edwin Perrin just mentioned, in which Perrin is shown full-bearded at about fifty years of age. My reasons for believing that the man with Carson is Frémont and not Perrin are as follows. Perrin was thirteen years younger than Carson and there does not appear to be that much difference in the ages of the two men in the picture. Carson does not appear to be over fifty years old, which he would have had to be, if he was photographed with Perrin. Perrin served under Carson's command just as Carson served under Frémont. There is every reason, therefore, why Carson should pose standing with Frémont seated, and every reason against his doing so with Perrin.

The first publication of this picture was in Blanche C. Grant's edition of Carson's memoirs, *Kit Carson's Own Story* (Taos, 1926), in which the picture is credited to the collection of Ralph E. Twitchell, the well-known authority on the history of New Mexico. It is reproduced in Estergren's biography of Carson by the "courtesy of Charles Carson." The Denver Public Library's copy, which is reproduced here, has a pencilled notation on the back stating that it was given to Dr. Francis W. Cragin by Mrs. Thomas J. Walton, of Mora, New Mexico. A reference to Mrs. Walton's possession of a picture of Carson is found in the F. W. Cragin Papers, Notebook VII, 41, dated February 23, 1908. There is a further notation, "Kit Carson and Fremont in 1839" on the back of this copy.

Since Daguerre first announced the details of his picture-making process in France in 1839, it is apparent that 1839 was written in error for 1849, possibly by Mrs. Walton herself. Moreover, Carson and Frémont did not become acquainted until 1842. For all these reasons I think it can be said quite definitely that the people in the picture are Carson and Frémont in 1849, and that prints continued to be available for several years in New Mexico because of the celebrity of the two men. Doubtless it was thus that Edwin Perrin acquired a picture of Carson, during the Civil War years in New Mexico.

Page 141: The daguerreotype of Carson wearing a beaver hat also presents some problems—and these incapable of so forthright a solution. Smith H. Simpson claimed that he and Carson had their pictures taken separately but at the same time in 1860, and that this is the picture of Carson made at that time. It is rather obvious that Carson is younger than fifty in this picture and that Simpson was mistaken in his recollection made many years later.

Mr. Jack K. Boyer, director of the Kit Carson Museum in Taos, believes that the picture was taken in Washington, either in 1847 or in 1848, when Carson was there. The coat and hat worn by Carson in the picture are certainly compatible with this view, and Mr. Boyer's opinion is entitled to careful consideration.

However, my own belief is that it was made about 1854, when Carson first entèred upon his duties as Indian agent. Smith Simpson did not know Carson before he was an Indian agent. He could have been right about Carson having the picture made during this period, and wrong about the year. It would be natural for Carson to have a picture made near the time he entered upon his new duties in this responsible position. My principal reason for believing that the picture was made in 1854 is to be found in the fact that Carson, though appearing younger than a date of 1860 would warrant, seems to be much fuller in the face and generally heavier than he appears in the picture with Frémont in 1849. He also seems more confident, as if he had faced a camera before. If the picture had been made in Washington in 1847 or 1848, I believe that Carson would have appeared leaner, perhaps even a little gaunt, during this hard-riding period of his overland journeys. The same might be true, in lesser degree, if the picture had been made during 1855, a year of hard Indian campaigns. The year 1856, when he completed his memoirs, is another time when he might have wanted a tintype of himself, but this is putting it rather late. If the picture was made as late as 1856, Carson may have been wearing the hat that Major Carleton ordered made for him.

None of my reasons is conclusive. It is quite possible that this is Carson's earliest picture, but there is no evidence to indicate it except that in his face. Mr. Boyer and I are agreed that it definitely should be dated before 1860. The question of how much earlier remains unanswered.

Page 155: The date for this photograph of Carson can only be approximated, but it can be approximated rather closely. The original was a tintype of Carson with Charley Boggs, son of Kit's close friend, Thomas O. Boggs, who married Rumalda Luna, niece of Carson's wife and step-daughter of Charles Bent. In the original picture, Charley Boggs appears to be about twelve years old, and since he was born in 1848, the date of the picture very likely is about the year 1860, when Carson was fifty years old. A copy of the original picture is in Sabin, *Kit Carson Days* (Chicago, 1914), opposite page 368. The tintype had been given by Carson's oldest daughter, Teresina, to J. S. Hough, and later it passed into other hands. The copy used here is from a photograph of the original picture, but shows only Carson. It bears out descriptions of Carson better than most of the pictures of him, and is undoubtedly a very good likeness.

Page 163: Colonel Carson in 1865 is a photograph that cannot be definitely assigned to that year on the basis of positive knowledge, and yet it is difficult to find any other time when it could have been made. Carson is dressed in the uniform of a colonel and appears to be heavier than in any other photograph. If the work is correctly attributed to Mathew B. Brady, the famous photographer of men and events of the Civil War (and there seems to be no reason to doubt it), the year 1865 is clearly indicated. The picture thus represents the only solid evidence that Carson visited Washington in the latter part of that year. A comparison of this photograph with Brewerton's earlier sketch reveals some facial similarities leading to the conclusion that the sketch has considerable merit.

Page 167: Brigadier General Carson in 1866 I consider to be the most handsome representation of Carson available. Sabin reproduced it as a copy of a crayon portrait owned by Mrs. William Carson. Mr. Jack K. Boyer believes that this crayon portrait is the one given to the Kit Carson Museum in Taos by her granddaughter, Mrs. Attie Provinzano, of Alamosa, Colorado. He also believes that the photograph reproduced here is from a photograph rather than from a crayon portrait. The Museum also has another crayon portrait of Carson, in the same uniform and pose but showing him with heavier jowls and more elongated face. I am inclined to think that the handsomer likeness shown here is from a photograph and that the other one, on page 171, is the original portrait or one of two made at the same time by an unknown artist, either from life or from the photograph, which was probably taken at Fort Garland.

Page 171: A comparison of this reproduction of a crayon portrait made at Fort Garland in 1866 with the photograph made at the same time reveals the deficiency of the unknown artist. The pose and costume are identical and the portrait may have been done from the photograph rather than from life. The artist has not done justice to Carson's breadth of shoulder or his piercing eye, and has shown him with heavier jowls and more elongated face than the photograph.

Page 173: This picture of Carson is from an oil painting once in the possession of William Gilpin, first territorial governor of Colorado, and now in the Colorado State Museum, in Denver. Gilpin had accompanied Frémont's second expedition, was a Carson admirer, and was a great Western enthusiast. The artist is unknown but the place of the sitting was undoubtedly Denver and the time either the fall of 1867 or the spring of 1868. The former time seems more probable than the latter. The artist could have been the unknown artist who painted Carson as a brigadier general.

Page 177: Although it differs greatly from the preceding painting, this painting by Charles S. Stobie was probably made at the same time. The collar and tie worn by Carson suggest this conclusion. This artist was well known in early Denver, and this and other examples of his work may be found in the Colorado State Museum, in that city. Both of these paintings deserve careful study and comparison with photographs of Carson, especially with his last photograph.

Page 180: This picture of Carson appears to belong to the period of his overland journeys as a courier for the federal government, since he is wearing a military coat. It is an unusual pose and a rather good likeness. The National Archives dates it *circa* 1849, but I would be inclined to place it no later than 1848.

Page 183: The equestrian statue by Henry Augustus Lukeman (1871–1935) and Frederick G. R. Roth (1872–1944) was unveiled at the dedication of Kit Carson Park in Trinidad, Colorado, June 1, 1913, by Amanda Carson and Leona Wood, two of Kit Carson's granddaughters. Lukeman, the more famous of the two sculptors, was commissioned to do the work, and Roth was associated with him because of his skill in portraying horses. The names of both sculptors appear on the work. It is a very fine bronze and deserves to be better known.

Daniel L. Taylor, who came to Trinidad in 1865, knew and admired Carson. Taylor contributed the land for the park and $5,000 toward the cost of the statue. In return for the land, the city of Trinidad contributed the remaining $10,000 of the cost of the statue.

Page 189: The Pioneer Monument in Denver's Civic Center was unveiled June 24, 1911. The equestrian statue of Kit Carson, which surmounts the entire monument, was the work of Frederick William MacMonnies (1863–1937), one of the most distinguished American sculptors. It is interesting that both Augustus Lukeman and MacMonnies used the same buckskin coat in making their Carson statues. The coat was on loan for the purpose from J. S. Hough, of Lake City, Colorado, and once belonged to Carson himself.

It is of incidental interest that the model for the well-known statue of Nathan Hale by MacMonnies in City Hall Park, New York, was William Theodore Peters, son of the Dr. D. C. Peters who was Carson's first biographer.

Page 211: Kit Carson's home in Taos was an adobe house which was rather more commodious than the average house in Taos at that time. The photograph on page 211 shows the portion that fronts upon the street as it appears today. A number of rooms have been added to the original house and there is an attractive patio between the front and rear sections. The Kit Carson Museum is located in the house at the present time.

Page 215: The map of Taos shows the location of the Kit Carson House in reference to the Plaza and the location of Carson's grave in the nearby Kit Carson Memorial Park. The Bent House, where Governor Charles Bent was killed during the Taos Revolt of 1847, is also shown. During Carson's time there were still houses, as well as shops, around the Plaza.

# Index